SOUND MANDARIN
for English Speakers

读拼音 学汉语

Chief editors
Liu Huaixi   Han Chusen

English proofreading
Bruce Julian（新西兰）   Matt Drew（英国）   Gong Yunfeng
Chinese proofreading
Wang Yunshi

外语教学与研究出版社
FOREIGN LANGUAGE TEACHING AND RESEARCH PRESS
北京 BEIJING

图书在版编目（CIP）数据

读拼音学汉语 ／ 刘怀玺，韩楚森主编. — 北京 ：外语教学与研究出版社，
2013.5（2014.8 重印）
ISBN 978-7-5135-3078-1

Ⅰ．①读… Ⅱ．①刘… ②韩… Ⅲ．①对外汉语教学－阅读教学 Ⅳ．① H195

中国版本图书馆 CIP 数据核字（2013）第 100028 号

出 版 人　蔡剑峰
责任编辑　颜　莉　刘虹艳
封面设计　高　蕾
出版发行　外语教学与研究出版社
社　　址　北京市西三环北路 19 号（100089）
网　　址　http://www.fltrp.com
印　　刷　北京京师印务有限公司
开　　本　889×1194　1/16
印　　张　18
版　　次　2013 年 6 月第 1 版 2014 年 8 月第 2 次印刷
书　　号　ISBN 978-7-5135-3078-1
定　　价　79.00 元（含 MP3 光盘一张）

购书咨询：（010）88819929　电子邮箱：club@fltrp.com
外研书店：http://www.fltrpstore.com
凡印刷、装订质量问题，请联系我社印制部
联系电话：（010）61207896　电子邮箱：zhijian@fltrp.com
凡侵权、盗版书籍线索，请联系我社法律事务部
举报电话：（010）88817519　电子邮箱：banquan@fltrp.com
法律顾问：立方律师事务所　刘旭东律师
　　　　　中咨律师事务所　殷　斌律师
物料号：230780001

Foreword

The book *Sound Mandarin for English Speakers* is designed for non-native beginners to study Chinese through mastering Pinyin so as to enable them to communicate in Chinese within a short period of time. The book consists of twenty units, with a brief introduction to the Pinyin system of Mandarin before the first unit. The vocabulary index, grammar outline, keys and audio scripts of exercises are also included in the book. These materials will help you pronounce and construct basic sentences. At the end of the book, there is a mini-dictionary providing a large amount of frequently used vocabulary in Chinese daily life. The book is not only for learners in class, it is also ideal for self-learners.

The book has the following features:

* The use of Chinese Pinyin is primary, and the use of Chinese characters is secondary. For every sentence we have provided English translation to help you grasp its meaning.
* We have put main vocabularies at the beginning of almost every unit, and also pictures to match up with them. You can speak by looking at the pictures.
* Each unit shows the comparative forms of Chinese and English, concisely and clearly laid out to give you a better understanding of the structural differences between the two languages.
* Speaking and listening exercises have been designed for each unit. These exercises are interesting and close to everyday use, such as listening to a story, matching pictures with words, listening to words then drawing a picture, and so on.
* The book is full of the atmosphere of Chinese culture. Chinese ancient poems and stories are included in the book and we have given their English translations. They are consistent with the substance of some units.
* An MP3 with the book is to help you to improve speaking and listening skills.
* The mini-dictionary is a collection of necessary words for living and traveling in China, including clothing (yī 衣), eating (shí 食), living (zhù 住) and going out (xíng 行).

In short, the book is for you to learn easily and be happy with your progress.

We would like to thank the following people for their support and assistance in writing this book: Troy Collings, Trin Lilananda, David Christian, Shen Lijiang (沈丽江), Qian Zhongxuan (钱钟选), Ying Jian (应坚), Liu Jianrong (刘剑戎), Dai Wentong (戴文潼) and Zheng Min (郑敏).

CONTENTS Mùlù（目录）

Vocabulary	Function	Cultural tip
1) Greetings 2) Polite expressions (1) 3) Personal pronouns	1) Greeting each other 2) Asking and saying names	Asking surnames
Countries and nationalities	1) Introducing yourself 2) Asking about and giving information about nationality	How happy we are, to meet friends from afar!
Family members	1) Talking about family members 2) Asking about and giving information about work	Chinese families
1) Stationery and books 2) Demonstrative pronouns	Talking about personal possession	The four treasures of study
1) Cardinal numbers 2) Ordinal numbers	1) Telling people where you live and your telephone number 2) Talking about means of transportation	Addresses
1) Items of fruit 2) Polite expressions (2)	1) Visiting a friend 2) Entertaining guests	Dropping in

Vocabulary	Function	Cultural tip
1) Specific measurement words 2) Specific position words (1)	1) Describing a room in your house 2) Talking about room furniture	Communities in the city
Expressions of time	1) Telling the time 2) Describing daily routines 3) Making an appointment by phone	Colorful evening life
Year, month and day	1) Talking about the year, month and day 2) Describing your birthday party	Birthday celebrations
1) Shops and public places 2) Specific position words (2)	1) Asking for locations and directions 2) Giving directions	Taking a bus
Verbs of action	Talking about things you can/can't do	Main transportation
1) Chinese currency 2) Main currencies of the world 3) Words used at banks and post offices	1) Depositing and withdrawing money 2) Sending letters and parcels at the post office	Saving and depositing money
1) Items of vegetables and other food 2) Chinese units of weight	Asking about prices and buying things	Food markets
1) Items of clothing and shoes 2) Colors	1) Describing goods and colors 2) Making comparisons	Chinese clothing
1) The four seasons 2) Days of a week and other words to express weeks	1) Describing the climate and scenery of the four seasons 2) Planning a trip	Traveling on holidays

Unit		Form
16. Nǐ qùguo Zhōngguó ma? Have you been to China? 你去过中国吗？	143	Expressing different tenses
17. Jīntiān tiānqì zěnmeyàng? What's the weather like today? 今天天气怎么样？	151	Nominal predicate Adjectival predicate
18. Duànliàn shēntǐ Do exercise 锻炼身体	159	lái 来 and qù 去 Two or more verbs (verbal phrases) in a sentence
19. Qǐng màn yòng! Take your time to enjoy the meal please! 请慢用！	167	Expressing the degree of extreme
20. Kàn yīshēng See a doctor 看医生	177	Verb reduplication Common ways of describing symptoms

Vocabulary	Function	Cultural tip
Some major cities and tourist attractions of China	Talking about your travel	Chinese traditional gardens
Weather forecast terms	1) Understanding the weather forecast 2) Talking about weather and what clothes to wear 3) Talking about your hometown	Adages of the weather
Sports	1) Talking about sports 2) Talking about your activities on the weekend	Physical exercise in early mornings and evenings
1) Items of tableware 2) Some staple food, dishes and beverages 3) Adjectives to describe senses of tastes 4) Adverbs to describe degrees	1) Asking and answering questions about different dishes 2) Ordering at a restaurant	Table manners
1) Main parts of the body 2) Symptoms of illness	1) Asking about symptoms 2) Describing symptoms 3) Understanding instructions for taking medicine	Going to see a doctor

Pīnyīn
PINYIN SYSTEM OF MANDARIN
拼音

I Initials and finals

The Pinyin System of Mandarin (Chinese phonetics) is a tool for learning characters and speaking Mandarin. If you want to learn Mandarin quickly, first of all you will need to know the Pinyin System well. The Pinyin System of Mandarin contains initials, finals and tones.

1. The 21 initials

Table of initials					
Unaspirated	Aspirated	Nasal	Voiceless fricative	Voiced fricative	Lateral
b	p	m	f		
d	t	n			l
g	k		h		
j	q		x		
zh	ch		sh	r	
z	c		s		

12 initials have almost the same pronunciation in English, 9 others have similar pronunciations in English.

Chinese initials	English equivalents	Chinese initials	English similarities
b	"b" in "black"	j	"jee" in "jeep"
p	"p" in "pen"	q	"chee" in "cheese"
m	"m" in "mother"	x	"sea"
f	"f" in "father"	zh	"ge" in "large"
d	"d" in "day"	ch	"ch" in "lunch"
t	"t" in "time"	sh	"sh" in "ship"
n	"n" in "now"	r	"r" in "raw"
l	"l" in "light"	z	"ds" in "words"
g	"g" in "go"	c	"ts" in "hats"
k	"k" in "desk"		
h	"h" in "high"		
s	"s" in "steel"		

读拼音学汉语

2. The 36 finals 🎧

Table of finals				
		i	u	ü
Singular finals	a	ia	ua	
	o		uo	
	e	ie		üe
Plural finals	ai		uai	
	ei		uei(-ui)	
	ao	iao		
	ou	iou(-iu)		
Nasal finals	an	ian	uan	üan
	en	in	uen(-un)	ün
	ang	iang	uang	
	eng	ing	ueng	
	ong	iong		
Special final	er			

The finals include singular, plural, nasal and special finals. Below is a table of intuitive pronunciation system.

Chinese finals	English similarities	Chinese finals	English similarities
a	"ar" in "arm"	ao	"ow" in "how"
o	"o" in "box"	ou	"o" in "go"
e	"ear" in "earth"	ia	"yar" in "yard"
i	"ea" in "eat"	ie	"ye" in "yes"
u	"wo" in "two"	iao	"ea" in "eat" + "ow" in "how"
ü			
ai	"i" in "high"	iou(-iu)	"ew" in "new"
ei	"a" in "age"	ua	"wa" in "waft"

拼音

Chinese finals	English similarities	Chinese finals	English similarities
uo	"war"	ing	"ing" in "learning"
uai	"why"	iong	"ea" in "eat" + "ong" in "long"
uei(-ui)	"wei" in "weight"		
üe	"ü" + "ye" in "yes"	uan	"wo" in "two" + "an" in "ant"
an	"an" in "ant"		
en	"en" in "men"	uen(-un)	"wen" in "went"
ang	"oung" in "young"	uang	"wo" in "two" + "oung" in "young"
eng			
ong	"ong" in "long"	ueng	
ian	"ea" in "eat" + "an" in "ant"	üan	"ü" + "an" in "ant"
		ün	"ü" + "en" in "men"
in	"in"	er	"er" in "younger"
iang	"young"		

Notes

How to pronounce "ü" :

When pronouncing "ü", lips are rounded and protruded. Extend the tip of the tongue to the front to touch the lower teeth, then aspirate.

II Combinations of initials and finals

1. The basic structure of Mandarin syllables

A Mandarin syllable usually consists of an initial, a final and a tone. Some syllables consist of only a final and a tone. (see "III Tones" , p9)

The initial and the final are conjoined, for example:

b+a → ba   m+a → ma
sh+u → shu   h+ei → hei

g+uo → guo   j+ie → jie
x+ian → xian   ch+uang → chuang

Notice: The final "i" in "zhi", "chi", "shi" and "ri" is pronounced as [ʅ]. The final "i" in "zi", "ci" and "si" is pronounced as [ɿ].

When the final section is "iou", "uei" or "uen" , it is written as "iu", "ui" or "un" , for example:

diu   gui   kun
liu   hui   chun

When the final "ü" is combined with the initials "j", "q" or "x" , they are written as "ju", "qu" or "xu". When combined with the initials "n" or "l" , they are written as "nü" or "lü" .

2. Syllables can be without initials

Notice:

(1) When the finals "i", "u" and "ü" serve as syllables without an initial before, they are written as:

yi   wu   yu

(2) When the finals begin with "i" , "i" is written as "y" or "yi" :

ya   ye   yao   you   yan   yin   yang   ying   yong

(3) When the finals begin with "u" , "u" is written as "w" :

wa   wo   wai   wei   wan   wen   wang   weng

(4) When the finals begin with "ü" , "ü" is written as "yu" :

yue   yuan   yun

(5) The special final "er" and nasal final "ueng" cannot be conjoined with any initials.

拼音

Addendum: Table of the Combinations of Initials and Finals (1)

	Singular finals						Special final	Plural finals					
	a	o	e	i (-i)	u	ü	er	ai	ei	ao	ou	ia	ie
	a	o	e	yi	wu	yu	er	ai	ei	ao	ou	ya	ye
b	ba	bo		bi	bu			bai	bei	bao			bie
p	pa	po		pi	pu			pai	pei	pao	pou		pie
m	ma	mo	me	mi	mu			mai	mei	mao	mou		mie
f	fa	fo			fu				fei		fou		
d	da		de	di	du			dai	dei	dao	dou		die
t	ta		te	ti	tu			tai		tao	tou		tie
n	na		ne	ni	nu	nü		nai	nei	nao	nou		nie
l	la		le	li	lu	lü		lai	lei	lao	lou	lia	lie
g	ga		ge		gu			gai	gei	gao	gou		
k	ka		ke		ku			kai	kei	kao	kou		
h	ha		he		hu			hai	hei	hao	hou		
j				ji		ju						jia	jie
q				qi		qu						qia	qie
x				xi		xu						xia	xie
zh	zha		zhe	zhi	zhu			zhai	zhei	zhao	zhou		
ch	cha		che	chi	chu			chai		chao	chou		
sh	sha		she	shi	shu			shai	shei	shao	shou		
r			re	ri	ru					rao	rou		
z	za		ze	zi	zu			zai	zei	zao	zou		
c	ca		ce	ci	cu			cai		cao	cou		
s	sa		se	si	su			sai		sao	sou		

拼音

	Plural finals							Nasal finals				
	iao	iou (-iu)	ua	uo	uai	uei (-ui)	üe	an	en	ian	in	uan
	yao	you	wa	wo	wai	wei	yue	an	en	yan	yin	wan
b	biao							ban	ben	bian	bin	
p	piao							pan	pen	pian	pin	
m	miao	miu						man	men	mian	min	
f								fan	fen			
d	diao	diu		duo		dui		dan	den	dian		duan
t	tiao			tuo		tui		tan		tian		tuan
n	niao	niu		nuo			nüe	nan	nen	nian	nin	nuan
l	liao	liu		luo			lüe	lan		lian	lin	luan
g			gua	guo	guai	gui		gan	gen			guan
k			kua	kuo	kuai	kui		kan	ken			kuan
h			hua	huo	huai	hui		han	hen			huan
j	jiao	jiu					jue			jian	jin	
q	qiao	qiu					que			qian	qin	
x	xiao	xiu					xue			xian	xin	
zh			zhua	zhuo	zhuai	zhui		zhan	zhen			zhuan
ch			chua	chuo	chuai	chui		chan	chen			chuan
sh			shua	shuo	shuai	shui		shan	shen			shuan
r			rua	ruo		rui		ran	ren			ruan
z				zuo		zui		zan	zen			zuan
c				cuo		cui		can	cen			cuan
s				suo		sui		san	sen			suan

	Nasal finals										
	uen (-un)	üan	ün	ang	eng	ong	iang	ing	iong	uang	ueng
	wen	yuan	yun	ang	eng		yang	ying	yong	wang	weng
b				bang	beng			bing			
p				pang	peng			ping			
m				mang	meng			ming			
f				fang	feng						
d	dun			dang	deng	dong		ding			
t	tun			tang	teng	tong		ting			
n				nang	neng	nong	niang	ning			
l	lun			lang	leng	long	liang	ling			
g	gun			gang	geng	gong				guang	
k	kun			kang	keng	kong				kuang	
h	hun			hang	heng	hong				huang	
j		juan	jun				jiang	jing	jiong		
q		quan	qun				qiang	qing	qiong		
x		xuan	xun				xiang	xing	xiong		
zh	zhun			zhang	zheng	zhong				zhuang	
ch	chun			chang	cheng	chong				chuang	
sh	shun			shang	sheng					shuang	
r	run			rang	reng	rong					
z	zun			zang	zeng	zong					
c	cun			cang	ceng	cong					
s	sun			sang	seng	song					

ᕕ Ⅲ Tones

The tones in Mandarin refer to the pitch variation within a syllable. Different tones indicate different meanings. There are four tones in Mandarin. They are called "The Four Sounds". The first tone is called "The High Tone", the second tone is called "The Rising Tone", the third tone is called "The Falling then Rising Tone" and the fourth tone is called "The Falling Tone" as shown in the figures below:

拼音

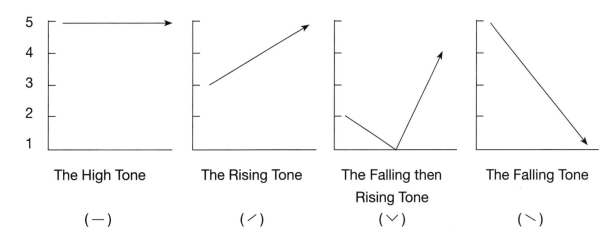

| The High Tone | The Rising Tone | The Falling then Rising Tone | The Falling Tone |
| (一) | (ˊ) | (ˇ) | (ˋ) |

For example: 🎧

The High Tone	The Rising Tone	The Falling then Rising Tone	The Falling Tone
bā *eight* 八	**bá** *uproot* 拔	**bǎ** *target* 靶	**bà** *father* 爸
shū *book* 书	**shú** *ripe* 熟	**shǔ** *rat* 鼠	**shù** *tree* 树
jiē *street* 街	**jié** *clean* 洁	**jiě** *sister* 姐	**jiè** *borrow* 借
guō *pot* 锅	**guó** *country* 国	**guǒ** *fruit* 果	**guò** *pass* 过
xiān *fresh* 鲜	**xián** *salty* 咸	**xiǎn** *dangerous* 险	**xiàn** *line* 线
chuāng *window* 窗	**chuáng** *bed* 床	**chuǎng** *rush* 闯	**chuàng** *initiate* 创

1. The place of tone marks

When a final has one vowel, the tone mark is written over the vowel, for example:

nǎ	gē	dì	tǔ	nǚ
kǎn	hěn	lín	jūn	
máng	děng	lóng	píng	

When a final has two vowels and the first vowel of the final is "a", "o" or "e", the tone mark is written over the first vowel, for example:

bái   měi   gāo   tóu

When a final has two or more vowels, and the first vowel of the final is "i", "u" or "ü", the tone mark is usually written over the second vowel of the final, for example:

jiā   qiē   piāo   liǔ
guā   duō   kuài   tuǐ   lüè
nián   guān   quān
xiǎng   qióng   chuáng

2. Syllable-dividing mark 🎧

When two syllables go together and the second syllable begins with "a", "o" or "e", a syllable-dividing mark " ' " is used in between, for example:

pí'ǎo *fur jacket* 皮袄   **píng'ān** *safe* 平安
ēn'ài *affectionate love* 恩爱   **nǚ'ér** *daughter* 女儿
shí'èr *12* 十二   **jī'è** *hungry* 饥饿
mù'ǒu *wooden image* 木偶   **hǎi'ōu** *seagull* 海鸥

⟲IV Pronunciation modification

1. The neutral tone 🎧

Some syllables are pronounced short and soft. This is called "the neutral tone". No tone mark is written over the neutral-tone syllable, for example:

wǒmen *we* 我们   **shétou** *tongue* 舌头
wǎnshang *evening* 晚上   **háizi** *child* 孩子
shénme *what* 什么   **chī le** *ate* 吃了
shíhou *time* 时候   **shìde** *yes* 是的
piàoliang *beautiful* 漂亮   **wǒ de shū** *my book* 我的书
lǐbian *inside* 里边   **duìbuqǐ** *sorry* 对不起
bàba *father* 爸爸   **hǎo ba** *OK* 好吧
shìshi *try on* 试试   **nǐ hǎo ma** *how are you* 你好吗

2. Tonal modification 🎧

(1) **yī** 一 *one*

"yī 一" is pronounced in the 1st tone when it indicates number counting, ordinal numbers, or is at the end of a word or expression, for example:

yī one 一

dì-yī first 第一

èrshíyī 21 二十一

tǒngyī unify 统一

When followed by a 1st, 2nd or 3rd tone syllable, "yī 一" is pronounced in the 4th tone, for example:

yì tiān whole day 一天

yìzhí straight 一直

yì nián one year 一年

yìqǐ together 一起

When it is followed by a 4th tone syllable, "yī" is pronounced in the 2nd tone, for example:

yídìng certainly 一定

yígòng total 一共

yílù-píng'ān have a safe trip 一路平安

(2) **bù** 不 no

Generally "**bù**" is pronounced in the 4th tone, for example:

bù chī don't eat 不吃

bù hǎo not good 不好

bù tián not sweet 不甜

bù xǐhuan don't like 不喜欢

But when followed by a 4th tone syllable, it changes to the 2nd tone, for example:

bú shì to be not 不是

bú kèqi you are welcome 不客气

bú yòng needn't 不用

(3) Modification of the 3rd tone

（ i ）3rd tone + 3rd tone. When two 3rd tones are put together, the first one should be pronounced in the 2nd tone, for example:

shuǐguǒ fruit 水果

bǎoxiǎn insurance 保险

lěngshuǐ cold water 冷水

kěyǐ can 可以

nǐ hǎo how are you 你好

xǐzǎo bathe 洗澡

（ii）3rd +1st/2nd/4th/neutral tone. Only the first half of the 3rd tone is to be pronounced together with the 1st/2nd/4th/neutral tone, for example:

guǒzhī fruit juice 果汁

yǐqián before 以前

měilì beautiful 美丽

wǎnshang evening 晚上

hǎibiān seaside 海边

lǚyóu travel 旅游

qǐng jìn come in 请进

yǎnjing eye 眼睛

3. R-final 🎧

The special final "er" cannot be combined with any initials.

But "er" can be used as a final ending, it is written as "r" and is called "R-final" (**érhuàyùn** 儿化韵), for example:

huā ér — **huār** flower 花儿

niǎo ér — **niǎor** bird 鸟儿

lǎotóu ér — lǎotóu<u>r</u> *old man* 老头儿

xiǎohái ér — xiǎohái<u>r</u> *child* 小孩儿

gōngyuán ér — gōngyuán<u>r</u> *park* 公园儿

miàntiáo ér — miàntiáo<u>r</u> *noodles* 面条儿

yìdiǎn ér — yìdiǎn<u>r</u> *a little* 一点儿

bàntiān ér — bàntiān<u>r</u> *half day* 半天儿

chàng gē ér — chàng gē<u>r</u> *sing a song* 唱歌儿

guǎi wān ér — guǎi wān<u>r</u> *turn* 拐弯儿

R-finals are generally used for something that is small, lovely or kind.

读拼音学汉语

1 Nín guìxìng?

What's your surname?

您 贵 姓?

Key points

1 "What" in Chinese
2 Greetings
3 Asking and saying names

⊃ Start here

Listen and repeat. 🎧

◁ Greetings

Nǐ hǎo. 你 好。	*Hello.*	**Wǎnshang hǎo.** 晚 上 好。	*Good evening.*

Zǎoshang hǎo. / Nín zǎo.
早 上 好。 您 早。 *Good morning.*

◁ Polite expressions (1)

guìxìng
贵 姓
(a polite expression used to ask about people's surnames) **guì** 贵 *honorable,* **xìng** 姓 *surname*

qǐngwèn
请 问
(a polite expression used for making inquiries) **qǐng** 请 *please,* **wèn** 问 *ask*

Xièxie.
谢 谢。 *Thanks.*

Bú kèqi.
不 客 气。 *You are welcome.*

Zàijiàn.
再 见。 *Goodbye.*

◁ Personal pronouns

Singular		Plural (singular + **men** 们)	
wǒ 我	*I*	**wǒmen** 我 们	*we*
nǐ 你	*you*	**nǐmen** 你 们	*you*
tā 他／她	*he / she*	**tāmen** 他 们／她们	*they*

> **Notes**
>
> **nín** 您 *is a polite form of* **nǐ** *you* 你 *used when addressing elder people or those in upper social status.*
>
> **men** 们 *is used after a personal pronoun or noun referring to a person to show plural form, e.g.* **wǒmen** *we* 我们, **nǚshìmen** *ladies* 女士们.
> *But you cannot add a quantity word before the plural form.*

1

A: **Nín hǎo! Wǒ jiào Lǐ Tāo. Qǐngwèn, nín guìxìng?**

Hello! I'm Li Tao. Excuse me, what's your surname?
您好！我叫李涛。请问，您贵姓?

B: **Wǒ xìng Wáng.**
My surname is Wang.
我姓王。

Wǒ jiào Wáng Liàng.
I'm Wang Liang.
我叫王亮。

Tā xìng Zhāng, jiào Lányīng.
Her surname is Zhang, and her first name is Lanying.
她姓张，叫兰英。

A: **Wáng xiānsheng、Zhāng nǚshì, nǐmen hǎo ma?**
Mr. Wang, Ms. Zhang, how are you?
王先生、张女士，你们好吗?

B: **Hěn hǎo. Xièxie.**
Fine. Thank you.
很好。谢谢。

hǎo 好	*good, fine*	
(**huài** 坏	*bad*)	
jiào 叫	*be called*	
xiānsheng 先 生	*Mr., gentleman*	
nǚshì 女 士	*Ms., lady, madam*	
ma 吗	*(mark of question)*	
(See "Grammar Outline", P202)		
hěn 很	*very*	

2

A: **Qǐngwèn, Lǐ xiānsheng, nín jiào shénme míngzi?**
Excuse me, what's your given name, Mr. Li?
请问，李先生，您叫什么名字?

B: **Wǒ jiào Zhìwén.**
My given name is Zhiwen.
我叫志文。

A: **Nín de nǚpéngyou jiào shénme?**
What's your girlfriend's name?
您的女朋友叫什么?

B: **Tā jiào Yùfēn.**
Her name is Yufen.
她叫玉芬。

A: **Tā hǎo ma?**
How is she?
她好吗?

shénme 什 么	*what*
míngzi 名 字	*full name, given name*
nǚ 女	*female*
péngyou 朋 友	*friend*

2

B: Tā hěn hǎo. Wáng nǚshì, nǐ de nánpéngyou jiào shénme?
She is fine. What's your boyfriend's name, Ms. Wang?
她很好。王女士，你的男朋友叫什么？

A: Tā jiào Liú Míng.
His name is Liu Ming.
他叫刘明。

B: Wèn tā hǎo!
Say hello to him for me, please.
问他好！

A: Xièxie nǐ de wènhòu.
Thanks for your regards.
谢谢你的问候。

B: Bú kèqi. Zàijiàn.
You are welcome. Goodbye.
不客气。再见。

A: Zàijiàn.
Goodbye.
再见。

nán 男	*male*
bù 不	*no, not*
wènhòu 问 候	*regards*

Notes

de 的 *is usually used after a noun or a pronoun to indicate a possessive relationship. It can be omitted when the relationship is clear, e.g.* **wǒ (de) péngyou** *my friend* 我(的)朋友.

3

A: Zǎoshang hǎo, Xiǎo Lǐ!
Good morning, Xiao Li !
早上好，小李！

B: Lǎo Wáng, nín zǎo!
Good morning, Lao Wang!
老王，您早！

A: Hǎojiǔ bú jiàn nǐ de péngyou Xiǎo Zhāng, tā hǎo ma?
I haven't seen your friend Xiao Zhang for a long time. How is he?
好久不见你的朋友小张，他好吗？

zǎoshang / zǎochen 早 上 ／ 早 晨	*early morning*
(**wǎnshang** 晚 上	*evening*)
hǎojiǔ 好 久	*a long time*
jiàn 见	*see*

16

B: **Tā hěn hǎo. Lǎo Wáng, nǐ hǎo ma?**
He's fine. How are you, Lao Wang?
他很好。老王，你好吗？

A: **Hěn hǎo. Xièxie.**
I'm fine. Thank you.
很好。谢谢。

Notes

xiǎo 小 *is used before someone's surname, usually an acquaintance who is younger than you, e.g.* **Xiǎo Lǐ** 小李.
lǎo 老 *is used before someone's surname, usually an acquaintance who is older than you, e.g.* **Lǎo Wáng** 老王.

Form

shénme 什么

	In Chinese	In English
Interrogative sentences	**shénme** 什么 *is positioned in the question in a way that tells where the answer is to be placed in the reply.* **Nǐ xìng shénme?** 你 姓 什 么？ **Tā jiào shénme (míngzi)?** 她 叫 什么 （名字）？	*"What" is usually positioned at the beginning of the sentence.* *What's your surname?* *What's her name?*
Answers	**Wǒ xìng Lǐ.** 我 姓 李。 **Tā jiào Lányīng.** 她 叫 兰 英。	*My surname is Li.* *Her name is Lanying.*
Short answers	**(Xìng) Lǐ.** （姓） 李。 **(Jiào) Lányīng.** （叫） 兰 英。	*(My surname is) Li .* *(Her name is) Lanying.*

⊃ Exercises

✎ 1. Fill in the blanks after listening. 🎧

A: _____, nín guìxìng?

B: Wǒ _____ Liú.

A: Nín jiào _____ ?

B: Wǒ _____ Liú Hǎi.

A: Tā jiào shénme _____?

B: Tā jiào Zhāng Jūn. Xiānsheng, nín _____?

A: Xìng _____.

B: Jiào shénme _____?

A: Lǐ Jiànguó.

✎ 2. Put the words in the correct order.

(1) Wǒ Zhāng xìng.

_____.

(2) Xiānsheng Huáng nín hǎo!

_____!

(3) Lǐ xiānsheng shénme míngzi nín jiào?

_____?

(4) Xiānsheng xìng guì nín?

_____?

(5) Wǒ jiào Wáng xìng Zhìqiáng.

_____.

✎ 3. Put the sentences in the correct order after listening. 🎧

(1) Tā hěn hǎo. Xièxie! Zàijiàn!

(2) Lǎo Liú, hǎojiǔ bú jiàn!

(3) Hǎo. Nǐ de péngyou Xiǎo Wú hǎo ma?

(4) Hǎojiǔ bú jiàn, Lǎo Zhāo. Nǐ hǎo ma?

(5) Zàijiàn!

( ) → ( ) → ( ) → ( ) → ( )

✎ 4. Circle the right answers after listening. 🎧

(1) Wǒ de hǎo péngyou xìng _____.

A. Liú   B. Qiú   C. Niú

(2) Lǐ nǚshì jiào Lǐ _____ .

    A. Yíngchūn   B. Yǎngchūn   C. Yīngshùn

(3) Zǎoshang hǎo, _____ xiānsheng!

    A. Cháng   B. Huáng   C. Wáng

(4) Tā nánpéngyou de míngzi jiào _____.

    A. Lǐ Dàjiān   B. Mǐ Dàshān   C. Lǔ Dàshuān

5. Choose the correct answers.

(1) Zǎoshang hao!

    A. Xièxie!   B. Nín zǎo!   C. Zàijiàn!

(2) Nín guìxìng?

    A. Wǒ xìng Xiǎohuá.   B. Wǒ xìng Huáng Xiǎohuá. C. Wǒ xìng Huáng.

(3) Tā xìng shénme?

    A. Wǒ xìng Lǐ.   B. Tā xìng Lǐ Yīng.   C. Tā xìng Lǐ.

(4) Nǐ jiào shénme míngzi?

    A. Wǒ jiào Jiànguó.   B. Wǒ jiào Zhāng.   C. Wǒ jiào Zhāng xiānsheng.

6. Write questions for the answers provided below.

(1) _____?

Wǒ xìng Wáng.

(2) _____?

Wǒ jiào Wáng Fāng.

(3) _____?

Tā xìng Zhāng.

(4) _____?

Zhào nǚshì jiào Zhào Huá.

(5) _____?

Liú xiānsheng hěn hǎo. Xièxie!

7. Ask and answer questions about each other's name.

读
拼
音
学
汉
语

Asking surnames

The English name pattern is: first name + middle name + surname.
The Chinese name pattern is: surname + given name.

*Unlike Westerners, Chinese put their surnames before given names and they tend to use "**Nín guìxìng?** 您贵姓？" to ask people's surnames. When you have known the person's surname, you can address him/her "**Wáng xiānsheng** 王先生", "**Lǐ nǚshì** 李女士", "**Zhāng xiǎojiě** 张小姐 (Miss)", etc. You can also use the surname before his/her title, such as "**Lǐ lǎoshī** 李老师 (teacher)", "**Liú jīnglǐ** 刘经理 (manager)", etc.*

*Chinese usually use "**lǎo** 老" which means "old" before surnames to address elder people to show respect and use "**xiǎo** 小" which means "young" before surnames to address younger people to show geniality.*

*In China, wives keep their own surnames after getting married. But their husbands' surnames will be used when the wives are called "**tàitai** 太太 (Mrs.)".*

*The most common Chinese surnames are: **Wáng** 王, **Lǐ** 李, **Zhāng** 张, **Liú** 刘, **Chén** 陈 and **Zhào** 赵, etc. A small number of surnames have two syllables, e.g. **Ōuyáng** 欧阳, **Zhūgě** 诸葛, etc.*

2 Nǐ shì nǎ guó rén?
What's your nationality?
你是哪国人？

Key points

1 "Who" in Chinese
2 Verb "be" in Chinese
3 Marks of question **ma** 吗 and **ne** 呢
4 Talking about nationalities

⊃ Start here

Listen and repeat. 🎧

China

UK

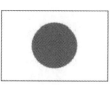

Japan

Australia

USA

Canada

South Korea

New Zealand

◁ Countries and nationalities

guó(jiā) 国（家）	country	**rén** 人	person
Zhōngguó 中 国	China	**Zhōngguórén** 中 国 人	Chinese
Měiguó 美 国	USA	**Měiguórén** 美 国 人	American
Yīngguó 英 国	UK	**Yīngguórén** 英 国 人	British
Jiānádà 加 拿 大	Canada	**Jiānádàrén** 加 拿 大 人	Canadian
Rìběn 日 本	Japan	**Rìběnrén** 日 本 人	Japanese
Hánguó 韩 国	South Korea	**Hánguórén** 韩 国 人	South Korean
Àodàlìyà 澳 大 利 亚	Australia	**Àodàlìyàrén** 澳 大 利 亚 人	Australian
Xīnxīlán 新 西 兰	New Zealand	**Xīnxīlánrén** 新 西 兰 人	New Zealander

1

T: **Tóngxuémen hǎo!**
Hello, everyone!
同学们好！

S: **Lǎoshī hǎo!**
Hello, sir/ma'am!
老师好！

T: **Wǒ xìng Liú, jiào Qǐmíng. Wǒ shì Zhōngguórén.**
My surname is Liu. My first name is Qiming.
I'm Chinese.
我姓刘，叫启明。我是中国人。

Nǐmen shì wǒ de xuésheng. Qǐng jièshào nǐmen zìjǐ.
You are my students. Please introduce yourselves.
你们是我的学生。请介绍你们自己。

A: **Wǒ jiào Dàwèi.**
My name is David.
我叫大卫。

T: **Dàwèi, nǐ shì nǎ guó rén?**
David, what's your nationality?
大卫，你是哪国人？

A: **Yīngguórén.**
British.
英国人。

B: **Wǒ shì Àodàlìyàrén, jiào Mǎlìyà.**
I'm Australian. My name is Maria.
我是澳大利亚人，叫玛丽亚。

C: **Wǒ jiào Líndá, shì Jiānádàrén.**
My name is Linda. I'm Canadian.
我叫琳达，是加拿大人。

D: **Wǒ yě shì Jiānádàrén, jiào Bǐ'ěr.**
I'm Canadian, too. My name is Bill.
我也是加拿大人，叫比尔。

T: **Nǐmen ne?**
How about you?
你们呢？

E: **Wǒ shì Hánguórén, xìng Piáo, jiào Piáo Jīnzhé.**
I'm South Korean. My surname is Park. My full name is Park Kimcher.
我是韩国人，姓朴，叫朴金哲。

tóngxué 同 学	classmate
lǎoshī / jiàoshī 老 师／教 师	teacher
shì 是	be
(**bú shì** 不 是	be not)
xuésheng 学 生	student
jièshào 介 绍	introduce
zìjǐ 自 己	oneself
nǎ 哪	which
yě 也	too
ne 呢	

(mark of question)
(See "Grammar Outline", P202)

1

F: **Wǒ shì Rìběnrén, xìng Shānběn, jiào Shānběn Yīláng.**
I'm Japanese. My surname is Yamamoto. My full name is Yamamoto Ichiro.
我是日本人，姓山本，叫山本一郎。

G: **Wǒ jiào Qiáoyī, shì Měiguórén.**
My name is Joy. I'm American.
我叫乔伊，是美国人。

2

A: **Xiǎo Wáng, zhè shì wǒ de péngyou Jiékè, Xīnxīlánrén.**
Xiao Wang, this is my friend Jack, a New Zealander.
小王，这是我的朋友杰克，新西兰人。

B: **Nǐ hǎo, Jiékè! Hěn gāoxìng rènshi nǐ.**
Hello, Jack! Nice to meet you.
你好，杰克！很高兴认识你。

A: **Jiékè, zhè shì wǒ de tóngshì Xiǎo Wáng, Zhōngguórén.**
Jack, this is my colleague Xiao Wang. He is Chinese.
杰克，这是我的同事小王，中国人。

C: **Rènshi nǐ wǒ yě hěn gāoxìng.**
Nice to meet you, too.
认识你我也很高兴。

gāoxìng	
高 兴	*glad, happy*
rènshi	
认 识	*know*
tóngshì	
同 事	*colleague*

3

A: **Shéi ya?**
Who?
谁呀？

B: **Wǒ.**
It's me.
我。

A: **Nǐ shì shéi?**
Who are you?
你是谁？

B: **Ānnà.**
Anna.
安娜。

shéi / shuí	
谁	*who*
ya	*(to show a tone*
呀	*of question)*

3

A: **Nǐ zhǎo shéi?**
Who are you looking for?
你找谁?

B: **Líndá.**
Linda.
琳达。

A: **Nǐ shì tā de tóngxué ma?**
Are you her classmate?
你是她的同学吗?

B: **Shì de.**
Yes, I am.
是的。

A: **Qǐng jìn.**
Come in, please.
请进。

zhǎo 找	*look for*
Qǐng jìn. 请进。	*Come in, please.*
jìn / jìnlái 进／进来	*come in*
(**chū / chūlái** 出／ 出来	*come out*)

2

你
是
哪
国
人
?

Notes

de 的 *is used at the end of a declarative sentence to show a tone of affirmation, e.g.* **Shì de.** *Yes.* 是的。 **Hǎo de.** *OK.* 好的。

 Form

shéi 谁

	In Chinese	In English
Interrogative sentences	**shéi** 谁 *is positioned in the question in a way that tells where the answer is to be placed in the reply.* **Nǐ shì <u>shéi</u>?** 你 是 谁? **<u>Shéi</u> shì lǎoshī?** 谁 是 老师?	*"Who" is usually positioned at the beginning of the sentence.* *Who are you?* *Who is the teacher?*

	In Chinese	In English
Answers	**Wǒ shì Xiǎo Wáng.** 我 是 小 王。 **Liú xiānsheng shì lǎoshī.** 刘 先生 是 老师。	*I am Xiao Wang.* *Mr. Liu is the teacher.*
Short answers	**Xiǎo Wáng.** 小 王。 **Liú xiānsheng.** 刘 先生。	*Xiao Wang.* *Mr. Liu.*

shì 是 and ma 吗

	In Chinese	In English
Interrogative sentences 1	*Declarative sentence with* **shì** 是 + ····· **ma** 吗 **Nǐ <u>shì</u> xuésheng <u>ma</u>?** 你 是 学 生 吗？ **Mǎkè <u>shì</u> nǐ de péngyou <u>ma</u>?** 马克 是你的 朋 友吗？	*The verb "be" is at the beginning of the sentence.* *Are you a student?* *Is Mark your friend?*
Interrogative sentences 2	*Noun/Pronoun* + **shì** 是 + **bú shì** 不是 + *noun* **Nǐ <u>shì</u> <u>bu</u> <u>shì</u> xuésheng?** 你 是 不 是 学 生？ **Mǎkè <u>shì</u> <u>bu</u> <u>shì</u> nǐ de** 马克 是 不 是 你 的 **péngyou?** 朋 友？	*Are you a student? /* *Are you a student or not?* *Is Mark your friend? /* *Is Mark your friend or not?*

	In Chinese	In English
Answers	*Positive:* **Wǒ <u>shì</u> xuésheng.** 我 是 学 生。 **Mǎkè <u>shì</u> wǒ de péngyou.** 马 克 是 我 的 朋 友。 *Negative:* **Wǒ <u>bú</u> <u>shì</u> xuésheng.** 我 不 是 学 生。 **Mǎkè <u>bú</u> <u>shì</u> wǒ de péngyou.** 马 克 不 是 我 的 朋 友。	*Positive:* *Yes, I am a student.* *Yes, Mark is my friend.* *Negative:* *No, I'm not a student.* *No, Mark isn't my friend.*
Short answers	**<u>Shì</u>.** 是。 **<u>Bú</u> <u>shì</u>.** 不 是。	*Yes, I am. / Yes, he is.* *No, I'm not. / No, he isn't.*

ne 呢

When the context is clear, we can omit the predicate of the previous sentence.

In Chinese	In English
Wǒ shì xuésheng, nǐ <u>ne</u>? 我 是 学 生，你 呢？ ⎛ **Wǒ shì xuésheng, nǐ <u>shì</u>** ＝ 我 是 学 生， 你 是 **<u>xuésheng ma</u>?** ⎞ 学 生 吗？ **Wǒ yě shì.** 我 也 是。	*I'm a student. How about you?* *I'm a student, too.*
Wrong	✕ **Nǐ shì xuésheng ne?**　✕ **Nǐ ma?**

⊃ Exercises

◁ 1. Substitution reading. 🎧

(1)

Nǐ	shì	xuésheng	ma?
你	是	学 生	吗?
Tā		Měiguórén	
她		美 国 人	
Xiǎo Liú		nǐ de tóngxué	
小 刘		你 的 同 学	
Lǐ xiānsheng		wǒmen de lǎoshī	
李 先 生		我 们 的 老 师	

(2)

Nǐ	shì bu shì	xìng Wáng?
你	是 不 是	姓 王?
Tā		nǐ de péngyou?
他		你 的 朋 友?
Xiǎo Jīn		Hánguórén?
小 金		韩 国 人?
Dàiwéi		nǐ de tóngshì?
戴 维		你 的 同 事?

(3)

Wǒ shì xuésheng,	nǐ	ne?
我 是 学 生,	你	呢?
Mǎ xiānsheng shì lǎoshī,	Wú nǚshì	
马 先 生 是 老师,	吴 女 士	
Wǒ rènshi Nínà,	nǐ	
我 认 识 尼娜,	你	
Tāmen hěn gāoxìng,	nǐmen	
他 们 很 高 兴,	你 们	

◁ 2. Choose the question words which best fit in these sentences.

ma 吗	shéi 谁	nǎ 哪	ne 呢
shì bu shì 是不是		shénme 什么	

(1) Tā shì _____?

(2) Nǐ jiào _____ míngzi?

(3) _____ shì wǒmen de lǎoshī?

(4) Nǐ rènshi wǒ de péngyou Zhāng Liàng _____ ?

(5) Lǐ Lányīng _____ nǐ de tóngshì?

(6) Lǎoshī xìng _____ ?

(7) Mǎlìyà shì _____ guó rén?

(8) Wáng Píng yě shì Rìběnrén _____ ?

(9) Tāmen shì Yīngguórén. Nǐ _____ ?

(10) Nǐ de péngyou _____ xìng Wáng?

3. Use suitable words to fill in the blanks, and then practice the dialogue.

A: _____ shì _____ ma?

B: Wǒ _____ xuésheng.

A: Tā _____ lǎoshī ma?

B: Bù, tā _____ lǎoshī.

A: _____ shì bu shì _____ ?

B: Shì de, wǒmen _____ tóngxué.

A: Tāmen _____ Àodàlìyàrén ?

B: _____ , _____ shì Xīnxīlánrén.

A: Nǐ _____ ?

B: Wǒ shì Zhōngguórén.

4. Listen to the passage and tell whether the statements are true (√) or false (×). 🎧

(1) Liú xiānsheng shì Zhōngguórén. ( )

(2) Líndá shì Àodàlìyàrén. ( )

(3) Mǎlìyà shì Liú lǎoshī de xuésheng. ( )

(4) Wǒ de tóngxué jiào Chálǐ. ( )

(5) Chálǐ shì Měiguórén. ( )

(6) Chálǐ yě shì Liú lǎoshī de xuésheng. ( )

5. Answer these questions after listening. 🎧

(1) Xiǎo Wáng jiào shénme míngzi? _____

(2) Xiǎo Wáng de tóngxué shì nǎ guó rén? _____

(3) Shéi shì tāmen de lǎoshī? _____

(4) Nǐnǎ hé Xiǎo Wáng shì bu shì tóngxué? _____

(5) Bǎoluó shì Yīngguórén ma? _____

(6) Xiǎo Wáng shì Zhōngguórén, Shānběn ne? _____

◁ 6. Introduce yourself.
(1) *What's your full name?*
(2) *What's your nationality?*

⊃ Cultural tip

How happy we are, to meet friends from afar !

More and more international students are coming to China since the "reform and opening up" policy took effect in the end of 1970s. There are more than 500 universities offering programs for international students and the number of overseas students reached more than 290,000 in 2011. They are from different countries and are friends of the Chinese. As the old saying states, "How happy we are, to meet friends from afar!" **(Yǒu péng zì yuǎnfāng lái, bú yì lè hu! 有朋自远方来，不亦乐乎！)**

3 Nǐ yǒu dìdi ma?

Have you got any younger brothers?

你有弟弟吗？

Key points

1 "Have" and "there + be" in Chinese
2 Talking about family

⊃ Start here

Listen and repeat. 🎧

⩘ Family members

bàba 爸爸	father	**mèimei** 妹妹	younger sister
māma 妈妈	mother	**zhàngfu** 丈夫	husband
yéye 爷爷	grandfather	**qīzi** 妻子	wife
nǎinai 奶奶	grandmother	**érzi** 儿子	son
gēge 哥哥	elder brother	**nǚ'ér** 女儿	daughter
jiějie 姐姐	elder sister	**sūnzi** 孙子	grandson
dìdi 弟弟	younger brother	**sūnnǚ** 孙女	granddaughter

⟶ Dialogues

1

A: **Zhè shì nǐ jiā de zhàopiàn ma?**
Is this the photo of your family?
这是你家的照片吗?

B: **Shì de.**
Yes, it is.
是的。

A: **Tāmen shì shéi?**
Who are they?
他们是谁?

B: **Wǒ de yéye、nǎinai、bàba、māma hé mèimei.**
They are my grandfather, grandmother, father, mother and younger sister.
我的爷爷、奶奶、爸爸、妈妈和妹妹。

A: **Nǐ yǒu dìdi ma?**
Have you got any younger brothers?
你有弟弟吗?

B: **Méiyǒu.**
No, I haven't.
没有。

A: **Yǒu gēge hé jiějie ma?**
Do you have any elder brothers or sisters?
有哥哥和姐姐吗?

B: **Yě méiyǒu.**
No, I don't.
也没有。

A: **Nǐ bàba zuò shénme gōngzuò?**
What does your father do?
你爸爸做什么工作?

B: **Wǒ bàba shì yīshēng, māma shì hùshi.**
My father is a doctor. My mother is a nurse.
我爸爸是医生,妈妈是护士。

Báitiān, tāmen qù yīyuàn shàngbān, wǒ hé mèimei qù shàngxué, yéye nǎinai zài jiā.
During the daytime they go to work in the hospital. My younger sister and I go to school. My grandfather and grandmother are at home.
白天,他们去医院上班,我和妹妹去上学,爷爷奶奶在家。

zhè 这		*this*
zhàopiàn 照片		*photo*
hé 和		*and*
yǒu 有		*have, there be*
méi(yǒu) 没(有)		*haven't, there be not*
zuò 做		*do*
gōngzuò 工作		*job, work*
yīshēng 医生		*doctor*
hùshi 护士		*nurse*
báitiān 白天		*daytime*
qù 去		*go*
(**lái** 来	*come*)	
(See "Grammar Outline", P215)		
yīyuàn 医院		*hospital*
shàngbān 上班		*go to work*
(**xiàbān** 下班	*finish work*)	
shàngxué 上学		*go to school*
(**xuéxiào** 学校	*school*)	
zài 在		*(similar to "be+on/at/in")*

1

Wǎnshang, wǒmen dàjiā zài yìqǐ, hěn kuàilè.
We are together in the evening and are very happy.
晚上，我们大家在一起，很快乐。

jiā 家	*home*
dàjiā 大家	*everybody*
yìqǐ 一起	*together*
kuàilè 快乐	*happy*

2

Nina: **Lùxī, nǐ de zhàngfu shì Xīméng ma?**
Lucy, is your husband Simon?
露西，你的丈夫是西蒙吗？

Lucy: **Shì de. Wǒmen shì dàxué tóngxué.**
Yes, he is. We used to be classmates when we were at university.
是的。我们是大学同学。

Nina: **Nǐmen zuò shénme gōngzuò?**
What do you do?
你们做什么工作？

Lucy: **Wǒ shì kuàijì, tā shì gōngchéngshī.**
I'm an accountant. He's an engineer.
我是会计，他是工程师。

Nina: **Nǐmen yǒu érzi ma?**
Do you have any sons?
你们有儿子吗？

Lucy: **Méiyǒu.**
No, we don't.
没有。

Nina: **Yǒu nǚ'ér ma?**
Do you have any daughters?
有女儿吗？

Lucy: **Yǒu yí gè nǚ'ér. Tā jiào Àimǎ, shì zhōng-xuéshēng. Wǒmen dōu ài tā.**
Yes, we have a daughter. Her name is Emma. She is a middle school student. We both love her.
有一个女儿。她叫艾玛，是中学生。我们都爱她。

dàxué 大学	*university*
kuàijì 会计	*accountant*
gōngchéngshī 工程师	*engineer*
gè 个	*(measurement word)*
zhōngxuéshēng 中学生 *middle school student* **zhōngxué** 中学 *middle school*	
dōu 都	*all*
ài 爱	*love, like*

⟳ Form

yǒu 有

	In Chinese	In English
Interrogative sentences 1	*Declarative sentence with* **yǒu** 有 + **ma** 吗 (1) **Nǐ yǒu dìdi ma?** 你 有 弟弟 吗? (2) **Nǐ jiā yǒu tā de zhàopiàn** 你 家 有 她 的 照 片 **ma?** 吗?	*Use "do" or move the verb "have" to the beginning of sentence.* (1) *Do you have any younger brothers?* *Have you got any younger brothers?* (2) *Are there any photos of hers in your home?*
Interrogative sentences 2	*Noun/Pronoun* + **yǒu** 有 + **méiyǒu** 没有 + *noun* (1) **Nǐ yǒu méiyǒu dìdi?** 你 有 没 有 弟弟? (2) **Nǐ jiā yǒu méiyǒu tā** 你 家 有 没 有 她 **de zhàopiàn?** 的 照 片?	(1) *Do you have any younger brothers? / Do you or don't you have any younger brothers?* *Have you got any younger brothers? / Have you or haven't you got any younger brothers?* (2) *Are there any photos of hers in your home?* *Are there or aren't there any photos of hers in your home?*
Answers	*Positive:* (1) **Wǒ yǒu dìdi.** 我 有 弟弟。 (2) **Wǒ jiā yǒu tā de zhàopiàn.** 我 家 有 她 的 照 片。 *Negative:* (1) **Wǒ méiyǒu dìdi.** 我 没 有 弟弟。	*Positive:* (1) *Yes, I've got a younger brother.* (2) *Yes, there are photos of hers in my home.* *Negative:* (1) *No, I haven't any younger brother.*

	In Chinese	In English
Answers	(2) **Wǒ jiā méiyǒu tā de** 我 家 没 有 她 的 **zhàopiàn.** 照 片。	(2) *No, there aren't any photos of hers in my home.*
Short answers	**Yǒu.** 有。 **Méiyǒu.** 没 有。	*Yes, I do/have.* *Yes, there are.* *No, I don't/haven't.* *No, there aren't.*

zài 在

It is used to indicate the situation about somebody or something. Its meaning is similar to "be + on/at/in…", but its grammatical function is equal to a verb.

In Chinese	In English
Nǐ gēge zài jiā ma? 你 哥哥 在 家 吗?	*Is your elder brother at home?*
Wǒ jiā zài Běijīng. 我 家 在 北京。	*My home is in Beijing.*
Wǒmen zài yìqǐ hěn kuàilè. 我 们 在 一起 很 快乐。	*We are very happy together.*

⟩ Exercises

◁ 1. Substitution reading. 🎧

(1) Tā yǒu
他　有

| gēge |
| 哥哥 |
| jiějie |
| 姐姐 |
| dìdi |
| 弟弟 |
| mèimei |
| 妹　妹 |

ma?
吗?

(2)

| Nǐ |
| 你 |
| Tā |
| 她 |
| Nǐ jiějie |
| 你　姐姐 |
| Tā gēge |
| 她　哥哥 |

yǒu méiyǒu
有　没　有

| zhàopiàn? |
| 照　片? |
| gōngzuò? |
| 工　作? |
| érzi? |
| 儿子? |
| nǚ'ér? |
| 女　儿? |

◁ 2. Look at the picture and write the relationship among the family members after listening. 🎧

(1) A shì B de _____.

(2) A hé B shì C de _____.

(3) D shì C de _____.

(4) E hé G shì C hé D de _____.

(5) F hé H shì C hé D de _____.

(6) E shì F、G hé H de _____.

(7) F shì G hé H de _____.

(8) G shì E hé F de _____.

(9) H shì E、F hé G de _____.

(10) A hé B shì E、F、G hé H de _____.

(11) E hé G shì A hé B de _____.

(12) F hé H shì A hé B de _____.

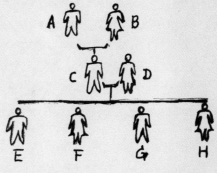

3. Choose the correct answers after listening. 🎧

(1) Mǎlìyà de gēge shì _____.

    A. lǎoshī   B. gōngchéngshī   C. kuàijì

(2) Jiékè yǒu _____.

    A. gēge   B. mèimei   C. dìdi

(3) Wǒ méiyǒu _____ tóngxué.

    A. Yīngguó   B. Zhōngguó   C. Měiguó

(4) Tā mèimei jiào _____.

    A. Fāngfang   B. Huáng Fāng   C. Wáng Fāng

(5) Xiǎo Wáng de _____ shì lǎoshī.

    A. bàba   B. māma   C. jiějie

(6) _____ xiānsheng shì wǒmen de lǎoshī.

    A. Liú   B. Niú   C. Lóu

4. Bring a photo of your family and introduce your family members to the classmates.

➲ Cultural tip

Chinese families

*Traditionally, Chinese families preferred having many children as they believed that the more children they had, the better life they would have. It was considered good fortune that four generations lived under one roof (**sì shì tóng táng** 四世同堂). The father or husband was in charge of the whole family. Children must obey their parents or other elders. For example, their marriage or careers were often arranged by parents. The treatment of females was inferior to males (**nán zūn nǚ bēi** 男尊女卑) and people brought up sons for their old age (**yǎng ér fáng lǎo** 养儿防老). These were the views of traditional families.*

Nowadays, the concept of family has changed. Generally, children will stay with their parents until marriage. Most young couples prefer living on their own after they get married.

In the 1980's, the "One Child" policy was introduced and only one child was allowed in each family. There are exceptions in minority groups, in areas where there is a labor shortage and in other special cases.

4 Zhè shì shéi de shūfáng?

Whose study is this?

这是谁的书房？

Key points

"Whose" and "whom" in Chinese

⤷ Start here

Listen and match the words with the pictures. 🎧

 1    2    3    4    5

 6   7    8   9    10

shū 书	*book*	( )	**zhǐ** 纸	*paper*	( )
zázhì 杂志	*magazine*	( )	**bào(zhǐ)** 报（纸）	*newspaper*	( )
cídiǎn 词典	*dictionary*	( )	**diànnǎo** 电脑	*computer*	( )
bǐ 笔	*pen*	( )	**qiānbǐ** 铅笔	*pencil*	( )
dìtú 地图	*map*	( )	**yuánzhūbǐ** 圆珠笔	*ballpoint pen*	( )

Listen and repeat. 🎧

Singular		Plural (singular + **xiē** 些)	
zhè 这	*this*	**zhèxiē** 这些	*these*
nà 那	*that*	**nàxiē** 那些	*those*

1

A: **Zhè shì shéi de shūfáng?**
Whose study is this?
这是谁的书房？

B: **Wǒmen de.**
It's ours.
我们的。

Wǒmen yǒu hěn duō shū, hái yǒu bù shǎo zázhì hé bàozhǐ.
We have many books, and also many magazines and newspapers.
我们有很多书，还有不少杂志和报纸。

A: **Zhèxiē Zhōngwénshū shì shéi de?**
To whom do these Chinese books belong?
这些中文书是谁的？

B: **Wǒ zhàngfu de.**
They're my husband's.
我丈夫的。

A: **Nàxiē Yīngwénshū shì shéi de?**
To whom do those English books belong?
那些英文书是谁的？

B: **Wǒ de. Wǒ hé zhàngfu xiàbān huílái, dōu xǐhuan dúshū kàn bào.**
They're mine. My husband and I like reading books and newspapers after coming back home from work.
我的。我和丈夫下班回来，都喜欢读书看报。

A: **Zhè shì shénme?**
What's this?
这是什么？

B: **Zhè shì cídiǎn. Nàxiē shì dìtú, yǒu Zhōngguó dìtú、Měiguó dìtú, hái yǒu shìjiè dìtú.**
This is a dictionary. Those are maps. There is a map of China, a map of the US and a map of the world.
这是词典。那些是地图，有中国地图、美国地图，还有世界地图。

shéi de 谁 的	whose
shūfáng 书 房	study
duō 多	many, much
shǎo 少	few, little
hái 还	also
Zhōngwén 中 文	Chinese (language)
Yīngwén 英 文	English
huílái 回 来	come back, return
xǐhuan 喜 欢	like
dúshū 读 书	read books, study
kàn bào 看 报	read newspapers
shìjiè 世 界	world

2

A: **Zhè diànnǎo shì shéi de?**
To whom does this computer belong?
这电脑是谁的？

B: **Wǒ de.**
It's mine.
我的。

Wǒ yòng tā shàngwǎng, zhǎo zīliào, shōufā diànzǐ yóujiàn.
I use it surfing the Net, looking up information, and receiving and sending E-mails.
我用它上网，找资料，收发电子邮件。

A: **Zhè běn 《Yīng–Zhōng Cídiǎn》 shì shéi de?**
To whom does the English-Chinese Dictionary belong?
这本《英中词典》是谁的？

B: **Wǒ qīzi de. Tā yòng tā xuéxí Yīngwén.**
It's my wife's. She uses it to learn English.
我妻子的。她用它学习英文。

A: **Zhèxiē zhǐ hé bǐ shì shéi de?**
To whom do these pieces of paper and pens belong?
这些纸和笔是谁的？

B: **Zhǐ shì wǒ nǚ'ér de, tā ài huà huàr; yuánzhūbǐ shì wǒ érzi de, tā xǐhuan xiě zì.**
The pieces of paper are my daughter's. She loves to draw pictures. The ballpoint pens are my son's. He loves to write Chinese characters.
纸是我女儿的，她爱画画儿；圆珠笔是我儿子的，他喜欢写字。

yòng 用	*use*	
tā 它	*it*	
shàngwǎng 上网	*surf the Net*	
zīliào 资料	*information*	
shōufā 收发	*receive and send* **shōu** 收 *receive*, **fā** 发 *send*	
diànzǐ yóujiàn 电子邮件	*E-mail*	
xué(xí) 学（习）	*learn*	
huà 画	*draw*	
huà(r) 画（儿）	*picture*	
xiě 写	*write*	
zì 字	*Chinese character*	

Notes

běn 本 *(measurement word) is used for book-like items, e.g.* **liǎng běn shū** *two books* 两本书, **yì běn zázhì** *a magazine* 一本杂志.

 Form

shéi de 谁的

	In Chinese	In English
Interrogative sentences	*The possessive question word* **shéi de**谁的 *is positioned in the sentence in a way that tells where the answer is to be placed in the reply.* **Zhè shì <u>shéi de</u> shū?** 这 是 谁 的 书? **Zhè shū shì <u>shéi de</u>?** 这 书 是 谁 的?	*The possessive question word is at the beginning of the sentence.* *Whose book is this?* *To whom does this book belong?*
	Wrong ✕ **Shéi de shū shì zhè?**	
Answers	**Zhè shì wǒ de shū.** 这 是 我 的 书。 **Zhè shū shì wǒ de.** 这 书 是 我 的。	*This is my book.* *This book is mine.*
Short sentences	*When the context is clear, some words in the sentence can be omitted.* **Shéi de?** 谁 的? *The answer can be shortened with only the possessive word left.* **Wǒ de.** 我 的。	*Whose book?* *It's mine.*

⊃ Exercises

↘ 1. Look at the pictures of "Start here" again and make a dialogue with a partner.

e.g. A: Zhè shì shénme?
What's this?
这是什么？

B: Zhè shì shū.
This is a book.
这是书。

A: Shéi de?
Whose book is this?
谁的？

B: Wǒ de.
It's mine.
我的。

A: Nàxiē shì shénme?
What are those?
那些是什么？

B: Nàxiē shì bàozhǐ.
Those are newspapers.
那些是报纸。

↘ 2. Substitution reading. 🎧

(1)
Zhè 这 Nà 那	shì shéi de 是 谁 的	qiānbǐ? 铅 笔? zázhì? 杂 志?

(2)
Zhè 这 Nà 那	shì 是	wǒ de 我 的 lǎoshī de 老 师 的	qiānbǐ. 铅 笔。 zázhì. 杂 志。

(3)
Zhè cídiǎn 这 词 典 Nà dìtú 那 地 图 Zhèxiē bǐ 这 些 笔 Nàxiē shū 那 些 书	shì shéi de? 是 谁 的?

(4) Zhè cídiǎn 这 词 典 Nà dìtú 那 地 图 Zhèxiē bǐ 这 些 笔 Nàxiē shū 那 些 书	shì 是	tā 他 gēge 哥 哥 yīshēng 医 生 tóngxué 同 学	de. 的。

3. Match the questions with the answers.

(1) Lǐ xiānsheng shì shéi de lǎoshī?
(2) Nǐ yǒu 《Zhōng-Yīng Cídiǎn》 ma?
(3) Xiǎo Wáng xǐhuan huà huàr ma?
(4) Dàwèi shì bu shì nǐ de tóngxué?
(5) Wǒ ài wǒ de jiā, nǐ ne?
(6) Zhè shì shìjiè dìtú ma?

a. Xǐhuan, tā yě xǐhuan xiě zì.
b. Bú shì, zhè shì Zhōngguó dìtú.
c. Méiyǒu, wǒ yǒu 《Yīng-Zhōng Cídiǎn》.
d. Tā shì wǒmen de lǎoshī.
e. Bú shì, tā shì Xiǎo Zhāng de tóngxué.
f. Wǒ yě ài wǒ de jiā.

4. Choose the correct words to fill in the blanks after listening.

lǎoshī	gēge	yīshēng	zhǐ
老 师	哥 哥	医 生	纸
zázhì	cídiǎn	yuánzhūbǐ	
杂 志	词 典	圆 珠 笔	
Zhōngwén bàozhǐ		Měiguó dìtú	
中 文 报 纸		美 国 地 图	

(1) Zhè shì yì běn _____.
(2) Nàxiē shì _____.
(3) Nàxiē _____ shì _____ de.
(4) Zhè shì _____ de _____.
(5) Nà běn _____ shì Lùxī de.
(6) Zhè běn _____ shì _____ de.

5. Draw pictures of the underlined items after listening.

(1) Zhào xiānsheng shì Yīngwén lǎoshī. Tā yǒu yì běn 《Yīng-Zhōng Cídiǎn》.
赵 先 生 是 英 文 老 师。他 有 一 本 《英 中 词 典》。

(2) Zhè shì yì zhāng wǒ hé qīzi de zhàopiàn, wǒ hěn xǐhuan.
这 是 一 张 我 和 妻 子 的 照 片，我 很 喜 欢。

(3) Xiǎo Lǐ ài xuéxí. Tā yǒu hěn duō shū.
小 李 爱 学 习。他 有 很 多 书。

(4) Zhèxiē bàozhǐ dōu shì Zhāng nǚshì de.
这 些 报纸 都 是 张 女士 的。

(5) Wǒ jiā yǒu hěn duō Yīngwén zázhì.
我 家 有 很 多 英 文 杂志。

(6) Zhè shì dìdi de qiānbǐ. Tā yòng tā huà huàr.
这 是 弟弟 的 铅笔。他 用 它 画 画儿。

(1)	(2)	(3)
(4)	(5)	(6)

⊃ Cultural tip

The four treasures of study

The writing brush, ink-stick, paper and ink-stone are called "the four treasures of study" **(wén fáng sì bǎo**文房四宝**)**. *They are Chinese-specific writing tools and are used to write books for either educational or recreational purposes. Different-sized brushes are used to create unique calligraphy as an art. The four treasures of study have a history of more than two thousand years.*

There are special places which are famous for producing the four treasures. For example, the brush Hubi **(Húbǐ** 湖笔**)** *is made in Huzhou in Zhejiang Province; the ink-stick Huimo* **(Huīmò** 徽墨**)** *is made in Huizhou in Anhui Province; the paper Xuanzhi* **(Xuānzhǐ** 宣纸**)** *is made in Xuancheng in Anhui Province and Duanyan* **(Duānyàn** 端砚**)** *is made in Zhaoqing Duanxi in Guangdong Province.*

5 Diànhuà hàomǎ shì duōshao?

What's the telephone number?

电话号码是多少？

Key points

1 Cardinal and ordinal numbers
2 **duōshao** 多少 and **jǐ** 几
3 "Where" in Chinese

Start here

Use hand language to express numbers.

yī 一 1	**èr** 二 2	**sān** 三 3	**sì** 四 4	**wǔ** 五 5
liù 六 6	**qī** 七 7	**bā** 八 8	**jiǔ** 九 9	**shí** 十 10

Listen and repeat. 🎧

↳ Cardinal numbers

(See "Grammar Outline", P218)

yī 一 1	**èrshí** 二十 20	**wàn** 万 10 thousand
èr 二 2	**sānshí** 三十 30	**shíwàn** 十万 100 thousand
sān 三 3	**sìshí** 四十 40	**bǎiwàn** 百万 million
sì 四 4	**wǔshí** 五十 50	**qiānwàn** 千万 10 million
wǔ 五 5	**liùshí** 六十 60	**yì** 亿 100 million
liù 六 6	**qīshí** 七十 70	**shíyì** 十亿 billion
qī 七 7	**bāshí** 八十 80	
bā 八 8	**jiǔshí** 九十 90	**líng** 零 zero
jiǔ 九 9	**bǎi** 百 hundred	**yāo** 幺 1
shí 十 10	**qiān** 千 thousand	**liǎng** 两 2

↖ Ordinal numbers

In Chinese, ordinal numbers are expressed by attaching the prefix **dì** 第 *to the cardinal numbers, e.g.*

dì–yī 第 一	*first*		**dì–shíyī** 第 十一	*eleventh*
dì–èr 第 二	*second*		**dì–shí'èr** 第 十二	*twelfth*
dì–sān 第 三	*third*		**dì–jiǔshíjiǔ** 第 九十九	*ninety-ninth*

⟳ Dialogues

1

A: **Xiǎo Zhōu, nǐ qù nǎr?**
Xiao Zhou, where are you going?
小周，你去哪儿？

B: **Wǒ qù Xiǎo Wáng jiā.**
I'm going to Xiao Wang's home.
我去小王家。

A: **Tā zhù zài nǎr?**
Where does he live?
他住在哪儿？

B: **Jiànguó Lù jiǔshíliù hào.**
Ninety-six Jianguo Road.
建国路九十六号。

A: **Wǒmen liǎ yìqǐ qí zìxíngchē qù, hǎo ma?**
Shall we go there together by bike?
我们俩一起骑自行车去，好吗？

B: **Bù, wǒmen zuò wǔshíqī lù gōngjiāochē qù ba.**
No, we'll go by bus No.57.
不，我们坐五十七路公交车去吧。

A: **Hǎo de. Xiān gěi tā dǎ yí gè diànhuà. Diànhuà hàomǎ shì duōshao?**
OK, but let's give him a call first. What's his telephone number?
好的。先给他打一个电话。电话号码是多少？

B: **Sì èr bā jiǔ sān líng yāo liù.**
42893016.
四二八九三零幺六。

A: **Wǒmen zǒu ba!**
Let's go!
我们走吧！

---

nǎr / nǎlǐ
哪儿／哪里 *where*

zhù
住   *live*

lù
路
road, route (It's also used for bus lines.)

hào
号
(used after numerals to indicate the number in a street)

liǎ
俩   *two*
(a fusion of **liǎng** 两 *and* **gè** 个*)*

qí
骑   *ride*

zìxíngchē
自 行 车 *bicycle, bike*
chē 车 *vehicle*

zuò / chéng	dǎ diànhuà
坐 / 乘	打 电 话　*make a call*
take (bus, taxi, plane, ship…)	**dǎ** 打 *make,* **diànhuà** 电话 *telephone*
gōngjiāochē / gōnggòng qìchē	**hàomǎ**
公 交 车 / 公 共 汽 车　*bus*	号 码　*number*
gōnggòng 公共 *public,* **qìchē** 汽车 *car*	**duōshao / jǐ**
xiān	多 少 / 几
先　　　*first*	*how many, how much, what number*
	(See "Grammar Outline", P206)
gěi	**zǒu**
给　　　*give*	走　　　*leave, go away*

Notes

ba 吧 *is used at the end of a declarative sentence to show a tone of consultation, request or acceptance, for example:*

Wǒmen zuò gōngjiāochē qù ba.
We'll go by bus.
我们坐公交车去吧。

Wǒmen zǒu ba!
Let's go!
我们走吧!

Hǎo ba!
OK!
好吧!

hǎo ma / hǎo bu hǎo
好 吗 / 好 不 好 *is usually put at the end of an interrogative sentence to ask for an opinion about a suggestion. The positive answer is* **hǎo** 好; *the negative answer is* **bù (hǎo)** 不(好).

2

A: **Wéi, chūzūchē gōngsī.**
Hello, this is the taxi company.
喂，出租车公司。

B: **Wǒ yào yí liàng chūzūchē.**
I need a taxi, please.
我要一辆出租车。

A: **Nín qù nǎr?**
Where are you going?
您去哪儿?

B: **Xiāngshān Gōngyuán.**
To Xiangshan Park.
香山公园。

A: **Qǐngwèn, nín zhù zài nǎr?**
Excuse me, where do you live?
请问，您住在哪儿?

B: **Wǒ zhù zài Xīnhuá Lù yìbǎi líng jiǔ hào.**
I live at 109 Xinhua Road .
我住在新华路一百零九号。

A: **Nín guìxìng?**
What's your surname?
您贵姓?

B: **Wǒ xìng Lǐ .**
My surname is Li.
我姓李。

A: **Nín de shǒujī hàomǎ shì duōshao?**
What's your mobile phone number?
您的手机号码是多少?

B: **Yāo sān liù sān jiǔ èr qī yāo sì wǔ liù.**
13639271456.
幺三六三九二七幺四五六。

A: **Qǐng shāo děng, chūzūchē yíhuìr dào.**
Wait a minute, please. The taxi will arrive soon.
请稍等，出租车一会儿到。

B: **Xièxie.**
Thanks.
谢谢。

wéi
喂 *hello*

chūzūchē
出租车 *taxi*

gōngsī
公司 *company*

yào
要 *want, need*

liàng
辆
(measurement word for vehicles)

gōngyuán
公园 *park*

shǒujī
手机 *mobile phone*

shāo děng
稍等 *wait a minute*

yíhuìr
一会儿 *soon*

dào
到 *arrive*

Form

duōshao 多少 / jǐ 几

	In Chinese	In English
Interrogative sentences	**duōshao** 多少 (+ noun / measurement word) **jǐ** 几 + measurement word **Tā de diànhuà hàomǎ shì** 他 的 电 话 号 码 是 **duōshao?** 多 少 ？	What's his telephone number?
	Nǐmen yīyuàn yǒu duōshao 你 们 医 院 有 多 少 **yīshēng?** 医 生 ？	How many doctors are there in your hospital?
	Nǐ jiā yǒu jǐ liàng qìchē? 你 家 有 几 辆 汽 车 ？	How many cars does your family have?
	Tā zhù zài Jiànguó Lù jǐ hào? 他 住 在 建 国 路 几 号 ？	What street number in Jianguo Road does he live at?
Answers	**Tā de diànhuà hàomǎ shì wǔ** 他 的 电 话 号 码 是 五 **sì bā yāo èr qī liù wǔ.** 四 八 幺 二 七 六 五 。	His telephone number is 54812765.
	Wǒmen yīyuàn yǒu liùshísān 我 们 医 院 有 六 十 三 **gè yīshēng.** 个 医 生 。	There are 63 doctors in our hospital.
	Wǒ jiā yǒu liǎng liàng qìchē. 我 家 有 两 辆 汽 车 。	We've got two cars in my family.
	Tā zhù zài Jiànguó Lù jiǔ hào. 他 住 在 建 国 路 九 号 。	He lives at 9 Jianguo Road.
Short answers	**Wǔ sì bā yāo èr qī liù wǔ.** 五 四 八 幺 二 七 六 五 。	54812765.
	Liùshísān gè. 六 十 三 个 。	63.
	Liǎng liàng. 两 辆 。	Two cars.
	Jiǔ hào. 九 号 。	The street number is nine.

52

nǎr 哪儿 / nǎlǐ 哪里

	In Chinese	In English
Interrogative sentences	**nǎr** 哪儿 *is positioned in the question in a way that tells where the answer is to be placed in the reply.* **Nǐ qù nǎr?** 你 去 哪儿？ **Tā shì nǎr de rén?** 她 是 哪儿的 人？ **Nǎr yǒu Zhōngwén cídiǎn?** 哪儿 有 中 文 词典？	*"Where" is usually positioned at the beginning of the sentence.* *Where are you going?* *Where does she come from?* *Where can I find a Chinese dictionary?*
	Wrong × **Nǎr nǐ qù?**	
Answers	**Wǒ qù Shànghǎi.** 我 去 上 海。 **Tā shì Běijīngrén.** 她 是 北 京 人。 **Wǒ de shūfáng yǒu Zhōngwén** 我 的 书 房 有 中 文 **cídiǎn.** 词 典。	*I'm going to Shanghai.* *She comes from Beijing.* *There is a Chinese dictionary in my study.*
Short answers	**(Qù) Shànghǎi.** （去） 上 海。 **Běijīngrén.** 北 京 人。 **Wǒ de shūfáng yǒu.** 我 的 书 房 有。	*Shanghai.* *From Beijing.* *In my study.*

➲ Exercises

↘1. Read the cardinal numbers after listening. 🎧

19 shíjiǔ
十九

100 yìbǎi
一百

605 liùbǎi líng wǔ
六 百 零 五

260 liǎng/èrbǎi liù(shí)
两 / 二百 六(十)

999 jiǔbǎi jiǔshíjiǔ
九 百 九 十 九

1,000 yìqiān
一 千

4,003 sìqiān líng sān
四 千 零 三

7,020 qīqiān líng èrshí
七 千 零 二十

8,500 bāqiān wǔ(bǎi)
八 千 五 (百)

9,600,000 jiǔbǎi liùshí wàn
九 百 六 十 万

23,000,000 liǎngqiān sānbǎi wàn
两 千 三 百 万

1,300,000,000 shísān yì
十 三 亿

↘2. Write down the Pinyin of numbers after listening. 🎧

(1) Wǒ jiā zhù zài Xīnhuá Lù _____ hào.

(2) Dāo lǎoshī jiā zuò _____ lù gōngjiāochē, bú zuò _____ lù.

(3) Zhāng yīshēng yǒu _____ běn Zhōngwén shū, _____ běn Yīngwén zázhì.

(4) Xiǎo Lǐ de diànhuà shì _____ .

(5) Wǒ yǒu _____ gè gēge, _____ gè jiějie hé _____ gè mèimei.

(6) Wǒmen xuéxiào yǒu _____ gè xuésheng.

↘3. Listen to the sentences and tell whether the answers are true (√) or false (✕). 🎧

(1) A: Xiǎo Wáng yǒu jǐ gè jiějie?   B: Sì gè.   ( )

(2) A: Lǎo Lǐ yǒu duōshao péngyou?   B: Sì gè.   ( )

(3) A: Rìběn yǒu duōshao rén?   B: 12,700,000 rén.   ( )

(4) A: Tā de diànhuà hàomǎ shì duōshao?   B: 35759478.   ( )

(5) A: Nǐ yǒu yì běn shénme cídiǎn?
B: 《Zhōng-Yīng Cídiǎn》 .   ( )

(6) A: Wǒmen xuéxiào yǒu duōshao xuésheng?   B: 1605 gè.   ( )

(7) A: Tā jiā zhù zài Zhōngshān Lù jǐ hào?   B: 68 hào.   ( )

(8) A: Wǒ de tóngxué Xiǎo Lǐ shì nǎlǐ rén?   B: Shànghǎirén.   ( )

(9) A: Tā māma zuò shénme gōngzuò?   B: Hùshi.   ( )

(10) A: Xiǎo Chén jiā yǒu jǐ kǒu rén?   B: Qī kǒu rén.   ( )

(11) A: Dàwèi yǒu duōshao běn Zhōngwén shū?   B: Qīshí běn.   ( )

(12) A: Zǎochen bàba chéng shénme chē qù shàngbān?

   B: Chūzūchē.   ( )

✑ 4. Tell people where you live and what your telephone number is.

✑ 5. Tongue twister. 🎧

Sì shì sì, shí shì shí.   *Four is four, ten is ten.*
四 是 四, 十 是 十。

Shísì shì shísì, sìshí shì sìshí.   *Fourteen is fourteen, forty is forty.*
十 四 是 十 四, 四 十 是 四 十。

Shísì bú shì sìshí, sìshí bú shì shísì.   *Fourteen is not forty, forty is not fourteen.*
十 四 不 是 四 十, 四 十 不 是 十 四。

Shéi bǎ shísì shuō sìshí,   *Those who speak fourteen as forty,*
谁 把 十 四 说 四 十,

jiù dǎ sìshísì gè dà bǎnzi.   *will be hit with the wooden ruler forty-four times.*
就 打 四 十 四 个 大 板 子。

⟳ Share the poem

Shāncūn yǒnghuái
山村　　咏怀　🎧

(Běi Sòng, Shào Yōng)
（北宋，邵雍）

Yí qù èr sān lǐ,
一 去 二 三 里，

yān cūn sì wǔ jiā.
烟　村 四 五 家。

Tíngtái liù qī zuò,
亭　台 六 七 座，

bā jiǔ shí zhī huā.
八 九 十 枝 花。

Express the feelings in a mountain village
*   (Northern Song Dynasty, Shao Yong)*
Two, three miles in a single walk,
Four, five smoky cottages in the village.
Six, seven pavilions along the path,
Eight, nine, ten flowers near the pavilions.

Cultural tip

Addresses

Speaking and writing addresses are different between English and Chinese.
In Chinese the order is from the biggest to the smallest:
country — city — district — street — lane — number.
In English the order is from the smallest to the biggest:
number — lane — street — district — city — country.

6 Zài péngyou jiā
At my friend's home
在朋友家

Key points

1 Declarative sentence + **ma** 吗
2 Alternative question

Start here

Listen and repeat. 🎧

⌐ Items of fruit

píngguǒ
苹　果 *apple*

xiāngjiāo
香　蕉 *bananas*

pútao
葡萄 *grapes*

xīguā
西 瓜 *watermelon*

lí
梨 *pear*

chéngzi
橙　子 *orange*

⌐ Polite expressions (2)

Qǐng zuò. 请　坐。	*Sit down, please.*	**Méi guānxi.** 没 关 系。	*Never mind.*
Duìbuqǐ. 对 不 起。	*Sorry.*	**Màn zǒu.** 慢　走。	*(a polite expression used when seeing a guest off which means "take care")*

Dialogues

1

A: **Qǐng jìn.**
Come in, please.
请进。

B: **Xiǎo Wáng, nǐ hǎo!**
Hi, Xiao Wang!
小王，你好！

A: **Xiǎo Lǐ, qǐng zuò! Hē diǎnr shénme, chá háishi kāfēi?**
Please sit down, Xiao Li! What would you like to drink, tea or coffee?
小李，请坐！喝点儿什么，茶还是咖啡？

B: **Wǒ xǐhuan hē kāfēi, bù jiā táng.**
I like coffee, without sugar.
我喜欢喝咖啡，不加糖。

A: **Chī diǎnr shuǐguǒ ba!**
Would you like to have some fruit?
吃点儿水果吧！

B: **Xièxie. Yǒu píngguǒ ma?**
Thanks. Do you have some apples?
谢谢。有苹果吗？

A: **Duìbuqǐ, méi píngguǒ le. Yǒu xiāngjiāo、chéngzi、lí、pútao hé xīguā.**
Sorry, I don't .There are some bananas, oranges, pears, grapes and watermelons.
对不起，没苹果了。有香蕉、橙子、梨、葡萄和西瓜。

B: **Méi guānxi. Wǒ chī gè chéngzi ba.**
Never mind. I'll have an orange.
没关系。我吃个橙子吧。

......

B: **Bù zǎo le, wǒ gāi zǒu le.**
It's getting late, I should leave now.
不早了，我该走了。

A: **Màn zǒu.**
Take care.
慢走。

B: **Zàijiàn.**
Goodbye.
再见。

hē 喝	drink	
diǎnr / yìdiǎnr 点儿／一点儿	a little	
chá 茶	tea	
háishi 还是	or	
kāfēi 咖啡	coffee	
jiā 加	put...in	
táng 糖	sugar	
chī 吃	eat	
shuǐguǒ 水果	fruit	
zǎo 早	early	
wǎn 晚	late	
gāi / yīnggāi 该／应该	should	

A: **Xiǎo Lǐ, wǎnshang hǎo!**
Good evening, Xiao Li!
小李，晚上好！

B: **Wǎnshang hǎo, Qiáoyī! Yìqǐ chī wǎnfàn hǎo ma?**
Good evening, Joy! Shall we have dinner together?
晚上好，乔伊！一起吃晚饭好吗？

A: **Xièxie, wǒ chī le.**
Thanks, but I have had dinner.
谢谢，我吃了。

B: **Hē diǎnr guǒzhī ba?**
Would you like some juice?
喝点儿果汁吧？

A: **Bù, wǒ xǐhuan hē shuǐ…Xiǎo Lǐ, wǒ yǒu nǚpéngyou le.**
No, I'd like some water please…I have a girlfriend now, Xiao Li.
不，我喜欢喝水……小李，我有女朋友了。

B: **Zhēn de ma? Tā jiào shénme míngzi?**
Really? What's her name?
真的吗？她叫什么名字？

A: **Wáng Fāng.**
Wang Fang.
王芳。

B: **Nǎlǐ rén?**
Where is she from?
哪里人？

A: **Shànghǎirén.**
She is from Shanghai.
上海人。

B: **Zuò shénme gōngzuò?**
What's her job?
做什么工作？

A: **Tā shì bàoshè jìzhě.**
She's a reporter in a newspaper office.
她是报社记者。

B: **Piàoliang ma?**
Is she pretty?
漂亮吗？

A: **Piàoliang.**
Yes, she is.
漂亮。

B: **Tài hǎo le! Zhùhè nǐ!**
Very nice! Congratulations!
太好了！祝贺你！

---

fàn 饭	meal
wǎnfàn 晚饭	supper, dinner
(**zǎofàn** 早饭	breakfast)
(**wǔfàn** 午饭	lunch)
guǒzhī 果汁	juice
shuǐ 水	water
zhēn 真	really
bàoshè 报社	newspaper office
jìzhě 记者	reporter
piàoliang 漂亮	beautiful, pretty
tài 太	very, too
zhùhè 祝贺	congratulate

Notes

le 了 *is used at the end of a sentence to emphasize that something has already changed or the emergence of a new situation, for example:*

Bù zǎo le, wǒ gāi zǒu le.

It's getting late. I should leave now.

不早了，我该走了。

Wǒ yǒu nǚpéngyou le.

I've got a girlfriend.

我有女朋友了。 *(See "Grammar Outline", P212)*

le 了 *can also be used after a verb or verbal phrase to express the action has been completed, for example:*

Nǐ chī fàn le ma?

Have you had meal?

你吃饭了吗?

Chī le.

Yes , I have.

吃了。 *(See "Grammar Outline", P211)*

Form

(shì)···háishi··· （是）······还是······

It is used in alternative questions, similar to "...or..." in English.

In Chinese	In English
Nǐ (shì) hē chá háishi (hē) kāfēi? 你（是）喝 茶 还是（喝）咖啡?	*Would you like a cup of tea or coffee?*
Nǐ (shì) chī píngguǒ háishi (chī) lí? 你（是）吃 苹 果 还是（吃）梨?	*Would you like to eat an apple or a pear?*
Nǐ (shì) yòng qiānbǐ háishi (yòng) 你（是）用 铅 笔 还是（用） **yuánzhūbǐ?** 圆 珠 笔?	*Would you like to use a pencil or a ballpoint pen?*
Nǐ (shì) xué Zhōngwén háishi (xué) 你（是）学 中 文 还是（学） **Yīngwén?** 英 文?	*Would you like to learn Chinese or English?*

The answer is to be chosen from one of the options.

Interrogative sentences with **ma** 吗 and alternative questions

	In Chinese	In English
Interrogative sentences 1	*Declarative sentence+***ma** 吗 **Nǐ hē chá <u>ma</u>?** 你 喝 茶 吗? **Xiǎo Lǐ qù Běijīng <u>ma</u>?** 小 李 去 北 京 吗?	Use an auxiliary verb "do", "be", "have", "will", etc. at the beginning of the sentence. *Would you like to drink a cup of tea?* *Is Xiao Li going to Beijing?*
Interrogative sentences 2	*Positive verb + negative verb* **Nǐ <u>hē bu hē</u> chá?** 你 喝 不 喝 茶? **Xiǎo Lǐ <u>qù bu qù</u> Běijīng?** 小 李 去 不 去 北 京?	*Would you like to drink a cup of tea? / Would you like to drink a cup of tea, or not?* *Is Xiao Li going to Beijing? / Is Xiao Li going to Beijing, or not?*
Answers	**Wǒ hē chá.** 我 喝 茶。 **Wǒ bù hē chá.** 我 不 喝 茶。 **Xiǎo Lǐ qù Běijīng.** 小 李 去 北 京。 **Xiǎo Lǐ bú qù Běijīng.** 小 李 不 去 北 京。	*Yes, I'd like to drink tea.* *No, I wouldn't like to drink tea.* *Yes, Xiao Li is going to Beijing.* *No, Xiao Li isn't going to Beijing.*
Short answers	**Hē. / Bù hē.** 喝。 / 不 喝。 **Qù. / Bú qù.** 去。 / 不 去。	*Yes, please. / No, thanks.* *Yes, he is. / No, he isn't.*

Exercises

1. Substitution reading. 🎧

(1)

Nǐ 你	ài 爱	nǐ de lǎoshī. 你的老师。
Tā 他		tā de jiā. 他的家。
Wǒ 我		xuéxí. 学习。
Wǒmen 我们		Zhōngguó. 中国。

(2) Nǐ shì 你是

Yīngguórén 英国人	háishi 还是	Měiguórén? 美国人?
xuésheng 学生		lǎoshī? 老师?
Xiǎofēn 小芬		Xiǎofāng? 小芳?
tā tóngxué 他同学		tā tóngshì? 他同事?

(3) Nǐ 你

xìng Wāng 姓王	háishi 还是	xìng Lǐ? 姓李?
hē guǒzhī 喝果汁		hē shuǐ? 喝水?
zuò gōngjiāochē 坐公交车		zuò chūzūchē? 坐出租车?
xǐhuan gēge 喜欢哥哥		xǐhuan dìdi? 喜欢弟弟?

2. Match the questions with the answers. (Every answer will be used twice.)

(1) Chī shuǐguǒ ma?   A. Chī. / Bù chī.

(2) Chī zǎofàn le ma?

(3) Chī bu chī xīguā?

(4) Chī méi chī wǎnfàn?   B. Chī le. / Méi(yǒu) chī.

(5) Hē guǒzhī·ma?

(6) Hē kāfēi le ma?   C. Hē. / Bù hē.

(7) Hē bu hē chá?

(8) Hē méi hē shuǐ?   D. Hē le. / Méi(yǒu) hē.

3. Choose the right words to fill in the blanks.

yǒu méiyǒu	méiyǒu	chī	háishi
有　没有	没有	吃	还是
shì bu shì	xǐhuan	hē	shì
是　不是	喜欢	喝	是

(1) Zhè _____ pútao ma?

(2) Nǐ _____ mèimei?

(3) Wǒ _____ kāfēi.

(4) Qǐng nín _____ júzi.

(5) Nǐ bàba _____ yīshēng?

(6) Wǒ _____ wǒ de tóngxué.

(7) Tā yǒu gēge, _____ jiějie.

(8) Tā shì xuésheng _____ lǎoshī?

4. Fill in the blanks after listening, then read the paragraph aloud. 🎧

Xiǎo Wáng shì _____. Tā de _____ Huáng Yīng shì

_____. Xiǎo Wáng wèn Huáng Yīng: "Wǒ de lǎo tóngxué Xiǎo

Lǐ yě shì diànnǎo gōngchéngshī. _____ wǒmen qù tā jiā, hǎo ma?"

Huáng Yīng wèn: "Tā jiā zài _____?" "_____ Zhōngshān Lù." Huáng Yīng

shuō: "Hǎo de, wǒmen yìqǐ_____ qù ba."

　　Dàole Xiǎo Lǐ jiā, Xiǎo Lǐ _____. Xiǎo Lǐ wèn tāmen xǐhuan

_____ shénme, chá、kāfēi, _____ guǒzhī. Xiǎo Wáng xǐhuan hē

_____, Huáng Yīng xǐhuan hē _____ de _____. Xiǎo

Lǐ _____ tāmen _____, yǒu píngguǒ、lí、chéngzi, _____

pútao. Xiǎo Wáng ài chī _____, Huáng Yīng ài chī _____. Xiǎo

Wáng wèn Xiǎo Lǐ: "Nǐ de _____ hé _____ zài jiā ma?" Xiǎo Lǐ

shuō: "Tāmen dōu zài shūfáng xuéxí. Nǚ'ér xǐhuan _____.

Érzi xǐhuan _____." Xiǎo Wáng shuō: "Tā liǎ dōu

shì _____."

5. Draw pictures of the fruit after listening. 🎧

6. What will you say?

(1) *When your friend visits you and knocks on your door, you open the door and what will you say?*

(2) *After you let him/her into the living room, what will you say?*

(3) *If you don't know what he/she wants to drink, what will you say?*

(4) *After you give him/her a drink, what will you say?*

(5) *If you don't know his wife's / her husband's name and you want to ask him/ her, what will you say?*

(6) *If your friend wants to leave, what will you say?*

➲ Cultural tip

Dropping in

Chinese enjoy dropping in as it is an important way of staying in touch with their relatives, friends and neighbours, especially during special occasions such as on New Year's Day and other festivals. They used to visit an acquaintance without having to make an appointment, but people today tend to make an appointment in advance.

When a guest drops in, the host would normally offer him or her some tea. If it is during meal time, the guest would be invited to have a meal with the host. Otherwise, the host would stop eating and chat with the guest.

*When seeing off the guest, the host would go to the outside till the gate and say "***màn zǒu** 慢走*", which means "take care". The guest normally says "* **liú bù** 留步*" which means "Stop here. Don't see me off too far."*

7 Xiǎo Wáng de wòshì
Xiao Wang's bedroom
小王的卧室

Key points

1 Specific measurement words
2 Specific position words

Start here

Listen and repeat. 🎧

⤓ Specific measurement words

gè
个
is a multi-purpose measurement word.

> **yí gè nǚháir/nánháir**
> 一 个 女孩儿／男 孩儿　　*one girl/boy*
>
> **sān gè chéngzi**
> 三 个 橙 子　　*three oranges*
>
> **liǎng gè xīngqī**
> 两 个 星 期　　*two weeks*

zhāng
张
is used when the item has an area.

> **yì zhāng yóupiào**
> 一 张 邮 票　　*one stamp*
>
> **liǎng zhāng zhuōzi**
> 两 张 桌 子　　*two tables*
>
> **sì zhāng zhàopiàn**
> 四 张 照 片　　*four photos*

bǎ
把
is used for items that have a handle, or for a handful of something.

> **yì bǎ sǎn**
> 一 把 伞　　*an umbrella*
>
> **liǎng bǎ yàoshi**
> 两 把 钥匙　　*two keys*
>
> **yì bǎ mǐ**
> 一 把 米　　*a handful of rice*

shuāng
双
is used for pairs of items.

> **yì shuāng xié**
> 一 双 鞋　　*a pair of shoes*
>
> **liǎng shuāng kuàizi**
> 两 双 筷 子　　*two pairs of chopsticks*
>
> **yì shuāng yǎnjing**
> 一 双 眼 睛　　*two eyes*

jiàn
件

is used for garments worn on the upper part of the body or on the whole body, or for some individual articles.

yí jiàn shàngyī
一　件　上 衣　　　　　　*a jacket*

yí jiàn dàyī
一　件　大衣　　　　　　*a coat*

sān jiàn xíngli
三　件　行李　　　*three pieces of luggage*

tiáo
条

is used for garments worn on the lower part of the body, or for items that are long and narrow.

yì tiáo kùzi
一　条　裤子　　　*a pair of trousers*

yì tiáo hé
一　条　河　　　　　*a river*

sì tiáo yú
四　条　鱼　　　　　*four fish*

zhī
支

is used for items that are stick-like.

yì zhī qiānbǐ
一　支　铅笔　　　*a pencil*

liǎng zhī làzhú
两　支 蜡烛　　　*two candles*

zhī
只

is used for certain animals and things, or for one of a pair of items.

yì zhī māo
一　只　猫　　　　*a cat*

yì zhī shǒu
一　只　手　　　　*a hand*

◁ Specific position words (1)

shàng(bian)　*on*　　**xià(bian)**　*under*　　**lǐ(bian)**　*inside*　　**wài(bian)**　*outside*
上　（边）　　　　下　（边）　　　　里　（边）　　　　外　（边）

读拼音学汉语

Reading

1

1. **Zhè shì Xiǎo Wáng de wòshì.**
   This is Xiao Wang's bedroom.
   这是小王的卧室。

2. **Wūzi li yǒu yì zhāng chuáng、yì zhāng zhuōzi、yì bǎ yǐzi hé yí gè xiǎo diànshì.**
   There is a bed, a table, a chair and a small television in the room.
   屋子里有一张床、一张桌子、一把椅子和一个小电视。

3. **Zhuōzi shang yǒu liǎng zhāng bàozhǐ、wǔ běn shū hé yì běn zázhì.**
   There are two newspapers, five books and one magazine on the table.
   桌子上有两张报纸、五本书和一本杂志。

4. **Chuáng shang yǒu sān jiàn yīfu, chuáng xià yǒu yì shuāng xié.**
   There are three pieces of clothing on the bed, and a pair of shoes under the bed.
   床上有三件衣服，床下有一双鞋。

5. **Qiáng shang guàzhe yì zhāng dà zhàopiàn.**
   There is a big photo hanging on the wall.
   墙上挂着一张大照片。

6. **Wūzi bú dà, dànshì hěn gānjìng.**
   His bedroom is not big but very clean.
   屋子不大，但是很干净。

wòshì 卧室	bedroom
wū (zi) 屋（子）	room
chuáng 床	bed
zhuō(zi) 桌（子）	table
yǐzi 椅子	chair
xiǎo 小	small
(**dà** 大	big)
diànshì(jī) 电视（机）	television
yīfu 衣服	clothes
qiáng 墙	wall
guà 挂	hang
dàn(shì) 但（是）	but
gānjìng 干净	clean
(**zāng** 脏	dirty)

Notes

zhe 着 *is usually used after the verb to indicate the continuity of an action or state, for example:*
Qiáng shang guàzhe yì zhāng Zhōngguó dìtú.
There is a map of China hanging on the wall.
墙上挂着一张中国地图。

(See "Grammar Outline", P210)

读拼音学汉语

1. **Zhè shì kètīng.**
   This is the living room.
   这是客厅。

2. **Kètīng li yǒu yí gè dà shūchú、yì zhāng shūzhuō、yì zhāng shāfā、 yì zhāng chájī hé yì zhǎn luòdìdēng.**
   There is a big bookcase, a desk, a sofa, a tea table and a floor lamp in the living room.
   客厅里有一个大书橱、一张书桌、一张沙发、一张茶几和一盏落地灯。

3. **Qiáng shang guàzhe yí gè zhōng hé yì běn niánlì.**
   A clock and a calendar are on the wall.
   墙上挂着一个钟和一本年历。

4. **Shūzhuō shang yǒu yì zhī shǒubiǎo、yì píng xiānhuā.**
   There is a watch and a vase of fresh flowers on the desk.
   书桌上有一只手表、一瓶鲜花。

5. **Shūzhuō xià wòzhe yì zhī māo.**
   A cat is lying under the desk.
   书桌下卧着一只猫。

6. **Chájī shang yǒu yí gè shuǐguǒpán.**
   There is a fruit plate on the tea table.
   茶几上有一个水果盘。

7. **Pánzi li yǒu píngguǒ、pútao、xiāngjiāo.**
   There are apples, grapes and bananas on the plate.
   盘子里有苹果、葡萄、香蕉。

8. **Pánzi wài yǒu yí gè dà xīguā、yì bǎ shuǐguǒdāo.**
   There is a big watermelon and a knife beside the plate.
   盘子外有一个大西瓜、一把水果刀。

9. **Luòdìchuāng wài shì yí gè dà yángtái.**
   There is a big balcony outside the French window.
   落地窗外是一个大阳台。

kètīng	客厅	living room
shūchú	书橱	bookcase
shūzhuō	书桌	desk
shāfā	沙发	sofa
chájī	茶几	tea table
luòdìdēng	落地灯	floor lamp
dēng	灯	lamp, light, lantern
zhōng	钟	clock
niánlì	年历	calendar
shǒubiǎo	手表	watch
píng(zi)	瓶（子）	vase, bottle
xiānhuā	鲜花	fresh flower
huā(r)	花（儿）	flower
wò	卧	lie
pán(zi)	盘（子）	plate
dāo(zi)	刀（子）	knife
luòdìchuāng	落地窗	French window
chuāng(hu)	窗（户）	window
yángtái	阳台	balcony

Notes

zhǎn 盏 *(measurement word) is used for items like a light, for example:* **yì zhǎn dēng** *a lamp* 一盏灯.

Form

Specific measurement words

(See "Grammar Outline", P219)

Numeral + specific measurement word + noun		
yì tiáo dà hé 一 条 大河 *a big river*	**liǎng jiàn yīfu** 两 件 衣服 *two pieces of clothes*	
liǎng gè nǚhái 两 个 女孩儿 *two girls*	**yì shuāng shǒu** 一 双 手 *two hands*	
yì bǎ dāo 一 把 刀 *one knife*	**sān běn shū** 三 本 书 *three books*	

Specific position words

(See "Grammar Outline", P220)

In Chinese	In English
Noun + specific position word	*Preposition + noun*
zhuōzi shang 桌 子 上	*on the table*
chuáng xià 床 下	*under the bed*
xuéxiào li 学 校 里	*in the school*
wū wài 屋 外	*outside the room*
Specific positional phrase + **yǒu** 有 *+ numeral + measurement word + noun*	*There is/are + numeral (+ measurement word) + noun + prepositional phrase*
Chuáng shang yǒu yí jiàn yīfu. 床 上 有 一 件 衣服。	*There is a dress on the bed.*
Chuáng xià yǒu yì shuāng xié. 床 下 有 一 双 鞋。	*There is a pair of shoes under the bed.*

7

小王的卧室

In Chinese	In English
Wū li yǒu yì zhāng zhuōzi. 屋 里 有 一 张 桌 子。	*There is a table in the room.*
Wū wài yǒu liǎng gè rén. 屋 外 有 两 个 人。	*There are two people outside the room.*
Wrong	× **Yǒu liǎng jiàn yīfu chuáng shang.** × **Yǒu liǎng gè rén wū wài.**

Exercises

◁ 1. Substitution reading.

(1)
| wǔ
五
liǎng
两
shí
十
sìshíbā
四十八 | gè
个 | rén
人
gēge
哥哥
xīguā
西瓜
guójiā
国家 |

(2)
| yìbǎi líng liù
一百零六
sān
三
shíjiǔ
十九
qī
七 | běn
本 | shū
书
dìtú
地图
zázhì
杂志
cídiǎn
词典 |

(3)
| liǎngbǎi wǔshí
两百五十
shí'èr
十二
yì
一
sì
四 | zhāng
张 | zhǐ
纸
zhàopiàn
照片
bàozhǐ
报纸
zhuōzi
桌子 |

(4)

yì 一	shuāng 双	shǒu 手
yì 一		yǎnjing 眼 睛
liǎng 两		xié 鞋
sān 三		kuàizi 筷 子

↘ 2. Describe the picture.

↘ 3. Describe your study.
Using the words below, add numerals and the correct measurement words, e.g.

bàozhǐ—sān zhāng bàozhǐ
报 纸 三 张 报 纸

yǐzi 椅子	shū 书	qiānbǐ 铅 笔	dāozi 刀 子
dēng 灯	yīfu 衣服	píngguǒ 苹 果	shūzhuō 书 桌

↘ 4. Listen and fill in the blanks. 🎧

(1) Jiàoshì li yǒu _____ zhuōzi, _____ yǐzi,_____ _____ dà diànshì.

(2) Qiáng shang yǒu _____ dìtú, _____ shì shìjiè dìtú, _____ shì Zhōngguó dìtú.

(3) Zhuōzi shang yǒu _____ shū, _____ cídiǎn, _____ _____ bàozhǐ, _____ yuánzhūbǐ.

(4) Yǐzi shang yǒu _____ shàngyī, yǐzi xià yǒu _____ māo.

5. Make questions with " jǐ 几"or "duōshao 多少".

Q: <u>Wūzi li yǒu jǐ zhǎn dēng?</u>

A: Wūzi li yǒu sān zhǎn dēng.

(1) Q: _____?

A: Xiǎo Zhāng zhù zài bā hào.

(2) Q: _____?

A: Qù lǎoshī jiā zuò sìshí'èr lù gōnggòng qìchē.

(3) Q: _____?

A: Jiějie de shǒujī hàomǎ shì 17306210895.

(4) Q: _____?

A: Wǒmen bān yǒu èrshíbā gè xuésheng.

⊃ Cultural tip

Communities in the city

The community is the basic organization of a residential area in the city. Communities are responsible for taking care of issues such as safety, environment protection and health. For example, there are security guards for each community and a medical service center in every residential area. There are many activities organised for both the elderly and children. They provide benefits for low-income families and elders. They are also responsible for mediating in family or neighbour disputes, etc.

8

Xiǎo Wáng de yì tiān
One day of Xiao Wang

小王的一天

Key points

Time of a day

⮕ Start here

读拼音学汉语

Listen and repeat. 🎧

⬐ During the day

zǎoshang / zǎochen 早 上 早 晨	early morning		**xiǎoshí** 小 时	hour
shàngwǔ 上 午	morning		**diǎn** 点	o'clock
zhōngwǔ 中 午	noon		**kè** 刻	quarter
xiàwǔ 下 午	afternoon		**fēn** 分	minute
wǎnshang 晚 上	evening		**miǎo** 秒	second
yè(li) 夜(里)	night			
zhěng 整	whole		**chà** 差	be short of
bàn 半	half			

⬐ Look at the clocks and tell the time

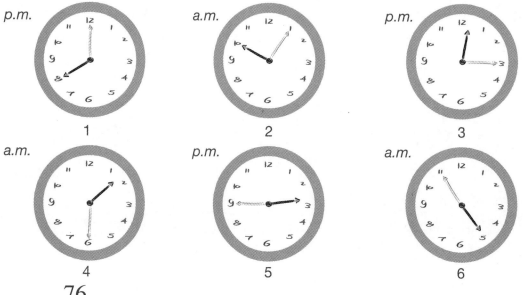

p.m. 1 a.m. 2 p.m. 3

a.m. 4 p.m. 5 a.m. 6

76

(1) **wǎnshang bā diǎn (zhěng)**
eight o'clock in the evening
晚上八点（整）

(2) **shàngwǔ shí diǎn líng wǔ (fēn)**
five past ten in the morning
上午十点零五（分）

(3) **zhōngwǔ shí'èr diǎn yí kè**
a quarter past twelve at noon
中午十二点一刻

zhōngwǔ shí'èr diǎn shíwǔ (fēn)
fifteen past twelve at noon
中午十二点十五（分）

(4) **yèli yī diǎn bàn**
half past one at night
夜里一点半

yèli yī diǎn sānshí (fēn)
one thirty at night
夜里一点三十（分）

(5) **xiàwǔ liǎng diǎn sìshíwǔ (fēn)**
two forty-five in the afternoon
下午两点四十五（分）

xiàwǔ liǎng diǎn sān kè
three quarters past two in the afternoon
下午两点三刻

xiàwǔ chà yí kè sān diǎn
a quarter to three in the afternoon
下午差一刻三点

(6) **zǎochen sì diǎn wǔshíwǔ (fēn)**
four fifty-five in the morning
早晨四点五十五（分）

zǎochen chà wǔ fēn wǔ diǎn
five to five in the morning
早晨差五分五点

Reading and dialogue

1

1. **Měi tiān zǎochen, Xiǎo Wáng qī diǎn qǐchuáng.**
Xiao Wang gets up at seven o'clock in the morning every day.
每天早晨，小王七点起床。

2. **Qī diǎn yí kè shuā yá xǐ liǎn.**
(He) brushes his teeth and washes his face at a quarter past seven.
七点一刻刷牙洗脸。

3. **Qī diǎn wǔshí chī zǎofàn.**
(He) has breakfast at seven fifty.
七点五十吃早饭。

4. **Jiǔ diǎn shàngbān.**
(He) starts working at nine o'clock.
九点上班。

5. **Gōngzuò sān gè xiǎoshí, shí'èr diǎn zuǒyòu chī wǔfàn.**
(He) works for three hours, then has lunch at about twelve o'clock.
工作三个小时，十二点左右吃午饭。

---

měi tiān
每 天　*every day*
měi 每 *every*

qǐchuáng
起 床　*get up*

shuā yá　*brush one's*
刷 牙　*teeth*
shuā 刷 *brush*

xǐ liǎn　*wash one's*
洗 脸　*face*
xǐ 洗 *wash*

zuǒyòu
左 右　*about*

1

6. **Wǔfàn yǐhòu xiūxi bàn xiǎoshí.**
(He) rests for half an hour after lunch.
午饭以后休息半小时。

7. **Xiàwǔ wǔ diǎn xiàbān.**
(He) finishes working at five o'clock in the afternoon.
下午五点下班。

8. **Liù diǎn bàn chī wǎnfàn.**
(He) has dinner at half past six.
六点半吃晚饭。

9. **Wǎnfàn yǐhòu chūqù sànbù.**
(He) goes out for a walk after dinner.
晚饭以后出去散步。

10. **Wǎnshang jiǔ diǎn kàn diànshì.**
(He) watches TV at nine o'clock in the evening.
晚上九点看电视。

11. **Shíyī diǎn yǐqián xǐzǎo.**
(He) takes a bath before eleven o'clock.
十一点以前洗澡。

12. **Xǐzǎo yǐhòu shàng chuáng shuìjiào.**
(He) goes to bed after taking a bath.
洗澡以后上床睡觉。

xiūxi 休息	rest
yǐhòu 以后	after
chūqù 出去	go out
sànbù 散步	walk
kàn 看	watch, see, look
yǐqián 以前	before
xǐzǎo 洗澡	take a bath
shàng 上	go up, come up
xià 下	go down, come down
shuìjiào 睡觉	sleep

2

A: **Qiáoyī, jīntiān wǎnshang nǐ shénme shíhou huílái?**
Joy, what time will you come back tonight?
乔伊，今天晚上你什么时候回来？

B: **Dàyuē liù diǎn. Yǒu shì ma?**
About six o'clock. What's the matter?
大约六点。有事吗？

A: **Wǒ hé péngyou qù tiàowǔ, nǐ qù bu qù?**
My friend and I are going to dance. Would you like to go with us?
我和朋友去跳舞，你去不去？

B: **Hǎo wa! Zài shénme dìfang?**
OK. Where?
好哇！在什么地方？

shíhou / shíjiān 时候／时间	time
dàyuē 大约	about
shì(qing) 事（情）	matter
tiàowǔ 跳舞	dance
wa 哇	modal particle

2

A: **Dàhuá wǔtīng.**
Dahua Dance Hall.
大华舞厅。

B: **Shénme shíjiān?**
What time?
什么时间?

A: **Dàhuá wǔtīng bā diǎn kāi mén.**
Dahua Dance Hall opens at 8 p.m.
大华舞厅八点开门。

B: **Hǎo. Bā diǎn zhěng, wǔtīng jiàn!**
OK, 8 p.m. See you at the dance hall.
好。八点整,舞厅见!

dìfang 地方	*place*
wǔtīng 舞厅	*dance hall*
kāi 开	*open*
guān 关	*close*
mén 门	*door*

 Form

Telling the time

	In Chinese	In English
Interrogative sentences	*Noun/Pronoun* + **jǐ** 几 + **diǎn** 点 + *verb / verbal phrase* **Nǐ jǐ diǎn qǐchuáng?** 你几点起床? *We can also use* **shénme shíhou** 什么时候 *to replace* **jǐ** 几 + **diǎn** 点. **Lǎo Lǐ měi tiān shénme shíhou xiàbān huí jiā?** 老李每天什么时候下班回家?	*What time do you get up?* *What time does Lao Li finish work and come back home every day?*

8 小王的一天

	In Chinese	In English
Answers	*The words or phrases of time are usually placed before the verbs.* **Wǒ qī diǎn qǐchuáng.** 我 七 点 起 床。 **Lǎo Lǐ měi tiān xiàwǔ wǔ** 老 李 每 天 下 午 五 **diǎn xiàbān huí jiā.** 点 下 班 回 家。	*The prepositional phrases of time are usually placed at the end of the sentences.* *I get up at seven o'clock.* *Lao Li finishes work and comes back home at five o'clock in the afternoon every day.*
	Wrong ✕**Wǒ qǐchuáng qī diǎn.**	
Short answers	**Qī diǎn.** 七 点。 **Xiàwǔ wǔ diǎn.** 下 午 五 点。	*Seven o'clock.* *Five o'clock in the afternoon.*
Before and after	**Zǎochen qī diǎn yǐqián.** 早 晨 七 点 以 前。 **Xiàwǔ wǔ diǎn yǐhòu.** 下 午 五 点 以 后。	*Before seven o'clock in the morning.* *After five o'clock in the afternoon.*
	Wrong ✕**Yǐqián qī diǎn zǎochen.**	

⊃ Exercises

◁ 1. Match the words in line A with the times in line B after listening. 🎧

A	B
zǎochen 早 晨	10:00
shàngwǔ 上 午	12:05
zhōngwǔ 中 午	2:55
xiàwǔ 下 午	6:15
wǎnshang 晚 上	1:45
yèli 夜里	9:30

◁ 2. Substitution reading. 🎧

(1) A: Nǐ jǐ diǎn
      你 几 点

| qǐchuáng?
起 床? |
| chéng gōngjiāochē?
乘 公 交 车? |
| shàngbān?
上 班? |
| kàn diànshì?
看 电 视? |

B:
| Qī diǎn.
七 点。 |
| Bā diǎn èrshí.
八 点 二 十。 |
| Jiǔ diǎn.
九 点。 |
| Wǎnshang shí diǎn.
晚 上 十 点。 |

(2) A: Nǐ
      你

| chīfàn yǐqián
吃 饭 以 前 |
| xiàbān yǐhòu
下 班 以 后 |
| wǎnfàn yǐhòu
晚 饭 以 后 |
| shuìjiào yǐqián
睡 觉 以 前 |

zuò shénme?
做 什 么?

B:
| Xǐshǒu.
洗 手。 |
| Xiūxi.
休 息。 |
| Sànbù.
散 步。 |
| Xǐzǎo.
洗 澡。 |

(3) A:
Mǎ lǎoshī 马 老师	
Xuéshengmen 学 生 们	jǐ diǎn 几 点
Hé yīshēng 何 医 生	
Lǐ kuàijì 李 会计	

qù xuéxiào? 去 学 校?
dúshū? 读书?
shàngbān? 上 班?
shàngwǎng? 上 网?

B:
Shàngwǔ jiǔ diǎn. 上 午 九 点。

3. Put the words below into the proper boxes.

kāfēi　　　　　dìtú　　　　　shuǐguǒ　　　　　diànshì
咖啡　　　　　地 图　　　　　水 果　　　　　电 视

chá　　　　　wǎnfàn　　　　　chē　　　　　shuǐ
茶　　　　　晚 饭　　　　　车　　　　　水

fàn　　　　　liǎn　　　　　bàozhǐ　　　　　lí
饭　　　　　脸　　　　　报 纸　　　　　梨

huàr　　　　　yīfu　　　　　pánzi　　　　　guǒzhī
画儿　　　　　衣服　　　　　盘 子　　　　　果 汁

chī
吃 [ ]

xǐ
洗 [ ]

hē
喝 [ ]

kàn
看 [ ]

4. Look at the pictures, tell the time and talk about what the boy is doing.

(1) _____.

(2) _____.

(3) _____.

(4) _____.

(5) _____.

(6) _____.

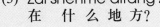 5. Make an appointment with your friend by phone.

Here are some details of the appointment.

(1) Zuò shénme?   *What are we going to do?*
    做　什　么？

(2) Shénme shíhou?   *What time?*
    什　么　时　候？

(3) Zài shénme dìfang?   *Where?*
    在　什　么　地　方？

⟳ Cultural tip

Colorful evening life

There are various entertainment places open at night in big or middle-sized cities such as dance halls, theaters, movie theaters, cafés, restaurants, bars, karaoke bars, saunas (**sāngná yùshì** 桑拿浴室), *tearooms* (**cháshì** 茶室), *and chess-and-card rooms* (**qípáishì** 棋牌室), *etc. They are open as late as 11:00 p.m. or even later in most big cities.*

If you go shopping at Nanjing Road in Shanghai or at Wangfujing in Beijing (both are well-known walkways in China), you can have many choices and enjoy yourself.

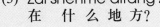

9 Zhù nǐ shēngrì kuàilè!

Happy birthday to you!

祝你生日快乐！

Key points

1 "When" and "which" in Chinese
2 Talking about the year, month and day

⟳ Start here

Listen and repeat. 🎧

↳ Year, month and day

nián 年：*year*

2008 nián	**1949 nián**
2008 年	1949 年

yuè 月：*month*

Yīyuè	一 月	January	**Qīyuè**	七 月	July
Èryuè	二 月	February	**Bāyuè**	八 月	August
Sānyuè	三 月	March	**Jiǔyuè**	九 月	September
Sìyuè	四 月	April	**Shíyuè**	十 月	October
Wǔyuè	五 月	May	**Shíyīyuè**	十 一 月	November
Liùyuè	六 月	June	**Shí'èryuè**	十 二 月	December

rì 日 / **hào** 号：*day*

Jīntiān shì jǐ hào?
What's the date today?
今天是几号？

Jīntiān shì Liùyuè shísān rì/hào.
Today is the 13th of June.
今天是六月十三日/号。

↳ Other expressions of year, month and day

zuótiān	昨 天	yesterday	**xià (gè) yuè**	下 （个）月	next month
jīntiān	今 天	today	**qùnián**	去 年	last year
míngtiān	明 天	tomorrow	**jīnnián**	今 年	this year
shàng (gè) yuè	上 （个）月	last month	**míngnián**	明 年	next year
zhè(ge) yuè	这 （个）月	this month			

Dialogue and reading

1

A: **Xiǎo Wáng, nǐ nǎ nián chūshēng de?**
In which year were you born, Xiao Wang?
小王，你哪年出生的？

B: **1989 nián, wǒ jīnnián èrshísì suì. Xiǎo Lǐ, nǐ ne?**
I was born in 1989. I'm twenty-four years old. How about you, Xiao Li?
一九八九年，我今年二十四岁。小李，你呢？

A: **Wǒ 1988 nián chūshēng.**
I was born in 1988.
我一九八八年出生。

B: **Nǐ de shēngrì shì nǎ tiān?**
When is your birthday?
你的生日是哪天？

A: **Shíyīyuè bā hào. Xiǎo Wáng, nǐ de shēngrì shì nǎ tiān?**
The eighth of November. How about you, Xiao Wang?
十一月八号。小王，你的生日是哪天？

B: **Xià gè yuè yī hào.**
The first of next month.
下个月一号。

A: **Jīntiān jǐ hào?**
What's the date today?
今天几号？

B: **Sìyuè sānshí hào.**
The thirtieth of April.
四月三十号。

A: **Ò! Míngtiān jiù shì Wǔyuè yī hào.**
Oh! It will be the first of May tomorrow.
哦！明天就是五月一号。

B: **Shì de. Huānyíng nǐ míngtiān cānjiā wǒ de shēngrì jùhuì.**
Yes. You are welcome to my birthday party tomorrow.
是的。欢迎你明天参加我的生日聚会。

A: **Hǎo de. Wǒmen wèi nǐ mǎi xiānhuā、diǎn làzhú、qiē dàngāo、chàng shēngrìgē, zhù nǐ shēngrì kuàilè!**
OK. We'll buy some flowers, light candles, cut the cake, sing the birthday song for you and wish you a happy birthday!
好的。我们为你买鲜花、点蜡烛、切蛋糕、唱生日歌，祝你生日快乐！

chūshēng / shēng	出 生 / 生	be born
suì	岁	year (of age)
shēngrì	生 日	birthday
tiān	天	day, date
ò	哦	oh
jiù	就	(indicating emphasis)
huānyíng	欢 迎	welcome
cānjiā	参 加	join
jùhuì	聚会	party
wèi	为	for
mǎi	买	buy
(mài	卖	sell)
diǎn	点	light
qiē	切	cut
dàngāo	蛋 糕	cake
chàng (gē)	唱 （歌）	sing
gē	歌	song
zhù	祝	wish

2

1. **Jīntiān shì nǎinai de qīshí dà shòu.**
   Today is my grandmother's seventieth big birthday.
   今天是奶奶的七十大寿。

2. **Wǒmen zhǔnbèile tā xǐhuan de shēngrì lǐwù.**
   We prepared the birthday presents that she likes.
   我们准备了她喜欢的生日礼物。

3. **Yéye mǎile yí gè dà dàngāo.**
   My grandfather bought a big cake.
   爷爷买了一个大蛋糕。

4. **Māma zuò chángshòumiàn, bàba dào jiǔ.**
   My mother made long-life noodles. My father poured wine for her.
   妈妈做长寿面，爸爸倒酒。

5. **Mèimei sòng xiānhuā, wǒ diǎn shēngrì làzhú.**
   My younger sister gave her a bunch of flowers. I lit birthday candles.
   妹妹送鲜花，我点生日蜡烛。

6. **Dàjiā chàng shēngrìgē, yìqǐ gānbēi, zhù nǎinai cháng shòu.**
   We sang the birthday song, drank a toast together and wished my grandmother a long life.
   大家唱生日歌，一起干杯，祝奶奶长寿。

7. **Nǎinai hěn gāoxìng, tā qiē shēngrì dàngāo, hé dàjiā fēnxiǎng.**
   My grandmother was very happy. She cut the birthday cake to share with us.
   奶奶很高兴，她切生日蛋糕，和大家分享。

dà shòu 大 寿	big birthday
zhǔnbèi 准 备	prepare
lǐwù 礼物	present
chángshòumiàn 长 寿 面	long-life noodles
chángshòu 长寿	long life
dào 倒	pour
jiǔ 酒	wine
sòng 送	give
gānbēi 干 杯	drink a toast
fēnxiǎng 分 享	share

9 祝你生日快乐！

➲ Form

Talking about the year, month and day

	In Chinese	In English
Interrogative sentences	*Noun/Pronoun* + **shénme shíhou** 什么时候 + *verb* (+ *noun*) (1)**Nǐ shénme shíhou qù** 你 什 么 时 候 去 **Měiguó?** 美 国?	(1)*When are you going to the U.S.?*

87

	In Chinese	In English
Interrogative sentences	(2) **Wǒmen bān tóngxué** 我们 班 同学 **shénme shíhou jùhuì?** 什么 时候 聚会? *We can also use question words* **nǎ** 哪+ **nián** 年/**yuè**月/**tiān** 天 *or* （**jǐ yuè** 几月+）**jǐ hào** 几号 *to replace* **shénme shíhou** 什么时候. (3) **Nǐ nǎ nián / gè yuè / tiān** 你哪年 / 个 月 / 天 **qù Měiguó?** 去 美 国? (4) **Wǒmen bān tóngxué** 我们 班 同学 **(jǐ yuè) jǐ hào jùhuì?** （几月）几号 聚会?	(2) *When are our classmates going to have a party?* (3) *In/On which year/month/day are you going to the U.S.?* (4) *On which day are our classmates going to have a party?*
	Wrong × **Nǐ jǐ nián qù Měiguó?**	
Answers	(1) **Wǒ míngnián Jiǔyuè** 我 明 年 九 月 **shíliù rì qù Měiguó.** 十六日去美 国。 (2) **Wǒmen bān tóngxué xià** 我们 班 同学下 **gè yuè wǔ hào jùhuì.** 个 月 五 号 聚会。 (3) **Wǒ jīnnián/Qīyuè/** 我 今年 / 七月 / **míngtiān qù Měiguó.** 明 天去美 国。 (4) **Wǒmen bān tóngxué** 我们 班 同学 **(Wǔyuè) sān hào jùhuì.** （五月）三 号 聚会。	(1) *I'm going to the U.S. on the sixteenth of September next year.* (2) *Our classmates are going to have a party on the fifth of next month.* (3) *I'm going to the U.S. this year / in July / tomorrow.* (4) *Our classmates are going to have a party on the third (of May).*

	In Chinese	In English
Short answers	(1) **Míngnián Jiǔyuè shíliù rì.** 明 年 九 月 十六日。	(1) *The sixteenth of September next year.*
	(2) **Xià gè yuè wǔ hào.** 下 个 月 五 号。	(2) *The fifth of next month.*
	(3) **Jīnnián./Qīyuè./** 今 年。/七 月。/ **Míngtiān.** 明 天。	(3) *This year. / July. / Tomorrow.*
	(4) **(Wǔyuè) Sān hào.** （五 月） 三 号。	(4) *The third (of May).*

The expression of dates in Chinese is year/month/day, but in English it is either day/month/ year or month/day/year.

Exercises

↘ 1. Read the dates. 🎧

03/06/1840	17/09/1894	16/08/1900	10/10/1911
04/05/1919	18/09/1931	07/07/1937	15/08/1945
01/10/1949	25/10/1971	08/08/2008	01/05/2010

↘ 2. Substitution reading. 🎧

(1)
Yīyuè wǔ rì 一 月 五 日	shì 是	wǒ de 我 的	shēngrì. 生 日。
Qīyuè sānshí rì 七 月 三 十 日		Chén lǎoshī de 陈 老师 的	
Shí'èryuè bā rì 十 二 月 八 日		Xiǎo Lǐ de 小 李 的	

(2)
Jīntiān 今 天	shì 是	Wǔyuè yī rì. 五 月 一 日。
Míngtiān 明 天		Wǔyuè èr rì. 五 月 二 日。
Zuótiān 昨 天		Sìyuè sānshí rì. 四 月 三 十 日。

(3)	Jīnnián 今 年	shì 是	èr líng yī sān nián. 二 零 一 三 年。
	Míngnián 明 年		èr líng yī sì nián. 二 零 一 四 年。
	Qùnián 去 年		èr líng yī èr nián. 二 零 一 二 年。

3. Tell whether the following sentences are right (√) or wrong (×).

(1) Zuótiān shì shíjiǔ hào, míngtiān shì èrshí hào.　　　　　( )

(2) Zhège yuè shì Bāyuè, xià gè yuè shì Jiǔyuè.　　　　　( )

(3) Qùnián shì 2012 nián, míngnián shì 2013 nián.　　　　　( )

(4) Qiáozhì qùnián méi qù Jiānádà, jīnnián qù le.　　　　　( )

(5) Tā míngtiān mǎi le sān běnr shū.　　　　　( )

(6) Zhāng lǎoshī qùnián qùle Xīnxīlán, tā qīzi jīnnián yě qù le.　　　( )

4. Draw a picture of your birthday party and describe it to your classmates.

Please use the expressions of date, time, food, and party decorations.

5. Fill in the blanks and repeat the sentences after listening. 🎧

(1) _____ nián _____ yuè _____ rì shì Xiǎo Mǎ de shēngrì.

(2) Tā qǐng péngyoumen cānjiā tā de _____.

(3) Péngyoumen sòng gěi tā hěn duō _____.

(4) Dàwèi _____, Nínà _____, Yīlāng _____, Xiǎo Wáng _____.

(5) Dàjiā yìqǐ _____, hé Xiǎo Mǎ _____, zhù tā shēngrì _____.

6. Sing a song.
   Zhù nǐ shēngrì kuàilè!
   祝 你 生 日 快 乐！
   Happy birthday to you!

Cultural tip

Birthday celebrations

The newly-born baby is very important for a family, because it is believed that the baby keeps the family blood stream running. The first event for the newly-born baby is the one-month-old celebration. In some areas, parents of the baby would offer boiled eggs dyed red to their relatives, friends and neighbours, because the shape and the red color of eggs are the symbols of a harmonious and happy life. In the evening, the baby's parents would also invite their relatives to a feast. The baby's one-year-old birthday is also an important event.

The sixtieth birthday is the first big birthday for the elderly, from then on, a big birthday will be celebrated for the elderly in each decade. People have various ways to celebrate birthdays and a dinner party is one of the most popular ways. It is considered inauspicious to give someone a clock as a gift, because "**sòng zhōng** 送 钟" *(give a clock as a gift) has the same sound as* "**sòngzhōng**送终" *(attend upon one's dying senior family member until he/she dies).*

Eating noodles on someone's birthday is a Chinese custom, as noodles are long, which symbolizes a long life. They are called "long-life noodles".

10 Zěnme zǒu?

How can I get there?

怎么走?

Key points

1 Asking for locations and directions and answering
2 Specific position words

⊃ Start here

Listen and fill in the brackets. 🎧

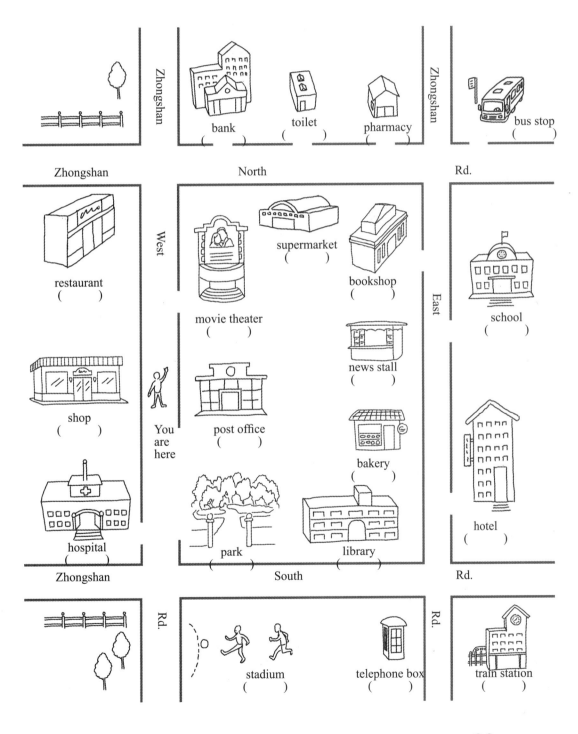

huǒchēzhàn
火 车 站   *train station*
huǒchē 火车 *train*

qìchēzhàn
汽 车 站   *bus stop*

yínháng
银 行   *bank*

túshūguǎn
图 书 馆   *library*

bīnguǎn / lǚguǎn
宾 馆 / 旅 馆   *hotel*

diànyǐngyuàn
电 影 院   *movie theater*
diànyǐng 电影 *movie*

tǐyùchǎng
体 育 场   *stadium*

diànhuàtíng
电 话 亭   *telephone box*

bàotíng
报 亭   *news stall*

shāngdiàn / diàn
商 店 / 店   *shop*

shūdiàn
书 店   *bookshop*

fàndiàn
饭 店   *restaurant*

miànbāodiàn
面 包 店   *bakery*
miànbāo 面包 *bread*

yàodiàn
药 店   *pharmacy*

chāoshì / chāojí shìchǎng
超 市 / 超 级 市 场 *supermarket*

yóujú
邮 局   *post office*

cèsuǒ
厕 所   *toilet*

Listen and repeat. 🎧

↘ Specific position words (2)

qián(bian)
前 （边）   *front*

hòu(bian)
后 （边）   *behind*

zuǒ(bian)
左 （边）   *left*

yòu(bian)
右 （边）   *right*

páng(biān)
旁 （边）   *next to*

zhōngjiān
中 间   *between*

duìmiàn
对 面   *opposite*

fùjìn
附近   *nearby*

dōng(bian)
东 （边）   *east / east side*

xī(bian)
西（边）   *west / west side*

nán(bian)
南 （边）   *south / south side*

běi(bian)
北（边）   *north / north side*

Dialogues

1

A: **Qǐngwèn, nǎr yǒu cèsuǒ?**
Excuse me, where is the toilet?
请问，哪儿有厕所？

B: **Zhōngshān Běilù.**
Zhongshan North Road.
中山北路。

A: **Zěnme zǒu?**
How can I get there?
怎么走？

B: **Cóng zhèr yìzhí wǎng qián, dào shízì lùkǒu, guò tiānqiáo yòu guǎi jiù kàndào le.**
Go straight ahead to the crossroads, cross an overhead walkway then turn right, you'll see a toilet.
从这儿一直往前，到十字路口，过天桥右拐就看到了。

Tā zài yínháng hé yàodiàn zhōngjiān, chāoshì duìmiàn.
It's between the bank and the pharmacy, opposite the supermarket.
它在银行和药店中间，超市对面。

A: **Yuǎn ma?**
Is it far?
远吗？

B: **Bù yuǎn.**
Not really.
不远。

zěnme 怎 么	*how*	
zǒu 走	*walk*	
cóng 从	*from*	
yìzhí 一直	*straight*	
wǎng 往	*go*	
shízì lùkǒu 十 字 路 口	*crossroads*	
guò 过	*to cross, to pass*	
tiānqiáo 天 桥	*overhead walkway*	
guǎi 拐	*turn*	
yuǎn 远	*far*	
(**jìn** 近	*near*)	

Notes

dào 到 *is used after the verb to express the result of an action, e.g.*

kàndào
saw
看到

shōudào
received
收到

读拼音学汉语

A: **Qǐngwèn, wǒ qù túshūguǎn, xūyào zuò gōngjiāochē ma?**
Excuse me, I'm going to the library. Do I need to take a bus?
请问，我去图书馆，需要坐公交车吗？

B: **Bú yòng. Nǐ wǎng huí zǒu, guòle gōngyuán wǎng dōng guǎi, nánbian shì tǐyùchǎng, běibian jiù shì túshūguǎn.**
No, you needn't. Go back this way, pass the park then turn east. There is a stadium on the south and the library is on the north.
不用。你往回走，过了公园往东拐，南边是体育场，北边就是图书馆。

A: **Xièxie.**
Thank you.
谢谢。

B: **Bú kèqi.**
You're welcome.
不客气。

xūyào 需要	*need*
bú yòng / bù xūyào 不 用／不 需 要	*needn't*
wǎng / xiàng 往 ／ 向	*toward, in the direction of*
huí 回	*back*

A: **Qǐngwèn, wǒ qù Shànghǎi, zài nǎr dēngjī?**
Excuse me, I'm going to Shanghai. Where is the boarding gate please?
请问，我去上海，在哪儿登机？

B: **Nǐ chéng nǎ cì hángbān?**
Which flight are you taking?
你乘哪次航班？

A: **Shànghǎi Hángkōng Gōngsī FM 9108 cì hángbān.**
The FM9108 flight of Shanghai Airlines.
上海航空公司FM9108次航班。

B: **12 hào dēngjīkǒu.**
Boarding Gate 12.
12号登机口。

A: **Wǎng nǎr zǒu?**
How can I get there?
往哪儿走？

B: **Cóng zhèr zuǒ guǎi, yìzhí wǎng qián, jìnle dàtīng jiù kàndào dēngjīkǒu le.**
Turn left from here, go straight ahead to the hall, then you'll see the boarding gate.
从这儿左拐，一直往前，进了大厅就看到登机口了。

dēngjī 登 机	*board a plane*
cì 次	*flight number*
hángbān 航 班	*scheduled flight*
hángkōng gōngsī 航 空 公 司	*airlines*
hángkōng 航空	*aviation*
dēngjīkǒu 登 机 口	*boarding gate*
dàtīng 大 厅	*hall*

⤶ Form

Expressing a location
(See "Grammar Outline", P220)

	In Chinese	In English
Interrogative sentences	**Diànyǐngyuàn zài nǎr?** 电 影 院 在 哪儿?	*Where is the movie theater?*
	Shūdiàn zài nǎr? 书 店 在 哪儿?	*Where is the bookshop?*
Answers	**zài** 在 + *noun + specific position word*	*A preposition / prepositional phrase is used between the two places*
	(Zài) Yóujú pángbiān. (在) 邮局 旁 边。	*The movie theater is next to the post office.*
	(Zài) Xuéxiào duìmiàn. (在) 学 校 对 面。	*The bookshop is opposite the school.*

Expressing the direction

⬈	⬉	⬆	⤵
yòu guǎi 右 拐 *turn right*	**zuǒ guǎi** 左 拐 *turn left*	**wǎng/xiàng qián zǒu** 往 / 向 前 走 *go straight ahead*	**wǎng huí zǒu** 往回走 *go back*

	In Chinese	In English
Interrogative sentences	**Zěnme zǒu?** 怎 么 走?	*How can I get there?*
Answers	*Preposition + specific position word + verb*	*Verb + adverb*
	Wǎng/Xiàng qián zǒu. 往 / 向 前 走。	*Go (straight) ahead.*
	Wǎng huí zǒu. 往 回 走。	*Go back (this way).*
	(Wǎng/Xiàng) Zuǒ guǎi. (往 / 向) 左 拐。	*Turn left.*
	(Wǎng/Xiàng) Yòu guǎi. (往 / 向) 右 拐。	*Turn right.*

Exercises

1. Look at the map on page 93. Suppose you're at the point marked "You are here", match the questions and answers after listening. 🎧

(1) Dàhuá Fàndiàn zài nǎr?	Zài Zhōngshān Běilù. Qiánbian shízì lùkǒu zuǒ guǎi, zuǒbian dì-yī jiā jiù shì.
(2) Huǒchēzhàn zài nǎr?	Wǎng qián zǒu, yòu guǎi, zài guò yí gè shízì lùkǒu, zuǒbian jiù shì.
(3) Qù tǐyùchǎng zěnme zǒu?	Zài Zhōngshān Dōnglù hé Zhōngshān Nánlù de shízì lùkǒu.
(4) Qù qìchēzhàn zěnme zǒu?	Wǎng huí zǒu, guòle shízì lùkǒu, jiù kànjiàn le.

2. Look at the map again. Listen to the recording and fill in the blanks. 🎧

(1) Qǐngwèn, chāoshì zài nǎr?

Zài Zhōngshān _____ lù, diànyǐngyuàn hé shūdiàn _____.

(2) Qǐngwèn, nǎr yǒu lǚguǎn ?

Zhōngshān _____ lù yǒu, zài xuéxiào _____.

(3) Qǐngwèn, túshūguǎn zài nǎr?

Zài Zhōngshān _____ lù, gōngyuán_____.

(4) Qǐngwèn, yīyuàn zài nǎr?

Zài Zhōngshān _____ lù, gōngyuán _____.

3. Look at the map again and answer the questions.

(1) Qù yàodiàn zěnme zǒu?

_____

(2) Qù huǒchēzhàn zěnme zǒu?

_____

(3) Qù gōngyuán zěnme zǒu?

_____

(4) Qù bàotíng zěnme zǒu?

_____

(5) Qù miànbāodiàn zěnme zǒu?

_____

4. Listen to the recording and draw a picture. 🎧

读拼音学汉语

98

⊃ Share the poem

Jiāngnán
江南

(Yuèfǔ míngē)
（乐府民歌）

Jiāngnán kě cǎi lián.
江　南　可　采　莲。

Liányè hé tiántián!
莲　叶　何　田　田！

Yú xì liányè jiān.
鱼　戏　莲　叶　间。

Yú xì liányè dōng,
鱼　戏　莲　叶　东，

yú xì liányè xī,
鱼　戏　莲　叶　西，

yú xì liányè nán,
鱼　戏　莲　叶　南，

yú xì liányè běi.
鱼　戏　莲　叶　北。

South of the Yangtze River

(Yuefu folk song)

Lotus can be picked in the south of the Yangtze River.
How thick the leaves are!
The fish are having fun amongst them.
They are playing eastward of lotus leaves,
they are playing westward of lotus leaves,
they are playing southward of lotus leaves,
they are playing northward of lotus leaves.

⊃ Cultural tip

Taking a bus

The bus is an important means of transportation in big cities in China. It is very convenient for people to take buses because detailed information is provided at each bus stop, including bus numbers, bus stop names, schedules and all stops along the way.

On buses in most big cities, there are announcements both in Chinese and English, telling passengers the details of each stop. The announcement is normally like "This is ×× stop and the next stop is ××. If you are getting off at the next stop, please get ready…"

When taking buses, passengers can use ticket cards or cashes. There are also boxes installed on some buses so that passengers can put the right amount of money in.

11

Nǐ néng jiāo wǒ ma?

Can you teach me?

你能教我吗？

Key points

Common modal verbs **huì** 会，
néng 能 and **kěyǐ** 可以

⟳ Start here

Listen and repeat. 🎧

tǎng 躺	lie
xiào 笑	smile, laugh
kū 哭	cry
zuò 坐	sit
pá 爬	crawl
zhàn 站	stand
pǎo 跑	run

tiào 跳	jump
shuō(huà) 说（话）	speak
yīng'ér 婴儿	baby
háizi 孩子	child
gāng 刚	just, newly
zhǐ 只	only

Listen and match the sentences with the pictures. 🎧

1

2

3

4

5

6

7

(1) **Gāng chūshēng de yīng'ér zhǐ huì tǎng zài chuáng shang. (　　)**
Newborn babies can only lie in bed.
刚出生的婴儿只会躺在床上。

(2) **Yīng'ér huì kū、huì xiào. (　　)**
Babies can cry and smile.
婴儿会哭、会笑。

(3) **Liù gè yuè de háizi huì zuò. (　　)**
Babies can sit at the age of six months.
六个月的孩子会坐。

(4) **Bā gè yuè de háizi huì pá. (　　)**
Babies can crawl at the age of eight months.
八个月的孩子会爬。

(5) **Shí gè yuè de háizi huì zhàn. (　　)**
Babies can stand at the age of ten months.
十个月的孩子会站。

(6) **Yí suì de háizi huì zǒu. (　　)**
Babies can walk at the age of one.
一岁的孩子会走。

(7) **Yí suì yǐhòu huì pǎo、huì tiào、huì shuōhuà. (　　)**
Children can run, jump and speak after the age of one.
一岁以后会跑、会跳、会说话。

Notes

huì 会, néng 能, kěyǐ 可以 *are modal verbs. They are used to express abilities and possibilities, and their meanings are similar to "can" in English.*
Negatives: **bú huì** 不会, **bù néng** 不能, **bù kěyǐ** 不可以.

⊃ Dialogues

1

A: **Xiǎo Lǐ, zhè shì shéi de qìchē?**
Xiao Li, whose car is it?
小李，这是谁的汽车？

B: **Wǒ de. Qiántiān cái mǎi de.**
It's mine. I just bought it the day before yesterday.
我的。前天才买的。

A: **Zhēn piàoliang! Wǒ yě xiǎng mǎi yí liàng qìchē. Nǐ néng bāng wǒ kànkan ma?**
How beautiful! I want to buy a car too. Can you help me to have a look?
真漂亮！我也想买一辆汽车。你能帮我看看吗？

B: **Kěyǐ. Nǐ huì kāi chē ma?**
Of course. Can you drive a car?
可以。你会开车吗？

A: **Bú huì. Nǐ néng jiāo wǒ ma?**
No , I can't. Can you teach me?
不会。你能教我吗？

B: **Néng. Shénme shíhou qù mǎi chē?**
Yes, I can. When shall we go to buy a car?
能。什么时候去买车？

A: **Míngtiān hǎo ma?**
How about tomorrow?
明天好吗？

qiántiān 前 天	*the day before yesterday*	
cái 才	*just*	
bāng(zhù) 帮 （助）	*help*	
kànkan 看 看	*(verb reduplication form)* (See "Grammar Outline", P217)	
kāi chē 开 车	*drive*	
jiāo 教	*teach*	

1

B: **Duìbuqǐ, míngtiān wǒ yǒu shìr. Hòutiān kěyǐ ma?**
Sorry, I will be occupied tomorrow. How about the day after tomorrow?
对不起，明天我有事儿。后天可以吗？

A: **Kěyǐ, xièxie nǐ.**
OK, thank you.
可以，谢谢你。

B: **Bú kèqi. Hòutiān jiàn.**
You are welcome. See you the day after tomorrow.
不客气。后天见。

hòutiān 后　天	*the day after tomorrow*

2

A: **Tián Fāng, xiàwǔ pá shān nǐ lèi ma?**
Tian Fang, were you tired from climbing the mountain this afternoon?
田芳，下午爬山你累吗？

B: **Bú lèi. Ānnà, nǐ huì shuō Pǔtōnghuà ma?**
I wasn't. Anna, can you speak Mandarin?
不累。安娜，你会说普通话吗？

A: **Zhǐ huì yìdiǎnr. Nǐ néng jiāo wǒ ma?**
Only a little. Could you teach me?
只会一点儿。你能教我吗？

B: **Néng. Wǒ jiāo nǐ Pǔtōnghuà, nǐ jiāo wǒ Yīngyǔ, hǎo ma?**
Yes, I can. I teach you Mandarin, and can you teach me English?
能。我教你普通话，你教我英语，好吗？

A: **Hǎo wa. Wǒ huì tiàowǔ, bú huì tán qín. Nǐ néng jiāo wǒ ma?**
OK. I can dance, but I can't play the piano. Could you teach me?
好哇。我会跳舞，不会弹琴。你能教我吗？

B: **Méi wèntí. Wǒ jiāo nǐ tán gāngqín, nǐ jiāo wǒ tiàowǔ.**
No problem. I teach you to play the piano and you teach me to dance.
没问题。我教你弹钢琴，你教我跳舞。

A: **Tài hǎo le! Tián Fāng, nǐ xǐhuan pǎobù ma?**
Wonderful! Do you like jogging, Tian Fang?
太好了！田芳，你喜欢跑步吗？

B: **Xǐhuan.**
Yes, I do.
喜欢。

A: **Wǒ yě xǐhuan. Xiàcì wǒmen yìqǐ pǎobù ba.**
I like jogging too. Let's go jogging together next time.
我也喜欢。下次我们一起跑步吧。

pá shān 爬　山	*climb mountains*
lèi 累	*tired*
Pǔtōnghuà 普　通　话	*Mandarin*
tán qín 弹　琴	*play the piano*
wèntí 问　题	*question, problem*
gāngqín 钢　琴	*piano*
pǎobù 跑　步	*run, jog*
xià (yí) cì 下（一）次	*next time*

A: **Qǐngwèn, jīn wǎn wǒ kěyǐ zhù zhège bīnguǎn ma?**
Excuse me, can I stay in this hotel tonight?
请问，今晚我可以住这个宾馆吗？

B: **Dāngrán kěyǐ. Nín shì Měiguórén ma?**
Sure. Are you American?
当然可以。您是美国人吗？

A: **Bù, wǒ shì Jiānádàrén.**
No, I'm Canadian.
不，我是加拿大人。

B: **Wǒ néng kànkan nín de zhèngjiàn ma?**
Could I have a look at your certificate?
我能看看您的证件吗？

A: **Zhè shì wǒ de hùzhào. Wǒ kěyǐ kànkan fángjiān ma?**
This is my passport. Could I have a look at the room?
这是我的护照。我可以看看房间吗？

B: **Kěyǐ. Qǐng suí wǒ lái.**
Yes, you can. Follow me please.
可以。请随我来。

A: **Zhèlǐ néng xīyān ma?**
Could I smoke here?
这里能吸烟吗？

B: **Bù néng, zhèlǐ shì wúyānqū.**
I'm afraid not. It's a smoke-free zone.
不能，这里是无烟区。

dāngrán 当 然	*of course, sure*
zhèngjiàn 证 件	*certificate*
hùzhào 护 照	*passport*
fángjiān 房 间	*room*
suí / gēn 随 / 跟	*follow*
xīyān 吸 烟	*smoke*
wúyānqū 无 烟 区	*smoke-free zone*

⤴ Form

Modal verbs: **huì** 会，**néng** 能，**kěyǐ** 可以

(See "Grammar Outline", P213)

	In Chinese	In English
Interrogative sentences	1. *Noun/Pronoun + modal verb + verb (+ noun/pronoun) +* **ma** 吗	*The modal verb "can" is at the beginning of the sentence.*
	Wǒ kěyǐ zuò ma? 我 可以 坐 吗？	*Can I sit down?*
	Tā huì shuō Pǔtōnghuà ma? 他 会 说 普 通 话 吗？	*Can he speak Mandarin?*

	In Chinese	In English
Interrogative sentences	**Nǐ néng jiāo wǒ ma?** 你 能 教 我 吗?	*Can you teach me?*
	2. *...positive modal verb + negative modal verb + verb...*	
	Wǒ kě(yǐ) bu kěyǐ zuò? 我 可(以) 不 可以 坐?	*Can I sit down?*
	Tā huì bu huì shuō Pǔtōnghuà? 他 会 不 会 说 普 通 话?	*Can he speak Mandarin?*
	Nǐ néng bu néng jiāo wǒ? 你 能 不 能 教 我?	*Can you teach me?*
Answers	**Nǐ kěyǐ / bù kěyǐ zuò.** 你 可以/ 不 可以 坐。	*Yes, you can sit down. /* *No, you can't sit down.*
	Tā huì / bú huì shuō Pǔtōnghuà. 他 会 /不 会 说 普 通 话。	*Yes, he can speak Mandarin. /* *No, he can't speak Mandarin.*
	Wǒ néng / bù néng jiāo nǐ. 我 能 / 不 能 教 你。	*Yes, I can teach you. /* *No, I can't teach you.*
Short answers	**Kěyǐ. / Bù kěyǐ.** 可以。/ 不 可以。	*Yes, you can. / No, you can't.*
	Huì. / Bú huì. 会。 / 不 会。	*Yes, he can. / No, he can't.*
	Néng. / Bù néng. 能。 / 不 能。	*Yes, I can. / No, I can't.*

⟳ Exercises

◁ 1. Substitution dialogues. 🎧

(1) Nǐ huì
你 会

kāi chē 开 车
shuō Pǔtōnghuà 说 普 通 话
chàng Zhōngwéngēr 唱 中 文 歌儿
tán gāngqín 弹 钢 琴

ma ?
吗?

Huì. / Bú huì. 会。 / 不 会。

(2) Nǐ néng
你 能

| bāng wǒ |
| 帮 我 |
| lái xuéxiào |
| 来 学 校 |
| mǎi yìdiǎnr shuǐguǒ |
| 买 一 点儿 水 果 |
| zǎodiǎnr qǐchuáng |
| 早 点儿 起 床 |

ma ?
吗?

| Néng. / Bù néng. |
| 能。 / 不 能。 |

(3) Wǒ kěyǐ
我 可以

| chéng chūzūchē |
| 乘 出租车 |
| hē diǎnr jiǔ |
| 喝 点儿 酒 |
| xīyān |
| 吸 烟 |
| xiūxi shí fēnzhōng |
| 休息 十 分 钟 |

ma?
吗?

| Kěyǐ. / Bù kěyǐ. |
| 可以。/不 可以。 |

2. Transform the declarative sentences to interrogative sentences.

e.g. Lǐ xiānsheng huì kāi chē.
Lǐ xiānsheng huì kāi chē ma?
Lǐ xiānsheng huì bu huì kāi chē?

(1) Chē shang bù kěyǐ xīyān.
_____?
_____?

(3) Tā de qīzi huì zuò dàngāo.
_____?
_____?

(2) Hǎilún néng kàn Zhōngwén zázhì.
_____?
_____?

(4) Xiǎo Zhāng huì tiàowǔ.
_____?
_____?

3. Listen to the passage and tell whether the statements are true (√) or false (×).

(1) Wǒ de péngyou jiào Zhāng Lì.   ( )
(2) Zhāng Lì bú huì shuō Yīngyǔ.   ( )
(3) Zhāng Lì de māma shì Yīngguórén.   ( )
(4) Zhāng Lì de bàba shì gāngqín lǎoshī.   ( )
(5) Zhāng Lì xué Yīngyǔ, wǒ xué tán gāngqín.   ( )
(6) Wǒ jiāo Zhāng Lì tán gāngqín, Zhāng Lì jiāo wǒ shuō Yīngyǔ. ( )
(7) Tā xǐhuan chàng gē, wǒ xǐhuan tiàowǔ.   ( )

(8) Tā kuàilè, wǒ yě kuàilè.　　　　　　　　　　　　　　( )

4. Read the explanation of "**huì**会", "**néng**能" and "**kěyǐ**可以" in "Grammar Outline" (P213), then fill in the blanks with them.

(1) Xiǎo Zhāng _____ chàng gē, bú _____ tiàowǔ.

(2) Zhèlǐ _____ xīyān ma?

(3) Wǒ bú _____ kāi chē, nǐ _____ jiāo wǒ ma?

(4) Chálǐ xuéle yì nián Zhōngwén, tā _____ shuō Zhōngguóhuà, _____ kàn Zhōngwénshū.

(5) Jīntiān wǒ yǒu shìr, bù _____ qù shàngbān le, míngtiān wǒ _____ qù.

(6) Wǒ yǒu chē, nǐ _____ zuò wǒ de chē qù túshūguǎn.

5. Talk about what you can do and what you cannot do.

chàng Zhōngwéngē / chàng Yīngwéngē 唱　中　文　歌 / 唱　英　文　歌	zuò dàngāo / zuò miàntiáo 做　蛋　糕 / 做　面　条
dú Zhōngwénshū / dú Yīngwén zázhì 读　中　文　书 / 读　英　文　杂志	shōufā diànzǐ yóujiàn / shàngwǎng 收　发　电子　邮　件 / 上　网
shuō Pǔtōnghuà / shuō Yīngyǔ 说　普　通　话 / 说　英　语	yòng shǒujī dǎ diànhuà / kàn shìjiè dìtú 用　手　机　打　电　话 / 看　世界　地图
xiě Zhōngguózì / huà huàr 写　中　国　字 / 画　画儿	kāi chē / xǐ yīfu 开　车 / 洗　衣服
tán gāngqín / tiàowǔ 弹　钢　琴 / 跳　舞	xīyān / hē jiǔ 吸　烟 / 喝　酒

⟳ Cultural tip

Main transportation

Bicycles are an important means of transportation for most Chinese people. There is at least one bicycle for each family on average. People ride bicycles to go to work, to go to school, and to go shopping. Electric bicycles and buses are also popular means of transportation. Subways develop very fast in big cities these years.

Cars were regarded as luxuries in the twentieth century but they are becoming more and more common. Nowadays, many families have their own cars. However, bicycles can never be replaced by cars due to the fact that they are much cheaper, more convenient, and pollution free. Of course, electric bicycles are becoming popular because they demand less effort for longer distance commute and are faster.

12 Zài yínháng

At the bank

在银行

Key points

1 Common modal verbs **yào** 要 and **xiǎng** 想
2 Chinese currency

➲ Start here

Listen and repeat. 🎧

◁ Chinese currency

qián 钱	*money*	**kuài / yuán** 块 ／ 元	*the basic unit of Chinese currency*
Rénmínbì 人 民 币	Renminbi *(RMB ¥)*	**máo / jiǎo** 毛 ／ 角	*one-tenth of one yuan*

◁ Main currencies of the world

wàibì 外 币	*foreign currency*	**Yīngbàng** 英 镑	*pound (GBP £)*
Měiyuán 美 元	*US dollar (USD $)*	**Rìyuán** 日 元	*Japanese yen (JPY ¥)*
Ōuyuán 欧 元	*euro (EUR €)*		

Listen and match the words with the pictures. 🎧

1	2	3	4	5	6

(1) **cúnzhé**
存 折   *bankbook*   (   )

(2) **zhīpiào**
支 票   *check*   (   )

(3) **xìnyòngkǎ**
信 用 卡   *credit card*   (   )

(4) **bāoguǒ**
包 裹   *parcel*   (   )

(5) **bāoguǒdān**
包 裹 单   *parcel form*   (   )

(6) **xìnfēng**
信 封   *envelope*   (   )

⊃ Reading and dialogues

1

1. **Zhèlǐ shì Zhōngguó Yínháng yíngyè dàtīng.**
   This is the business hall of the Bank of China.
   这里是中国银行营业大厅。

2. **Wǒ xiǎng shēnqǐng yì zhāng xìnyòngkǎ.**
   I'd like to apply for a credit card.
   我想申请一张信用卡。

3. **Líndá yào cún qián.**
   Linda wants to deposit some money.
   琳达要存钱。

4. **Mǎlìyà yào qǔ qián.**
   Maria wants to withdraw some money.
   玛丽娅要取钱。

5. **Xiǎo Lǐ yào duìxiàn zhīpiào.**
   Xiao Li wants to cash the check.
   小李要兑现支票。

6. **Jiékè yào yòng Měiyuán duìhuàn Rénmínbì.**
   Jack wants to exchange US dollars for Renminbi.
   杰克要用美元兑换人民币。

yíngyè 营业	do business
shēnqǐng 申请	apply for
cún qián / cún kuǎn 存钱 / 存款	deposit
cún(fàng) 存（放）	leave sth in sb's care
qǔ qián / qǔ kuǎn 取钱 / 取款	withdraw
qǔ 取	take
duìxiàn 兑现	cash a check
duìhuàn / huàn 兑换 / 换	exchange

Notes

yào 要 *and* **xiǎng** 想 *are modal verbs, which have meanings similar to "want", "will", "would", etc. They are used to express needs, demands and wishes.* *Negatives:* **bú yào** 不要, **bù xiǎng** 不想.

2

A: **Qǐngwèn, jīntiān Měiyuán de huìlǜ shì duōshao?**
   Excuse me, what is today's exchange rate for US dollars?
   请问，今天美元的汇率是多少？

B: **Nǐ yào mǎi háishi yào mài?**
   Do you want to buy or sell?
   你要买还是要卖？

huìlǜ 汇率	exchange rate
yígòng / zǒnggòng 一共 / 总共	in total, altogether

2

A: **Měiyuán huàn Rénmínbì.**
I want to sell US dollars, and buy Renminbi.
美元换人民币。

B: **6.31. Nǐ huàn duōshao?**
6.31. How many dollars do you want to sell?
六点三一。你换多少?

A: **Wǔbǎi Měiyuán.**
$ 500.
五百美元。

B: **Yígòng sānqiān yībǎi wǔshíwǔ yuán Rénmínbì.**
That's ¥ 3155 in total.
一共三千一百五十五元人民币。

3

A: **Xiānsheng, wǒ yào wǎng Huìlíngdùn jì yí gè bāoguǒ.**
Sir, I want to send a parcel to Wellington.
先生,我要往惠灵顿寄一个包裹。

B: **Bāoguǒ li shì shénme, kěyǐ kànkan ma?**
What's in the parcel? Could I have a look?
包裹里是什么,可以看看吗?

A: **Dāngrán kěyǐ.**
Sure.
当然可以。

B: **Qǐng tiánxiě bāoguǒdān.**
Please fill in the parcel form.
请填写包裹单。

A: **Yóufèi duōshao?**
How much is the postage, please?
邮费多少?

B: **Yìbǎi sānshíbā yuán.**
¥ 138.
一百三十八元。

A: **Wǒ hái xiǎng mǎi yì zhāng Shèngdànkǎ, jì yì fēng hángkōngxìn.**
And I'd like to buy a Christmas card and send an air letter.
我还想买一张圣诞卡,寄一封航空信。

B: **Wǎng nǎr jì ?**
Where would you like to send it?
往哪儿寄?

A: **Xīní.**
To Sydney.
悉尼。

jì / yóujì
寄／邮寄　*send, post*

tián(xiě)
填（写）　*fill in*

yóufèi
邮费　*postage*

Shèngdànkǎ
圣诞卡 *Christmas card*

Shèngdàn 圣诞 *Christmas*

fēng
封　*(measurement word used for letters)*

hángkōngxìn
航空信 *air letter*

xìn 信 *letter*

111

Form

Modal verbs: **yào** 要，**xiǎng** 想
(See "Grammar Outline", P214)

	In Chinese	In English
Interrogative sentences	1. *Noun/Pronoun + modal verb + verb (+noun/pronoun) +* **ma** 吗 **Nǐ yào xiūxi ma?** 你 要 休息 吗？ **Jiǎn xiǎng huí Yīngguó ma?** 简 想 回 英 国 吗？	Modal verbs "would", "will" or auxiliary verbs "do", "does" etc. are at the beginning of the sentences. *Would you like to have a rest?* *Does Jane want to go back to Britain?*
	2. *...positive modal verb + negative modal verb + verb ...* **Nǐ yào bu yào xiūxi?** 你 要 不 要 休息？ **Jiǎn xiǎng bu xiǎng huí Yīngguó ?** 简 想 不 想 回 英 国？	*Would you like to have a rest?* *Does Jane want to go back to Britain?*
Answers	**Wǒ yào / bú yào xiūxi.** 我 要／ 不 要 休息。 **Jiǎn/Tā xiǎng / bù xiǎng huí Yīngguó.** 简 ／她 想／ 不 想 回 英 国。	*Yes, I'd like to have a rest. /* *No, I wouldn't like to have a rest.* *Yes, Jane/she wants to go back to Britain. /* *No, Jane/she doesn't want to go back to Britain.*
Short answers	**Yào. / Bú yào.** 要。／ 不 要。 **Xiǎng. / Bù xiǎng.** 想。 ／ 不 想。	*Yes, I'd like to. / No, I wouldn't.* *Yes, she does. / No, she doesn't.*

yào 要，**xiǎng** 想 *are also verbs*

In Chinese	In English
Wǒ yào yì bēi shuǐ. 我 要 一 杯 水。	*I want a glass of water.*
Wǒ xiǎng wǒ de māma. 我 想 我 的 妈 妈。	*I miss my mother.*

Another meaning of **yào** 要

In Chinese	In English
Chéng gōngjiāochē yào mǎi piào. 乘 公 交 车 要 买 票。	*Everybody has to buy a ticket to take a bus.*
Wǒmen měi tiān yào shuā yá. 我 们 每 天 要 刷 牙。	*We must brush our teeth everyday.*

⊃ Exercises

◁ 1. Substitution reading. 🎧

	jì 寄	yì fēng xìn. 一 封 信。 yí jiàn bāoguǒ. 一 件 包 裹。
Wǒ xiǎng 我 想	qǔ 取	yì fēng xìn. 一 封 信。 kuǎn. 款。
	mǎi 买	yì zhāng yóupiào. 一 张 邮 票。 shí gè xìnfēng. 十 个 信 封。

| Wǒ yào
我　要 | kāfēi.
咖啡。
gānjìng de fángjiān.
干　净　的　房　间。 |

| Wǒ xiǎng
我　想 | jiā.
家。
wǒ de péngyoumen.
我　的　朋　友　们。 |

| Shēnqǐng xìnyòngkǎ
申　请　信　用　卡
Guò shēngrì
过　生　日 | yào
要 | dài zhèngjiàn.
带　证　件。
chī chángshòumiàn.
吃　长　寿　面。 |

◁ **2. Choose the correct answers after listening.** 🎧

(1) *What did Xiao Wang receive?* (　　)

    A. Yí jiān bāoguǒ.

    B. Yì zhāng Shèngdànkǎ.

    C. Yì fēng xìn.

(2) *What did Charlie ask?* (　　)

    A. Měiyuán de huìlǜ.

    B. Rìyuán de huìlǜ.

    C. Ōuyuán de huìlǜ.

(3) *What did he do in the afternoon?* (　　)

    A. Qǔ qián.   B. Jì qián.   C. Cún qián.

(4) *Who did I call in the morning?* (　　)

    A. Fàndiàn.   B. Bīnguǎn.   C. Túshūguǎn.

(5) *How much* Renminbi *did Li Ming exchange?* (　　)

    A. Liǎngqiān èrbǎi wǔshísì yuán.

    B. Liǎngqiān wǔbǎi wǔshí'èr yuán.

    C. Liǎngqiān wǔbǎi èrshísì yuán.

3. Match A. with B. (Every A. verbal phrase will be used more than once.)

	A.	B.
Wǒ xiǎng 我 想	qù yínháng (1) 去 银 行 qù yóujú (2) 去 邮局 qù chāoshì (3) 去 超 市	duìxiàn zhīpiào. (1) 兑 现 支 票。 mǎi diǎnr shuǐguǒ. (2) 买 点儿 水 果。 jì xìn. (3) 寄 信。 qǔ bāoguǒ. (4) 取 包 裹。 cún kuǎn. (5) 存 款。 mǎi (yí) gè shǒujī. (6) 买 (一) 个 手 机。 qǔ qián. (7) 取 钱。 duìhuàn wàibì. (8) 兑 换 外 币。 mǎi (yì) píng jiǔ. (9) 买 (一) 瓶 酒。 mǎi yóupiào. (10) 买 邮 票。 mǎi xìnfēng. (11) 买 信 封。 mǎi (yì) tiáo kùzi. (12) 买 (一) 条 裤子。

➲ Cultural tip

Saving and depositing money

Chinese, especially the elderly, like to save and deposit money. It is a traditional custom, as the old saying goes: "Success in life comes from being hardworking and thrifty; failure in life comes from being extravagant." **(Chéng yóu qínjiǎn bài yóu shē 成由勤俭败由奢)** *"Be prepared for danger in times of safety." (Jū'ān–sīwēi 居安思危)*

People save and deposit money to prepare for expenditure when they are old or sick. Although the government offers them social insurance, many people are still worried about their old age and being unable to work.

People also save and deposit money for their children, helping them with their marriage, careers and other important events.

Nowadays, young people tend to spend money rather than save as they want to enjoy life. They spend money on travelling and on entertainment.

13

Duōshao qián yì jīn?
How much is it for half a kilo?
多少钱一斤？

Key points

1 Selling and buying
2 Units of weight

→ Start here

Listen and repeat.

⬿ Items of vegetables and other food

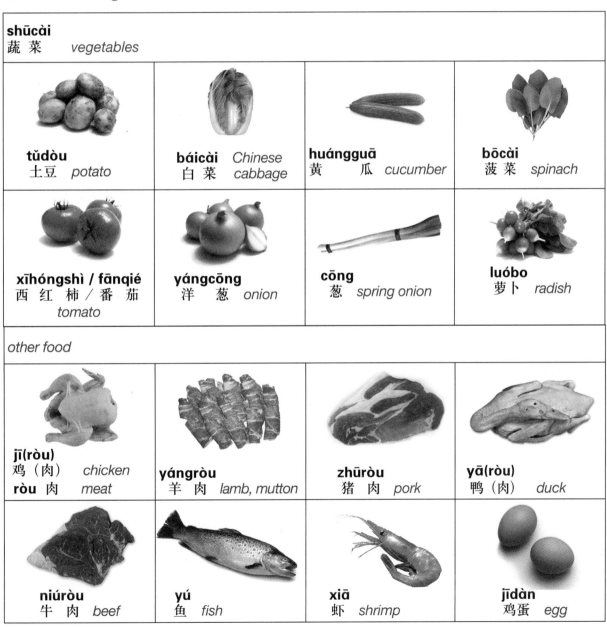

shūcài
蔬菜　*vegetables*

tǔdòu 土豆　*potato*	**báicài**　*Chinese* 白菜　*cabbage*	**huángguā** 黄　瓜　*cucumber*	**bōcài** 菠菜　*spinach*
xīhóngshì / fānqié 西红柿／番茄 *tomato*	**yángcōng** 洋　葱　*onion*	**cōng** 葱　*spring onion*	**luóbo** 萝卜　*radish*

other food

jī(ròu) 鸡（肉）　*chicken* **ròu** 肉　*meat*	**yángròu** 羊　肉　*lamb, mutton*	**zhūròu** 猪　肉　*pork*	**yā(ròu)** 鸭（肉）　*duck*
niúròu 牛　肉　*beef*	**yú** 鱼　*fish*	**xiā** 虾　*shrimp*	**jīdàn** 鸡蛋　*egg*

⬿ Chinese units of weight

jīn 斤	*(equal to half a kilogram)*	**liǎng** 两

*(One **liǎng** 两 is one-tenth of a **jīn** 斤.)*

⟳ Dialogues

1

A: **Nín yào mǎi shénme?**
What would you like to buy?
您要买什么？

B: **Hǎo xīnxiān de huángguā!**
Oh, how fresh the cucumbers are!
好新鲜的黄瓜！

A: **Dāngrán, zǎoshang gāng zhāi de. Nín yào duōshao?**
Of course, they were just picked this morning. How many do you want?
当然，早上刚摘的。您要多少？

B: **Wǒ yào liǎng gēn. Duōshao qián?**
Can I have two please? How much are they?
我要两根。多少钱？

A: **Yí kuài bā. Hái yào shénme?**
¥1.8. Anything else?
一块八。还要什么？

B: **Xīhóngshì duōshao qián yì jīn?**
How much is it for half a kilo of tomatoes?
西红柿多少钱一斤？

A: **Liǎng kuài yī.**
¥2.1.
两块一。

B: **Tǔdòu ne?**
And the potatoes?
土豆呢？

A: **Yí kuài èr yì jīn.**
¥1.2 for half a kilo.
一块二一斤。

B: **Wǒ měi yàng yào yì jīn.**
I'd like half a kilo of each, please.
我每样要一斤。

A: **Hǎo de, yígòng wǔ kuài yī.**
OK, ¥5.1 altogether.
好的，一共五块一。

B: **Zài yào yì kē dàbáicài hé yìxiē cōng.**
I also want a Chinese cabbage and some spring onions, please.
再要一棵大白菜和一些葱。

hǎo 好		*(used before an adjective to emphasize it)*
xīnxiān 新鲜	*fresh*	
zhāi 摘	*pick*	
zài 再	*again, in addition*	
yìxiē / xiē 一些／些	*some*	
zhǎo (qián) 找 （钱）	*give change*	

读拼音学汉语

1

A: **Dàbáicài liù máo yì jīn, cōng liǎng kuài qián yì bǎ. Zhè kē báicài sì jīn.**
It's six mao for half a kilo of Chineses cabbages and two kuai for a handful of spring onions. This Chinese cabbage is two kilos.
大白菜六毛一斤，葱两块钱一把。这棵白菜四斤。

B: **Yígòng duōshao qián?**
How much are these in total?
一共多少钱？

A: **Jiǔ kuài wǔ.**
¥9.5.
九块五。

B: **Gěi nín shí kuài.**
Here is ¥10.
给您十块。

A: **Zhǎo nín wǔ máo.**
Here's your ¥0.5 change.
找您五毛。

Notes

de 的 *is used after an adjective or adjectival phrase to indicate a modifier,*
e.g. **xīnxiān de huángguā** *fresh cucumbers* 新鲜的黄瓜.

gēn 根 *(measurement word) is used for items that are long and thin,*
e.g. **yì gēn huángguā** *a cucumber* 一根黄瓜, **liǎng gēn guǎizhàng** *two*
walking sticks 两根拐杖.

yàng/zhǒng 样/种 *(measurement words) are used to indicate different*
types of items, e.g. **liǎng zhǒng shuǐguǒ** *two types of fruit* 两种水果,
sān yàng shūcài *three types of vegetables* 三样蔬菜.

kē 棵 *(measurement word) is used with plants,*
e.g. **sān kē báicài** *three Chinese cabbages* 三棵白菜.

2

A: **Hǎo dà de jīdàn! Duōshao qián yì jīn?**
How big the eggs are! How much is it for half a kilo?
好大的鸡蛋！多少钱一斤？

B: **Sì kuài bā. Nín yào duōshao?**
¥4.8. How many would you like to buy?
四块八。您要多少？

guì 贵	expensive, high price
piányi 便宜	cheap, low price
xíng 行	okay

读拼音学汉语

A: **Hǎo guì! Zhūròu ne?**
So expensive! How about the pork?
好贵！猪肉呢？

B: **Shí kuài jiǔ.**
¥ 10.9.
十块九。

A: **Yě guì. Piányi diǎnr xíng ma?**
That's expensive, too. Can they be cheaper, please?
也贵。便宜点儿行吗？

B: **Xíng. Jīdàn sì kuài liù, zhūròu shí kuài wǔ, zěnmeyàng?**
Okay. ¥ 4.6 for eggs and ¥ 10.5 for pork. Is that OK?
行。鸡蛋四块六，猪肉十块五，怎么样？

A: **Liǎng jīn jīdàn, yì jīn shòu zhūròu.**
One kilo of eggs and half a kilo of lean pork.
两斤鸡蛋，一斤瘦猪肉。

B: **Hái yào shénme? Huó yú wǔ kuài qián yì jīn, nín yào ma?**
Anything else? The live fish are ¥ 5 for half a kilo. Would you like to have some?
还要什么？活鱼五块钱一斤，您要吗？

A: **Hǎo wa. Wǒ yào zhè tiáo dà de.**
Okay. I'd like to buy this bigger one.
好哇。我要这条大的。

B: **Yì jīn bā liǎng, jiǔ kuài qián. Yígòng èrshíbā kuài qī.**
0.9 kilo, the cost of the fish is ¥ 9. That's ¥ 28.7 in total.
一斤八两，九块钱。一共二十八块七。

A: **Ò, jīntiān huā qián tài duō le!**
Oh, I've spent a lot of money today!
哦，今天花钱太多了！

zěnmeyàng 怎 么 样	*is that OK*	
shòu 瘦	*lean*	
(**féi** 肥	*fat*	)
huó 活	*live*	
(**sǐ** 死	*dead*	)
huā 花	*spend*	

Form

Selling and buying

Interrogative sentences and short answers

1. *Noun/Pronoun +* **(yào) mǎi** (要)买 **/ yào** 要 **+ shénme** 什么

   Nǐ (yào) mǎi / yào shénme?   *What would you like to buy?*
   你（要）买 / 要 什么?

   Xīhóngshì.   *Tomatoes.*
   西 红 柿。

2. *Noun/Pronoun +* **(yào) mǎi** (要)买 **/ yào** 要 **+ duōshao** 多少
   Noun/Pronoun + **(yào) mǎi** (要)买 **/ yào** 要 **+ jǐ** 几 *+ measurement word*

   Nǐ (yào) mǎi / yào duōshao?   *How many do you want?*
   你（要）买 / 要 多少?

   Liǎng jīn.   *One kilo.*
   两 斤。

   Nǐ (yào) mǎi / yào jǐ jīn?   *How many half kilos do you want?*
   你（要）买 / 要 几斤?

   Liǎng jīn.   *I want one kilo.*
   两 斤。

3. **duōshao qián** 多少钱 **+ yī** 一 *+ measurement word*

   Duōshao qián yì jīn?   *How much is it for half a kilo?*
   多 少 钱 一 斤?

   Yí kuài èr.   *¥ 1.2.*
   一 块 二。

   The measurement word can be omitted when the interrogative word is **duōshao**多少*, but the measurement word cannot be omitted when the interrogative word is* **jǐ**几*.*

   Wrong   ✗ **Nǐ mǎi jǐ?**

Adverb **hǎo** 好

hǎo 好 *+ adjective (+* **de**的 *+ noun) is similar to the exclamatory sentence form "how + adjective" in English.*

Hǎo piányi de huángguā!   *How cheap these cucumbers are!*
好 便宜 的 黄 瓜!

Hǎo gānjìng de wūzi!   *How clean the room is!*
好 干 净 的 屋子!

Hǎo guì!   *How expensive!*
好 贵!

⊃ **Exercises**

↘ 1. Substitution dialogue. 🎧

A: Nǐ yào mǎi shénme?
你 要 买 什 么?

B: Wǒ yào mǎi
我 要 买

cōng. 葱。
báicài. 白 菜。
niúròu. 牛 肉。
yā. 鸭。

Duōshao qián
多 少 钱

yì bǎ? 一 把?
yì kē? 一 棵?
yì jīn? 一 斤?
yì zhī? 一 只?

A:
Liǎng kuài èr yì bǎ. 两 块 二 一 把。
Yí kuài yī yì kē. 一 块 一 一 棵。
Shí bā kuài wǔ yì jīn. 十 八 块 五 一 斤。
Èrshí liù kuài yì zhī. 二 十 六 块 一 只。

Nǐ yào duōshao?
你 要 多 少?

B:
Liǎng bǎ. 两 把。
Liǎng kē. 两 棵。
Sān jīn. 三 斤。
Yì zhī. 一 只。

A:
Sì kuài sì. 四 块 四。
Liǎng kuài èr. 两 块 二。
Wǔshí wǔ kuài wǔ. 五 十 五 块 五。
Èrshí liù kuài . 二 十 六 块。

↘ 2. Read dialogue 1 on pages 118-119, then make a shopping list and answer the questions.

(1) B mǎile yìxiē shénme?
B 买了 一些 什么?

(2) Měi yàng huāle duōshao qián?
每 样 花了 多 少 钱?

(3) B yígòng huāle duōshao qián?
B 一共 花了 多 少 钱?

(4) B gěile A duōshao qián?

　　B 给了 A 多 少　钱?

(5) A zhǎole B duōshao qián?

　　A 找了 B 多 少　钱?

B's shopping list		
Name	How many	How much
huángguā	2 gēn	¥ 1.8
	Total:	

⊴ 3.　Listen and repeat. 🎧

Hǎo xīnxiān de　　　shuǐguǒ! / báicài! / yú! / niúròu!
好　新　鲜　的　　　水　果! /白　菜! /鱼! /牛　肉!

Hǎo dà de　　　　　gōnggòng qìchē! / shǒu! / xīhóngshì!
好　大　的　　　　　公　　共　汽　车! /手! /西　红　柿!

Hǎo gānjìng de　　　xiǎo nǚháir! / yīfu! / wūzi! / xuéxiào!
好　干　净　的　　　小　女孩儿! /衣服! /屋子! /学　校!

⊴ 4.　Fill in the blanks after listening. 🎧

(1) Jīntiān _____ hěn piányi.

(2) Wǒ mǎile _____ píngguǒ, huāle _____ .

(3) Mǎile _____ jīn chéngzi, huāle _____ qián.

(4) Dìnà huāle _____ , mǎile _____ xiāngjiāo.

(5) Tā gěile _____ qián, zhǎole tā _____ .

⊃ Cultural tip

Food markets

There are daily food markets in all cities, selling a variety of foods every day such as live chickens, ducks, fish, shrimp, fresh meat, vegetables and fruit, etc. You are able to buy food from all over the country. You can negotiate the price with the sellers.

14 Zài fúzhuāngdiàn
In a clothing shop
在服装店

Key points

1 Comparative sentence
2 Adjective + **de** 的

Start here

Listen and repeat. 🎧

◁ Items of clothing and shoes

jiākè
夹 克   *jacket*

chènshān
衬 衫   *shirt*

niúzǎikù
牛 仔 裤   *jeans*

kùzi
裤子   *pants*

qúnzi
裙 子   *dress, skirt*

xié
鞋   *shoes*

1. **Zhè jiàn jiākè dà, nà jiàn jiākè xiǎo.**
   This jacket is big, and that jacket is small.
   这件夹克大，那件夹克小。

2. **Zhè shuāng xié xīn, nà shuāng xié jiù.**
   This pair of shoes is new, and that pair of shoes is used.
   这双鞋新，那双鞋旧。

3. **Zhè jiàn chènshān guì, nà jiàn chènshān piányi.**
   This shirt is expensive, and that shirt is cheap.
   这件衬衫贵，那件衬衫便宜。

4. **Zhè tiáo kùzi féidà, nà tiáo kùzi shòuxiǎo.**
   This pair of pants is loose, and that pair of pants is tight.
   这条裤子肥大，那条裤子瘦小。

5. **Zhè tiáo qúnzi piàoliang, nà tiáo qúnzi nánkàn.**
   This skirt is beautiful, and that skirt is ugly.
   这条裙子漂亮，那条裙子难看。

6. **Zhè tiáo niúzǎikù cháng, nà tiáo niúzǎikù duǎn.**
   This pair of jeans is long, and that pair of jeans is short.
   这条牛仔裤长，那条牛仔裤短。

fúzhuāngdiàn			**shòu(xiǎo)**		
服 装 店	*clothing shop*		瘦 （小）	*tight*	
xīn			**cháng**		
新	*new*		长	*long*	
jiù			**duǎn**		
旧	*old, used, worn*		短	*short*	
féi(dà)					
肥 （大）	*loose*				

⊿ Colors

hóng(sè)			**huáng(sè)**		
红 （色）	*red*		黄 （色）	*yellow*	
lán(sè)			**lǜ(sè)**		
蓝 （色）	*blue*		绿 （色）	*green*	
zōng(sè)			**chéng(sè)**		
棕 （色）	*brown*		橙 （色）	*orange*	
hēi(sè)			**bái(sè)**		
黑 （色）	*black*		白 （色）	*white*	

Notes

bǐ 比 *is used in comparative sentences when comparing two or more items. The adjective form remains the same. The word order in the sentence is A + **bǐ** 比 + B+ adjective.*

Zhè jiàn jiākè bǐ nà jiàn jiākè dà.
This jacket is bigger than that one.
这件夹克比那件夹克大。

A: **Xīnnián kuài dào le. Wǒ xiǎng mǎi tiáo kùzi.**
New Year is coming. I want to buy a pair of pants.
新年快到了。我想买条裤子。

B: **Zhèr yǒu hěn duō kùzi zhèngzài jiǎn jià, wǒmen qù kànkan!**
There're a lot of pants on sale in this shop. Let's go and have a look!
这儿有很多裤子正在减价，我们去看看！

A: **Zhè tiáo huáng de hěn hǎokàn. Wǒ néng shìshi ma?**
The yellow one is very beautiful. Could I try it on, please?
这条黄的很好看。我能试试吗？

C: **Kěyǐ.**
Of course.
可以。

A: **Yǒu diǎnr cháng, yǒu duǎn diǎnr de ma?**
It's a little long for me. Have you got a shorter one?
有点儿长，有短点儿的吗？

C: **Zhè tiáo lán de zěnmeyàng?**
How about this blue one?
这条蓝的怎么样？

B: **Lán de gèng piàoliang, chángduǎn yě héshì.**
This blue one is even nicer than the yellow one. The size suits you well.
蓝的更漂亮，长短也合适。

A: **Duōshao qián yì tiáo?**
How much is it?
多少钱一条？

C: **Wǔshíbā kuài.**
¥ 58.
五十八块。

A: **Hǎo ba, wǒ yào zhè tiáo.**
OK, I'll take it.
好吧，我要这条。

xīnnián 新 年	*New Year*
zhèngzài / zhèng 正 在 / 正	*(indicating an action in progress)*
jiǎn jià 减 价	*on sale, cut the price*
hǎokàn 好 看	*beautiful*
(**nánkàn** 难看	*ugly*)
shì 试	*try on*
chángduǎn / dàxiǎo 长 短 / 大 小	*size*
gèng 更	*even more*
héshì 合 适	*suit, fit*

2

A: **Nín yào mǎi shénme xié?**
What sort of shoes would you like to buy?
您要买什么鞋？

B: **Wǒ xiǎng mǎi yì shuāng hēi píxié.**
I'd like to buy a pair of black leather shoes.
我想买一双黑皮鞋。

A: **Zhèxiē píxié shì gāng dào de. Nín kěyǐ shìshi.**
These leather shoes are new arrivals. You can try them on.
这些皮鞋是刚到的。您可以试试。

B: **Ō, shìyàng hái búcuò. Wǒ shìshi zhè shuāng zōngsè de.**
The style is good. I'll try on the brown ones.
噢，式样还不错。我试试这双棕色的。

A: **Tā bǐ hēi de piàoliang de duō.**
They are much nicer than the black ones.
它比黑的漂亮得多。

B: **Dàxiǎo yě héshì. Jiàqián yíyàng ma?**
The size fits me well. Are the prices the same?
大小也合适。价钱一样吗？

A: **Zōng de bǐ hēi de shāo guì yìdiǎnr, sānbǎi bāshíjiǔ yuán.**
The brown ones are a bit more expensive than the black ones. They are ¥389.
棕的比黑的稍贵一点儿，三百八十九元。

B: **Néng piányi diǎnr ma?**
Could you sell them a little cheaper to me?
能便宜点儿吗？

A: **Duìbuqǐ, xiānsheng, wǒmen diàn bǐ bié de diàn piányi de duō, bú xìn, nín kěyǐ dào duìmiàn kànkan.**
Sorry, sir, our prices are much cheaper than those in other shops. If you don't believe me, you can go to the shop opposite and have a look.
对不起，先生，我们店比别的店便宜得多，不信，您可以到对面看看。

píxié 皮鞋	leather shoes
ō 噢	oh
shìyàng / yàngshì 式样／样式	pattern, style
búcuò 不错	good
bǐ 比	than
jià(qián) 价（钱）	price
yíyàng 一样	the same
shāo(wēi) 稍（微）	slightly
xìn / xiāngxìn 信／相信	believe

Notes

de 得 *is used after an adjective to link a complement of degree, e.g.*
Zhè shuāng xié dà de duō!
This pair of shoes is much bigger.
这双鞋大得多！

Comparative sentences
(See "Grammar Outline", P224)

Some words are often used in comparative sentences to indicate the degree of differences.

▶ *To indicate a slight difference*

yìdiǎnr 一 点儿	*a little*

A bǐ B dà yìdiǎnr.   *A is a little bigger than B.*
A 比 B 大 一 点儿。

shāowēi / shāo 稍 微 / 稍	*slightly*

shāowēi 稍微 + *adjective* + **yìdiǎnr** 一点儿

A bǐ C shāowēi dà yìdiǎnr.   *A is slightly bigger than C.*
A 比 C 稍   微 大 一 点儿。

▶ *To indicate a big difference*

adjective + **de duō** 得多 / **duō le** 多了

A bǐ D dà de duō.   *A is much bigger than D.*
A 比 D 大 得 多。

▶ *When two or more things are the same, the pattern is:*

A+ **hé** 和 + *E*+ **yíyàng** 一样 + *adjective*

A hé E yíyàng dà.   *A is as big as E.*
A 和 E 一 样   大。

Adjective + **de** 的

Its grammatical function is equal to a noun.

hóng de 红 的	**huáng de** 黄 的
piàoliang de 漂 亮 的	**nánkàn de** 难 看 的
cháng de 长 的	**duǎn de** 短 的
shòu (yì)diǎnr de 瘦 (一) 点儿 的	**féi (yì)diǎnr de** 肥 (一) 点儿 的
guì de 贵 的	**piányi de** 便 宜 的
gānjìng (yì)diǎnr de 干 净 (一) 点 的	**zāng (yì)diǎnr de** 脏 (一) 点儿 的

When the context is clear, the noun can be omitted. The grammatical function of "adjective + **de** *的" is equal to a noun.*

Tā mǎile xīn fángzi, zhè xīn de bǐ jiù de dà.
He bought a new house. The new house is bigger than the old one.
他买了新房子，这新的比旧的大。

⊃ Exercises

✎ 1. Repeat the sentences after Listening. 🎧

(1) Gēge de shū bǐ wǒ duō.
   哥哥 的 书 比 我 多。

(2) Hēi kùzi bǐ lán kùzi féidà.
   黑 裤子 比 蓝 裤子 肥大。

(3) Zhè shuāng xié bǐ nà shuāng xié xiǎo yìdiǎnr.
   这 双 鞋 比 那 双 鞋 小 一 点儿。

(4) Yángròu bǐ niúròu piányi yìdiǎnr.
   羊 肉 比 牛 肉 便宜 一 点儿。

(5) Qù gōngyuánr bǐ qù xuéxiào yuǎn yìdiǎnr.
   去 公 园儿 比 去 学校 远 一 点儿。

(6) Zhè liàng chē bǐ nà liàng chē shāowēi guì yìdiǎnr.
   这 辆 车 比 那 辆 车 稍 微 贵 一 点儿。

(7) Huǒchēzhàn bǐ qìchēzhàn dà de duō.
   火 车 站 比 汽车 站 大 得 多。

(8) Zhōngshān Lù bǐ Jiànguó Lù cháng de duō.
   中 山 路 比 建国 路 长 得 多。

(9) Mèimei hé jiějie yíyàng piàoliang.
   妹 妹 和 姐姐 一 样 漂 亮。

(10) Wūli hé wūwài yíyàng gānjìng.
   屋 里 和 屋 外 一 样 干 净。

✎ 2. Choose the right words to fill in the blanks from the box below.

xīnxiān 新 鲜	gèng⋯ 更⋯⋯
xiǎo 小	yíyàng⋯ 一 样⋯⋯
guì 贵	shāowēi⋯yìdiǎnr 稍 微⋯⋯一 点儿
duō 多	⋯yìdiǎnr ⋯⋯一 点儿
gānjìng 干 净	⋯de duō ⋯⋯得 多

(1) Huǒchē bǐ gōnggòng qìchē dà, gōnggòng qìchē bǐ xiǎo qìchē dà, xiǎo qìchē bǐ huǒchē _____.

(2) Zhè shì sān jīn yī liǎng yángròu, nà shì sān jīn niúròu, yángròu bǐ niúròu _____.

(3) Kètīng hěn gānjìng, wòshì yě hěn gānjìng, kètīng hé wòshì _____.

(4) Luóbo yí kuài qián yì jīn, hěn guì; báicài yí kuài wǔ yì jīn, báicài bǐ luóbo _____.

(5) Hóng pútao shì shàngwǔ zhāi de, lǜ pútao shì zhōngwǔ zhāi de, lǜ pútao bǐ hóng pútao _____.

⬦ 3. Use comparative form to say 5 sentences about yourself.

e.g. Wǒ shíbā suì, dìdi shíliù suì, wǒ bǐ dìdi dà liǎng suì.

⬦ 4. Complete the sentences, using the words in the box below.

xīn de 新 的	guì de 贵 的	huáng de 黄 的	bái de 白 的
nán de 男 的	hóng de 红 的	jiù de 旧 的	lán de 蓝 的
nǚ de 女 的	piányi de 便 宜 的		

(1) Gōngyuán li yǒu gè zhǒng yánsè de huār, wǒ xǐhuan _____、
_____、_____, bù xǐhuan _____.

(2) Qǐngwèn, píxié duōshao qián yì shuāng?
_____ wǔshí duō, _____ wǔbǎi duō.

(3) Zhèxiē yīfu shì shéi de?
Nà jiàn _____ shì wǒ de, zhè jiàn _____ shì wǒ dìdi de.

(4) Nà liǎng gè rén shì shéi?
_____ shì Xiǎo Lǐ, _____ shì tā gēge.

⬦ 5. Listen and repeat the story. 🎧

Kǒng Róng Ràng Lí
Kǒng Róng shì gè sì suì de háizi.
Quán jiā zài yìqǐ chī lí de shíhou,
tā nále yí gè zuì xiǎo de. Tā shuō:
"Gēgemen dōu bǐ wǒ dà, tāmen
yīnggāi chī dà de. Wǒ zuì xiǎo,
yīnggāi chī xiǎo de."

孔融让梨

孔融是个四岁的孩子。全家在一起吃梨的时候，他拿了一个最小的。他说："哥哥们都比我大，他们应该吃大的。我最小，应该吃小的。"

Kong Rong Spared Big Pears for His Brothers
Kong Rong was a four-year-old child. When the whole family were sharing pears, he chose the smallest one. He said: "Brothers are all older than me. I am the youngest, so I should eat the smallest pear."

⟳ Cultural tip

Chinese clothing

Nowadays many Chinese young people love wearing famous brand clothes and the latest fashionable shoes.

*Cheongsam（**qípáo**旗袍）and Chinese tunic suit（**zhōngshānzhuāng**中山装）are typical Chinese clothes. Cheongsam originated from Man ethnic group（**Mǎnzú**满族）. It became popular among ladies of noble families in the Qing Dynasty. The style of Cheongsam has changed many times and it still holds great attraction to many ladies, not only to Chinese ladies but also to ladies from all over the world.*

Chinese tunic suit is a kind of male attire. It is named after Sun Zhongshan, who liked to wear the suit and initiated the fashion. The suit combines the features of both Chinese and Western suits. It became popular in China since the Revolution of 1911 and is deemed as typical modern clothes of China.

15 Yílù–píng'ān!
Have a safe trip!
一路平安！

Key points

1 Talking about the seasons and days of a week
2 Planning a trip

⟳ Start here

Listen and repeat. 🎧

⟨ The four seasons

jì(jié)
季（节）　　*season*

sìjì
四季　　*the four seasons*

chūn(tiān)
春　（天）　　*spring*

xià(tiān)
夏　（天）　　*summer*

qiū(tiān)
秋　（天）　　*autumn, fall*

dōng(tiān)
冬　（天）　　*winter*

⟨ Days of a week

Xīngqīrì / Lǐbàitiān 星　期日／礼拜天	*Sunday*	**Xīngqīsì** 星　期四	*Thursday*
Xīngqīyī 星　期一	*Monday*	**Xīngqīwǔ** 星　期五	*Friday*
Xīngqī'èr 星　期二	*Tuesday*	**Xīngqīliù** 星　期六	*Saturday*
Xīngqīsān 星　期三	*Wednesday*		

⟨ Other words to express weeks

xīngqī / zhōu
星　期／周　　*week*

zhè(ge) xīngqī / zhè zhōu　*this*
这（个）星　期／这　周　*week*

shàng (gè) xīngqī / shàng zhōu *last*
上　（个）星　期／上　周　*week*

xià (gè) xīngqī / xià zhōu　*next*
下　（个）星　期／下　周　*week*

134

读拼音学汉语

A: **Tàiyáng chūlái le, tiānqì zhēn hǎo.**
The sun is rising. The weather is really good.
太阳出来了，天气真好。

B: **Chūntiān lái le, wǒ xiǎng qù lǚyóu.**
Spring is coming. I want to go travelling.
春天来了，我想去旅游。

A: **Qù nǎr?**
Where are you going?
去哪儿？

B: **Àokèlán.**
To Auckland.
奥克兰。

A: **Ō, nàlǐ chūntiān yídìng hěn měi.**
Oh, it's certainly beautiful there in spring.
噢，那里春天一定很美。

B: **Bù, xiànzài zhèlǐ shì chūntiān, nàlǐ shì qiūtiān.**
No, it's spring here now, but it's autumn there.
不，现在这里是春天，那里是秋天。

A: **Nàlǐ qiūtiān měi ma?**
Is it beautiful in autumn there?
那里秋天美吗？

B: **Měi, nàlǐ yìnián-sìjì dōu hěn měi.**
Yes. All the seasons are very beautiful there.
美，那里一年四季都很美。

A: **Shénme shíhou qù?**
When are you going?
什么时候去？

B: **Xià gè yuè wǒmen fàngjià.**
I'll have a holiday next month.
下个月我们放假。

tàiyáng 太阳	*sun*	
tiānqì 天气	*weather*	
lǚyóu 旅游	*travel*	
Àokèlán 奥克兰	*Auckland*	
nàr / nàlǐ 那儿/那里	*there*	
zhèr / zhèlǐ 这儿／这里	*here*	
yídìng 一定	*certainly*	
xiànzài 现在	*now*	
měi(lì) 美（丽）	*beautiful*	
fàngjià 放假	*have a holiday*	
jià(rì) 假（日）	*holiday*	

1

A: **Jǐ hào?**
What date is it?
几号？

B: **Xià gè yuè sān hào, Xīngqīliù.**
Saturday, the third of next month.
下个月三号，星期六。

A: **Hé shéi yìqǐ qù?**
Who are you going with?
和谁一起去？

B: **Wǒ qīzi.**
My wife.
我妻子。

A: **Qù duō jiǔ?**
How long will you stay there?
去多久？

B: **Sān gè xīngqī.**
Three weeks.
三个星期。

A: **Zhù nǐmen lǚtú yúkuài, yílù–píng'ān!**
I hope you have a nice time and a safe trip!
祝你们旅途愉快，一路平安！

duō jiǔ 多 久	*how long*	
lǚtú 旅途	*trip, journey*	
yúkuài 愉 快	*happy*	
yílù–píng'ān 一路 平 安	*have a safe trip*	

2

A: **Nǐ xǐhuan nǎge jìjié?**
Which season do you like?
你喜欢哪个季节？

B: **Chūntiān.**
Spring.
春天。

A: **Wèishénme?**
Why?
为什么？

B: **Tiānshang piāozhe bái yún. Dìshang cǎo lǜ le. Shù fāyá le. Huār kāi le, hóng de、huáng de、lán de, duō měi ya!**
The white clouds are floating in the sky. The grass is turning green on the ground. The trees are sprouting. The red, yellow and blue flowers are blooming. How beautiful it is!
天上飘着白云。地上草绿了。树发芽了。花儿开了，红的、黄的、蓝的，多美呀！

wèishénme 为 什 么	*why*
tiān 天	*sky*
piāo 飘	*float*
yún 云	*cloud*
dì 地	*ground*
cǎo 草	*grass*
shù 树	*tree*
fāyá 发芽	*sprout*
kāi (huār) 开（花儿）	*bloom*

2

A: **Wǒ gèng xǐhuan qiūtiān. Shùyè huáng le. Guǒshí chéngshú le. Rénmen gāogāoxìngxìng mángzhe shōuhuò.**

I prefer autumn. The leaves are turning yellow. The fruits are becoming ripe. People are very happily and busily harvesting.

我更喜欢秋天。树叶黄了。果实成熟了。人们高高兴兴忙着收获。

B: **Wǒ yě xǐhuan dōngtiān, màn shān shì xuě. Wǒ xǐhuan huáxuě.**

I like winter, too. The mountains are covered with snow. I like to ski.

我也喜欢冬天，漫山是雪。我喜欢滑雪。

(shù)yè		
（树）叶	leaf	
guǒshí		
果实	fruit	
chéngshú		
成熟	ripe	
gāogāoxìngxìng		
高高兴兴		
(adjective reduplication)		
(See "Grammar Outline", P224)		
máng		
忙	busy	
shōuhuò		
收获	harvest	
màn shān	all over the	
漫山	mountain	
shān 山 hill, mountain		
xuě		
雪	snow	
huáxuě		
滑雪	ski	

15 一路平安！

Notes

duō 多 *is used before adjective in the exclamatory sentence to indicate extreme degree.*
Duō piányi!
How cheap it is!
多便宜！
(See "Grammar Outline", P223)

3

读拼音学汉语

A: **Wǒ xiǎng dìng liǎng zhāng jīpiào. Zhè shì wǒ hé wǒ qīzi de hùzhào.**
I'd like to book two airplane tickets. These are my and my wife's passports.
我想订两张机票。这是我和我妻子的护照。

B: **Hǎo, Lǐ xiānsheng nín qù nǎr?**
OK. Mr. Li, where are you going?
好，李先生您去哪儿？

A: **Shànghǎi.**
To Shanghai.
上海。

B: **Shénme shíhou?**
When are you going?
什么时候？

A: **Shíyuè èrshíwǔ rì.**
The twenty fifth of October.
十月二十五日。

B: **Fēi wǎng Shànghǎi yǒu sì gè hángbān.**
There are four flights to Shanghai.
飞往上海有四个航班。

Zǎochen qī diǎn wǔ fēn, shàngwǔ jiǔ diǎn yí kè, xiàwǔ sān diǎn bàn hé wǎnshang jiǔ diǎn sìshíwǔ fēn.
The 7:05 flight and 9:15 flight in the morning. The 3:30 flight in the afternoon and the 9:45 flight in the evening.
早晨七点五分，上午九点一刻，下午三点半和晚上九点四十五分。

Nín chéng nǎ yì bān?
Which one will you take?
您乘哪一班？

A: **Xiàwǔ sān diǎn bàn de. Shénme shíhou dào Shànghǎi?**
The 3:30 p.m. flight please. What time will we arrive in Shanghai?
下午三点半的。什么时候到上海？

B: **Xiàwǔ wǔ diǎn èrshí.**
5:20 p.m.
下午五点二十。

dìng	
订	*book*
jīpiào	
机票	*airplane ticket*
fēi	
飞	*fly*
fēijī	
飞机	*airplane, plane*

Planning a trip

	In Chinese	In English
Interrogative sentences	1. **Nín qù nǎr?** 您 去 哪儿？	1. *Where are you going?*
	2. **Hé shéi yìqǐ qù?** 和 谁 一起 去？	2. *Who are you going with?*
	3. **Shénme shíhou qù?** 什 么 时 候 去？	3. *When are you going?*
	4. **Zěnme qù?** 怎 么 去？	4. *How will you get there?*
	5. **Qù duō cháng shíjiān?** 去 多 长 时 间？	5. *How long will you stay there?*
	6. **Shénme shíhou huílái?** 什 么 时 候 回来？	6. *When will you come back?*
Short answers	1. **Qù Běijīng.** 去 北 京。	1. *To Beijing.*
	2. **Hé wǒ nánpéngyou yìqǐ qù.** 和 我 男 朋 友 一起 去。	2. *With my boyfriend.*
	3. (1) **Míngnián.** 明 年。	3. (1) *Next year.*
	Èr líng yī sì nián. 二 零 一 四 年。	*In 2014.*
	Xiàbànnián. 下 半 年。	*In the second half of the year.*
	(2) **Qiūtiān.** 秋 天。	(2) *In autumn.*
	Xià gè yuè. 下 个 月。	*Next month.*
	Bāyuè. 八 月。	*In August.*
	(3) **Míngtiān.** 明 天	(3) *Tomorrow.*

	In Chinese	In English
	Xīngqīliù. 星 期六。	*Saturday.*
	Bāyuè wǔ hào. 八 月 五 号。	*The fifth of August.*
	4. **Chéng fēijī.** 乘 飞机。	4. *By air.*
	Chéng huǒchē. 乘 火 车。	*By train.*
	Zuò qìchē. 坐 汽 车。	*By bus.*
Short answers	5. **Bàn nián.** 半 年。	5. *Six months.*
	Sān gè yuè. 三 个 月。	*Three months.*
	Yí gè xīngqī. 一 个 星 期。	*One week.*
	6. **Míngnián Sānyuè.** 明 年 三 月。	6. *Next March.*
	Shí'èryuè wǔ hào. 十 二 月 五 号。	*The fifth of December.*
	Xià gè xīngqī. 下 个 星 期。	*Next week.*

Exercises

1. Look at the calendar of October and fill in the blanks.

Shíyuè 十月 October						
SUN	MON	TUE	WED	THU	FRI	SAT
		1	2	3	4	5
6	7	8	9	10	11	12
13	14	15	16	17	18	19
20	21	22	23	24	25	26
27	28	29	30	31		

读拼音学汉语

(1) Jīntiān shì èr líng yī sān nián Shíyuè shíliù rì, Xīngqīsān.

(2) _____ shì shíqī rì, Xīngqīsì.

(3) Hòutiān shì shíbā rì, _____.

(4) Zuótiān shì _____, Xīngqī'èr.

(5) Qiántiān shì shísì rì, _____.

(6) Shàng zhōu Xīngqīyī shì _____ hào.

(7) _____ Xīngqīliù shì èrshíliù hào.

(8) Shàng gè yuè shì Jiǔyuè, _____ shì Shíyīyuè.

(9) _____ shì èr líng yī èr nián.

(10) _____ shì èr líng yī sì nián.

2. Choose the right answers after listening. 🎧

(1) Mǎlì de shēngrì shì _____.
   A. Yīyuè 30 hào   B. Èryuè 1 hào   C. Yīyuè 31 hào

(2) Xiǎo Wáng jīnnián _____ qùle Jiānádà.
   A. Shíyuè   B. Qīyuè   C. Sìyuè

(3) Wǒmen _____ jùhuì.
   A. míngtiān   B. hòutiān   C. qiántiān

(4) Wǒmen _____ qù Shànghǎi lǚyóu.
   A. shàng xīngqī   B. zhè xīngqī   C. xià xīngqī

(5) Wǒ bù xǐhuan Běijīng de _____.
   A. chūntiān   B. xiàtiān   C. dōngtiān

3. Read dialogue 3 on page 138, then answer the questions.

(1) Lǐ xiānsheng xiǎng qù nǎlǐ?_____

(2) Tā dìngle nǎ yì tiān de jīpiào?_____

(3) Dìngle jǐ zhāng?_____

(4) Fēijī jǐ diǎn qǐfēi?_____

(5) Shénme shíhou dào Shànghǎi?_____

(6) Dào Shànghǎi yào duō cháng shíjiān?_____

4. What do you say?

(1) *When you attend a friend's birthday party, what do you say?*

(2) *Your friend is going to travel, and you see him off at the airport. What do you say to him?*

(3) *New Year is coming. What do you say to your friends?*

(4) *Christmas is coming. What do you say to your friends?*

读拼音学汉语

↘ 5. Talk about going away for a holiday.

⊃ Cultural tip

Traveling on holidays

The main holidays in China are:

New Year's Day (**Yuándàn** 元旦，*the first of January)*

Spring Festival (**Chūnjié** 春节，*the first day of the first month in the lunar calendar)*

Tomb Sweeping Day (**Qīngmíngjié** 清明节，*about the fifth of April)*

Labor Day (**Láodòngjié** 劳动节，*the first of May)*

Dragon Boat Festival (**Duānwǔjié** 端午节，*the fifth day of the fifth month in the lunar calendar)*

Mid-Autumn Festival (**Zhōngqiūjié** 中秋节，*the fifteenth day of the eighth month in the lunar calendar)*

National Day (**Guóqìngjié** 国庆节，*the first of October)*

In the past, the Chinese liked to spend holidays at home, meeting relatives and friends, and entertaining guests. Nowadays many Chinese prefer going away for holidays, especially during long holidays such as the National Day and the Spring Festival. Traveling has become popular too.

142

16 Nǐ qùguo Zhōngguó ma?

Have you been to China?

你去过中国吗?

Key points

Expressing different tenses

⟳ Start here

Listen and repeat. 🎧

⟨ Some major cities and tourist attractions of China

Běijīng 北 京	*Beijing*		**Kūnmíng** 昆 明	*Kunming*
Shànghǎi 上 海	*Shanghai*		**Xiānggǎng** 香 港	*Hong Kong*
Hā'ěrbīn 哈 尔 滨	*Harbin*		**Cháng Jiāng** 长 江	*the Yangtze River*
Nánjīng 南 京	*Nanjing*		**Huáng Hé** 黄 河	*the Yellow River*
Guǎngzhōu 广 州	*Guangzhou*			

⟳ Dialogues

1

A: **Zhège jiàqī qù nǎr lǚyóu le?**
Where did you go for travelling during the holidays?
这个假期去哪儿旅游了？

B: **Zhōngguó. Wǒ gāng cóng nàr huílái.**
China. I've just come back from there.
中国。我刚从那儿回来。

A: **Ō, Zhōngguó hěn dà, kěyǐ yóulǎn de dìfang hěn duō. Nǐ yóulǎnle nǎxiē dìfang?**
Oh, China is spacious. There are many places to visit. Where did you go?
噢，中国很大，可以游览的地方很多。你游览了哪些地方？

jiàqī
假期　　*holidays*

yóulǎn
游 览
visit, go sightseeing (It is used when visiting a scenic or historical site.)

1

B: **Wǒ qùle Běijīng、Shànghǎi hé Guǎngzhōu. Nǐ qùguo Zhōngguó ma?**
I went to Beijing, Shanghai and Guangzhou. Have you been to China?
我去了北京、上海和广州。你去过中国吗?

A: **Wǒ zhǐ qùguo Běijīng, yóulǎnle Yíhé Yuán hé Chángchéng.**
I've only been to Beijing. I visited the Summer Palace and the Great Wall.
我只去过北京,游览了颐和园和长城。

B: **Chángchéng hěn xióngwěi! Xiàcì wǒ hái yào qù.**
The Great Wall is grand! I'll go there again next time.
长城很雄伟!下次我还要去。

Yíhé Yuán 颐 和 园	the Summer Palace
Chángchéng 长 城	the Great Wall
xióngwěi 雄 伟	grand

Notes

guo 过 *is used after a verb to indicate the action is past.*
Wǒ qùguo Zhōngguó. *I have been to China.*
我去过中国。
(See "Grammar Outline", P212)

2

A: **Dàwèi, nǐ dāi zài Zhōngguó de shíhou, qùguo wǒ de jiāxiāng Nánjīng ma?**
Did you go to my hometown Nanjing when you stayed in China, David?
大卫,你呆在中国的时候,去过我的家乡南京吗?

dāi 呆	stay
jiāxiāng 家 乡	hometown

读拼音学汉语

B: **Qù le. Wǒ zài nàr dāile sān tiān, cānguānle Zhōngshān Líng、Fūzǐ Miào, yóulǎnle Qínhuái Hé.**
Yes, I did. I stayed there for three days and visited the Zhongshan Mausoleum, the Confucius Temple and the Qinhuai River.
去了。我在那儿呆了三天，参观了中山陵、夫子庙，游览了秦淮河。

A: **Nǐ zuì gǎn xìngqù de shì nǎr?**
Which place were you most interested in?
你最感兴趣的是哪儿？

B: **Wǒ zuì xǐhuan Qínhuái Hé.**
I loved Qinhuai River the most.
我最喜欢秦淮河。

A: **Nǐ zuò "Dēngchuán" le ma?**
Did you take the "Floating Light" boat?
你坐"灯船"了吗？

B: **Shénme "Dēngchuán"?**
Sorry, what's that?
什么"灯船"？

A: **Jiù shì guàzhe yí chuànchuàn dàhóng dēnglong de yóuchuán.**
The "Floating Light" is a boat that is hung with strings of red lanterns.
就是挂着一串串大红灯笼的游船。

B: **Ò, míngbai le! Wǒ zuò le. Zuò zài "Dēngchuán" shang, chī Nánjīng xiǎochī, hē lǜchá, tīng yīnyuè, liáotiānr, hǎo jí le.**
Oh, I see! Yes, I did. I had Nanjing snacks, drank some green tea, listened to the music and chatted while I was sitting on the boat. How wonderful it was!
哦，明白了！我坐了。坐在"灯船"上，吃南京小吃，喝绿茶，听音乐，聊天儿，好极了。

---

cānguān
参观 *visit*
(It is used when visiting a historical site, building, school, factory, museum and exhibition, etc.)

Zhōngshān Líng
中山陵
Zhongshan Mausoleum

Fūzǐ Miào the Confucius
夫子庙 Temple

Qínhuái Hé the Qinhuai
秦淮河 River

zuì
最 *most*

gǎn
感 *feel*

xìngqù
兴趣 *interest*

Dēngchuán
灯船
"Floating Light" boat
chuán 船 *ship, boat, yacht, etc.*

chuàn
串 *string*

dēnglong
灯笼 *lantern*

yóuchuán
游船 *pleasure boat*

míngbai
明白 *understand*

xiǎochī
小吃 *snack*

lǜchá
绿茶 *green tea*

tīng
听 *listen*

yīnyuè
音乐 *music*

liáotiān(r)
聊天(儿) *chat*

jí
极 *extremely*

Notes

chuànchuàn 串串 *is a form of measurement word reduplication to show many strings.* (See "Grammar Outline", P220)

3

A: **Mǎkè, nǐ yào qù nǎr?**
Mark, where are you going?
马克，你要去哪儿？

B: **Guǎngzhōu.**
Guangzhou.
广州。

A: **Mǎi fēijīpiào le ma?**
Have you bought a plane ticket?
买飞机票了吗？

B: **Méiyǒu, wǒ mǎile huǒchēpiào.**
No, I haven't. I've bought a train ticket.
没有，我买了火车票。

A: **Wèishénme yào zuò huǒchē?**
Why will you go there by train?
为什么要坐火车？

B: **Piányi, shūfu, hái kěyǐ guānshǎng yántú fēngjǐng.**
It's cheaper, more comfortable and we can enjoy the scenery on the way as well.
便宜，舒服，还可以观赏沿途风景。

A: **Nǐ zuò nǎ cì chē?**
Which train are you taking?
你坐哪次车？

B: **T15 tèkuài lièchē. Èrshí gè xiǎoshí jiù dào Guǎngzhōu le.**
The T15 express train. It takes 20 hours to get to Guangzhou from here.
T15特快列车。二十个小时就到广州了。

A: **Èrshí gè xiǎoshí! Duō lèi ya!**
Oh, 20 hours! You'll be tired!
二十个小时！多累呀！

B: **Wǒ mǎile ruǎnwòpiào, bú lèi.**
I've bought the ticket of a soft-sleeper so I should be fine.
我买了软卧票，不累。

shūfu 舒服 *comfortable*
nánshòu 难受 *uncomfortable*
guānshǎng 观赏 *see and enjoy*
yántú 沿途 *on the way*
fēngjǐng 风景 *scenery, view*
tèkuài lièchē 特快列车 *express train*
lièchē 列车 *train*
ruǎnwò 软卧 *soft sleeper*
wòpù 卧铺 *sleeper*
yìngwò 硬卧 *hard sleeper*

⊃ Form

Expressing different tenses

(See "Grammar Outline", P210)

	In Chinese	In English
Verb + zhe 着	**zhe** 着 *is used after verbs to indicate continuity of an action or state.* **Wǒmen hē__zhe__ chá liáotiānr.** 我 们 喝 着 茶 聊 天 儿。 **Tā tīng__zhe__ yīnyuè kāi chē.** 她 听 着 音 乐 开 车。	*Similar to present continuous.* *We're drinking tea and chatting.* *She's listening to the music and driving the car.*
	We can also put the word **zhèng** 正/**zhèngzài**正在 *before the verb to emphasize the action is in progress.* **Wǒ __zhèngzài__ hē chá.** 我 正 在 喝 茶。 **Wǒ __zhèng__ hē__zhe__ chá.** 我 正 喝 着 茶。 **Tā __zhèngzài__ tīng yīnyuè.** 她 正 在 听 音 乐。 **Tā __zhèng__ tīng__zhe__ yīnyuè.** 她 正 听 着 音 乐。	 *I'm drinking tea.* *She's listening to the music.*
Verb + le 了	**le** 了 *is used after a verb or verbal phrase to indicate the action is complete.* **Shàngwǔ wǒ hē__le__ chá.** 上 午 我 喝 了 茶。 **Zuótiān tā tīng__le__ yīnyuè.** 昨 天 她 听 了 音 乐。	*Similar to simple past tense.* *I drank tea in the morning.* *She listened to the music yesterday.*
	Negative: **Shàngwǔ wǒ méi(yǒu) hē chá.** 上 午 我 没（有）喝 茶。 **Zuótiān tā méi(yǒu) tīng** 昨 天 她 没（有）听 **yīnyuè.** 音 乐。	 *I didn't drink tea in the morning.* *She didn't listen to the music yesterday.*

	In Chinese	In English
Verb + **guo** 过	**guo** 过 *is used after a verb to indicate the action is past and to emphasize the past experience.* **Wǒ hēguo chá.** 我 喝 过 茶。 **Tā tīngguo yīnyuè.** 她 听 过 音乐。 *Negative:* **Wǒ méi hēguo chá.** 我 没 喝 过 茶。 **Tā méi tīngguo yīnyuè.** 她 没 听 过 音乐。	*Use present perfect tense.* *I've drunk tea.* *She has listened to the music.* *I haven't drunk tea.* *She hasn't listened to the music.*

⊃ Exercises

⊴ 1. Match the words.

(1)
zuòzhe	shuǐguǒ
A. 坐 着	a. 水 果
jiàozhe	péngyou de míngzi
B. 叫 着	b. 朋 友 的 名 字
chīzhe	nà běn zázhì
C. 吃 着	c. 那 本 杂 志
kànzhe	qìchē
D. 看 着	d. 汽 车

(2)
dàole	tóngxué
A. 到 了	a. 同 学
jiànle	yì zhāng huàr
B. 见 了	b. 一 张 画 儿
hēle	xuéxiào
C. 喝 了	c. 学 校
huàle	yì bēi chá
D. 画 了	d. 一 杯 茶

(3)
jiāoguo	Zhōngwén
A. 教 过	a. 中 文
sòngguo	zǎofàn
B. 送 过	b. 早 饭
yóulǎnguo	xiānhuā
C. 游览 过	c. 鲜 花
chīguo	Chángchéng
D. 吃 过	d. 长 城

⊴ 2. Put the words "zhe 着", "le 了" and "guo 过" into the correct places.

(1) Wǒ xiǎng xià A̲ bān qù B̲ mǎi C̲ shuǐguǒ. (le)　　　　　　　　　(　)

(2) Wǒ lái A̲ de shíhou tā zhèngzài B̲ shāfā shang zuò C̲. (zhe)　　(　)

(3) Tā méiyǒu A̲ qù B̲ Běijīng C̲. (guo)　　　　　　　　　　　　　(　)

149

(4) Jīntiān zǎoshang <u>A</u> tā hē <u>B</u> yì bēi guǒzhī <u>C</u>. (le)　　　　　(　　)

(5) Xiǎo Lǐ <u>A</u> shàngwǔ qù <u>B</u> mǎi <u>C</u> yóupiào. (guo)　　　　　(　　)

(6) Tā de zhàopiàn dōu <u>A</u> zài <u>B</u> qiáng shang guà <u>C</u>. (zhe)　　　(　　)

3. Fill in the blanks with "**zhe**着", "**le**了" or "**guo**过" after listening. 🎧

Tuōní méi qù＿＿＿＿＿ Xiǎo Lǐ jiā. Xīngqīliù xiàwǔ, wǒmen liǎ qù＿＿＿＿＿
Xiǎo Lǐ jiā. Mén zhèng kāi＿＿＿＿＿. Xiǎo Lǐ jiàn＿＿＿＿＿ wǒmen hěn gāoxìng.
Tā qǐng wǒmen jìn wū zuòxià, xiào＿＿＿＿＿ wèn: "Hē＿＿＿＿＿ Lóngjǐng chá
ma?" Wǒmen shuō: "Méi hē＿＿＿＿＿." Tā qǐng wǒmen hē. Wǒmen hē＿＿＿＿＿ chá
liáotiānr. Zuò dào hěn wǎn, wǒmen cái zǒu.

4. Speaking.

(1) *Would you like to go to China for a holiday? Explain why or why not.*

(2) *Describe a place of China.*

(3) *If you have two days in China, which place do you want to visit? Give reasons for your choice.*

⊃ Cultural tip

Chinese traditional gardens

*There are many ancient imperial and private gardens in China. Most former imperial gardens are in Beijing. For example, the Yuanming Yuan (**Yuánmíng Yuán** 圆明园) and the Summer Palace (**Yíhé Yuán** 颐和园). The Summer Village (**Bìshǔ Shānzhuāng** 避暑山庄) in Chengde of Hebei Province is also famous.*

There are many former private gardens located in Suzhou of Jiangsu Province as well. The gardens' owners used to be bureaucrats, rich merchants and other important people. The gardens were their residences too. There are miniature mountains and rockeries, fish ponds filled with lotuses in blossom, various beautiful flowers and grasses, and winding verandas in the gardens. All landscapes show unusual ingenuity and implicit charm.

Moreover, there are monastic gardens and garden architectures in scenic spots in many places.

17 Jīntiān tiānqì zěnmeyàng?

What's the weather like today?

今天天气怎么样？

Key points

1 Nominal and adjectival predicate
2 Weather forecast

⊃ Start here

Listen and match the words with the pictures. 🎧

⌐ Weather forecast terms

1	2	3	4	5	6
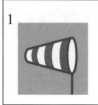					

qíng
( ) 晴　　　*sunny*

yīn
( ) 阴　　　*overcast*

yǔ
( ) 雨　　　*rainy*　　　**xià yǔ**　　　下　雨　　　*rain*

xuě
( ) 雪　　　*snowy*　　　**xià xuě**　　　下　雪　　　*snow*

duōyún
( ) 多　云　　　*cloudy*

fēng
( ) 风　　　*windy*　　　**guā fēng**　　　刮　风　　　*blow*

⊃ Reading and dialogues

1

1.

Tiānqì yùbào
Weather forecast
天气预报

Běijīng, qíng, xīběifēng èr dào sān jí, zuì gāo wēndù (Shèshì) shíwǔ dù, zuì dī wēndù wǔ dù.
Beijing, sunny, with 2 to 3 grades northwest wind. The highest temperature is 15°C, and the lowest temperature is 5°C.
北京，晴，西北风二到三级，最高温度（摄氏）十五度，最低温度五度。

yùbào
预报　　*forecast*
jí
级　　*level, grade*
wēndù
温　度　　*temperature*
gāo
高　　*high*
dī
低　　*low*

1

2. **Shànghǎi, duōyún, zuì gāo wēndù èrshí dù, zuì dī wēndù shí dù.**
   Shanghai, cloudy. The highest temperature is 20°C, and the lowest temperature is 10°C.
   上海，多云，最高温度二十度，最低温度十度。

3. **Hā'ěrbīn, xuě, zuì gāo wēndù qī dù, zuì dī wēndù líng xià liù dù.**
   Harbin, snowy. The highest temperature is 7°C, and the lowest temperature is −6°C.
   哈尔滨，雪，最高温度七度，最低温度零下六度。

4. **Guǎngzhōu, yǔ, zuì gāo wēndù èrshísān dù, zuì dī wēndù shíliù dù.**
   Guangzhou, rainy. The highest temperature is 23°C, and the lowest temperature is 16°C.
   广州，雨，最高温度二十三度，最低温度十六度。

5. **Xiānggǎng, duōyún zhuǎn qíng, zuì gāo wēndù èrshíwǔ dù, zuì dī wēndù shíwǔ dù.**
   Hong Kong, cloudy turns to sunny. The highest temperature is 25°C, and the lowest temperature is 15°C.
   香港，多云转晴，最高温度二十五度，最低温度十五度。

dù 度	degree
Shèshì 摄 氏	Centigrade (°C)
[**Huáshì** 华 氏	Fahrenheit (°F)]
língxià 零 下	below zero
zhuǎn 转	change, turn

2

A: **Jīntiān shàngwǔ xià xuě, xiàwǔ guā fēng, tiānqì hěn lěng.**
   It's snowy in the morning, windy in the afternoon, and very cold.
   今天上午下雪，下午刮风，天气很冷。

B: **Nǐ de jiāxiāng Kūnmíng, dōngtiān yě xià xuě ma?**
   Does it also snow in your hometown Kunming in winter?
   你的家乡昆明，冬天也下雪吗？

A: **Dōngtiān hěn shǎo xià xuě, xiàtiān cháng xià yǔ. Rénmen jiào tā "Chūnchéng".**
   Seldom. It always rains in summer. It is called "Spring City".
   冬天很少下雪，夏天常下雨。人们叫它"春城"。

B: **Wèishénme jiào "Chūnchéng"?**
   Why is it called "Spring City"?
   为什么叫"春城"？

yīnwèi 因 为	because
qìhòu 气 候	climate
wēnnuǎn / nuǎnhuo 温 暖／ 暖 和 *warm, temperate*	
lěng 冷	cold
rè 热	hot
xiàng 像	like
suǒyǐ 所 以	so

2

A: **Yīnwèi nàlǐ qìhòu wēnnuǎn, dōngtiān bù lěng, xiàtiān bú rè, yìnián–sìjì dōu xiàng chūntiān, suǒyǐ jiào "Chūnchéng".**
Kunming has a temperate climate. It's not very cold in winter, not very hot in summer. It is like in spring throughout the whole year, so it is called "Spring City".
因为那里气候温暖，冬天不冷，夏天不热，一年四季都像春天，所以叫"春城"。

B: **Jīnnián hánjià, wǒ yào qù Kūnmíng lǚyóu.**
I will go to Kunming during the winter holiday this year.
今年寒假，我要去昆明旅游。

hánjià 寒假	winter holiday
shǔjià 暑假	summer holiday

3

A: **Nǐ yào qù nǎr?**
Where are you going?
你要去哪儿？

B: **Wǒ xiān qù Běijīng, zài qù Shànghǎi hé Guǎngzhōu.**
I'm going to Beijing first, then to Shanghai and Guangzhou.
我先去北京，再去上海和广州。

A: **Wǔyuè de Běijīng hái yǒu diǎnr lěng, yǒushí zǎochen qìwēn Shèshì shí dù zuǒyòu, xūyào chuān wàitào.**
It is a little cold in Beijing in May. Sometimes the temperature is about 10°C in the morning. You need to wear a coat.
五月的北京还有点儿冷，有时早晨气温摄氏十度左右，需要穿外套。

B: **Shànghǎi ne?**
How about Shanghai?
上海呢？

A: **Bǐ Běijīng nuǎnhuo duō le. Qìwēn èrshísān dù zuǒyòu, kěyǐ chuān qúnzi.**
Shanghai is much warmer than Beijing. The temperature is about 23°C. You can wear a dress.
比北京暖和多了。气温二十三度左右，可以穿裙子。

B: **Cháng xià yǔ ma?**
Does it often rain?
常下雨吗？

A: **Cháng xià, tiānqì cháoshī, chūmén yào dài yǔsǎn.**
Yes, it does. It is wet. If you go out, you need to take an umbrella.
常下，天气潮湿，出门要带雨伞。

xiān… zài… 先……再……	first…then…
yǒushí 有时	sometimes
qìwēn 气温	air temperature
chuān 穿	wear, put on
wàitào 外套	overcoat
cháng / jīngcháng 常 / 经常	often, always
cháoshī 潮湿	wet
gānzào 干燥	dry
dài 带	take
yǔsǎn / sǎn 雨伞 / 伞	umbrella

B: **Guǎngzhōu zěnmeyàng?**
How about Guangzhou?
广州怎么样？

A: **Guǎngzhōu bǐ Shànghǎi rè.**
Guangzhou is hotter than Shanghai.
广州比上海热。

B: **Yǒu duō rè?**
How hot is it in Guangzhou?
有多热？

A: **Èrshíbā dù zuǒyòu, kěyǐ chuān duǎnqún.**
About 28°C. You can wear a short skirt.
二十八度左右，可以穿短裙。

duǎnqún
短 裙   *short skirt*

Notes

duō 多

1. *much* It is used after the adjective to show a high degree with comparison.

gānjìng duō le
much cleaner
干净多了

nuǎnhuo duō le
much warmer
暖和多了

2. It is used before the adjective to ask about degree.
Guǎngzhōu yǒu duō rè? *How hot is it in Guangzhou?* 广州有多热？
(See "Grammar Outline", P223)

Form

Nominal predicate

(See "Grammar Outline", P222)

In Chinese, nouns, noun phrases, quantifiers, etc. can directly follow the subject in sentences, and the verb "be" can be omitted. They're often used to express nationality, age, time, date, weather, price, etc. In English, similar sentences must have the verb "be".

Tā Měiguórén, shíbā suì.
他 美 国 人，十 八 岁。
He's American, eighteen years old.

Xiànzài yī diǎn bàn.
现 在 一 点 半。
It's one thirty now.

Míngtiān Jiǔyuè bā rì, Xīngqīliù.
明 天 九 月 八 日，星 期 六。
It will be the 8th of September, Saturday, tomorrow.

Jīntiān qíngtiān.
今 天 晴 天。
It's sunny today.

Qiānbǐ yí kuài qián yì zhī.
铅 笔 一 块 钱 一 支。
The pencils are ¥1.00 for one.

Adjectival predicate

(See "Grammar Outline", P223)

Adjectives can directly follow the subject in the sentences. They're usually used to describe someone or something. In English, similar sentences must have the verb "be".

Tā hěn piàoliang.
她 很 漂 亮。
She's pretty.

Dàjiā dōu hěn gāoxìng.
大 家 都 很 高 兴。
Everybody is very happy.

Tiānqì liángkuài.
天 气 凉 快。
It's cool.

Wūzi gānjìng.
屋 子 干 净。
The house is clean.

Yīfu piányi, xié yě bú guì.
衣 服 便 宜，鞋 也 不 贵。
Clothes are cheap and shoes are cheap too.

Exercises

◁ 1. Substitution reading. 🎧

(1) Jīntiān
今 天

| Jiǔyuè yī hào. |
| 九 月 一 号。 |
| Xīngqīliù. |
| 星 期六。 |
| yīntiān. |
| 阴 天。 |
| hěn lěng. |
| 很 冷。 |

(2) Wǒmen xuéxiào
我 们 学 校

| hěn dà. |
| 很 大。 |
| gānjìng. |
| 干 净。 |
| bū yuǎn. |
| 不 远。 |
| xuésheng hěn duō. |
| 学 生 很 多。 |

(3) Mǎlì
玛丽

| èrshísān suì. |
| 二 十 三 岁。 |
| hěn piāoliang. |
| 很 漂 亮。 |

2. Correct the sentences.

(1) Wǒ de yīfu yǒu zāng, nǐ de yīfu hěn gānjìng.

_____

(2) Zhè běnr shū mǎi hěn guì, nà běnr shū hěn piányi.

_____

(3) Chūntiān méiyǒu lěng, qiūtiān bú rè.

_____

(4) Túshūguǎn shì dà, shū hěn duō.

_____

(5) Shàngwǔ qíngtiān, xiàwǔ yǒu xià yǔ.

_____

(6) Nǐ lěng bu lěng? Wǒ yǒu lěng.

_____

3. Describe your feelings to match the weather forecast in the text.
e.g. Hā'ěrbīn hěn lěng (哈尔滨很冷).

4. Talk about your hometown with the following passage as an example. 🎧

Kūnmíng shì wǒ de jiāxiāng. Nàlǐ fēngjǐng měilì, qìhòu hǎo. Chūntiān wēnnuǎn, qiūtiān liángshuǎng, dōngtiān bù lěng, xiàtiān bú rè. Yìnián-sìjì, cǎo cháng lǜ, huā cháng kāi, suǒyǐ rénmen jiào tā "Chūnchéng". Wǒ ài wǒ de jiāxiāng — Kūnmíng.

昆明是我的家乡。那里风景美丽,气候好。春天温暖,秋天凉爽,冬天不冷,夏天不热。一年四季,草常绿,花常开,所以人们叫它"春城"。我爱我的家乡——昆明。

5. Fill in the blanks and read the weather forecast aloud after listening. 🎧
Tiānqì yùbào:

Qīyuè shísān rì, Xīngqīsì. Shàngwǔ _____, xiàwǔ _____, yèli yǒu _____. Zuì gāo _____ èrshíbā dù, zuì dī wēndù _____.
Qīyuè shísì rì, Xīngqīwǔ. _____. Zuì gāo wēndù _____, zuì dī _____ èrshísì dù.

157

⊃ Share the poem

Jìng yè sī
静夜思
                    (Táng, Lǐ Bái)
                    （唐，李白）

Chuáng qián míng yuè guāng,
床　　前　明　月　光，
yí shì dì shang shuāng.
疑是地上　　霜。
Jǔ tóu wàng míngyuè,
举头　望　　明　月，
dī tóu sī gùxiāng.
低头思故乡。

Missing homeland on a quiet night
                    (Tang Dynasty, Li Bai)
There is bright moonlight ahead of my bed,
Like frost on the ground.
Raising my head I look at the bright moon,
Lowering my head I miss my homeland.

⊃ Cultural tip

Adages of the weather

Zhāo xiá bù chūmén, wǎn xiá xíng qiān lǐ. 朝霞不出门，晚霞行千里。
Do not leave home if the rosy clouds of dawn show as it is going to rain;
go out as far as you can when sunset clouds are rosy as it is going to be fine.

Jiǔ qíng dà wù yīn, jiǔ yǔ dà wù qíng. 久晴大雾阴，久雨大雾晴。
Thick fog after a lot of sunny days indicates it is going to be cloudy;
thick fog after a lot of rainy days indicates it is going to be sunny.

Qíngtiān bú jiàn shān, xià yǔ sān wǔ tiān. 晴天不见山，下雨三五天。
If mountains can't be seen on a sunny day, it will rain for a long time.

Zǎo yǔ yí rì qíng, wǎn yǔ dào tiān míng. 早雨一日晴，晚雨到天明。
Rain in the morning, sunny all day; rain in the evening, rainy all night.

18 Duànliàn shēntǐ

Do exercise

锻炼身体

Key points

1 "Come" and "go" in Chinese
2 Two or more verbs (verbal phrases) in a sentence
3 Talk about sports

⊃ Start here

Listen and match the words with the pictures. 🎧

⬐ Sports

yóuyǒng
游　泳　　　　　*swim*

tiánjìng yùndòng　*track and field*
田　径　运　动　　*sports*

dǎ lánqiú
打　篮　球　　　　*play basketball*

dǎ páiqiú
打　排　球　　　　*play volleyball*

tī zúqiú
踢　足　球　　　　*play football*

dǎ wǎngqiú
打　网　球　　　　*play tennis*

dǎ yǔmáoqiú
打　羽　毛　球　　*play badminton*

dǎ pīngpāngqiú
打　乒　乓　球　　*play table tennis*

yùndòng
运　动　*sports*

tī
踢　*kick, play*

dǎ
打　　　*play*

dǎ qiú
打　球　*play a ball game by hand*

Dialogue and reading

1

A: **Nǐ qù kàn dì-èrshíjiǔ jiè Àolínpǐkè Yùndònghuì le ma?**
Did you go to watch the 29th Olympic Games?
你去看第二十九届奥林匹克运动会了吗？

B: **Nǐ shuō de shì 2008 nián Běijīng Àoyùnhuì ma?**
You mean the 2008 Beijing Olympic Games?
你说的是2008年北京奥运会吗？

A: **Shì de.**
Yes, that's right.
是的。

B: **Dāngrán, wǒ qù kàn tiánjìng bǐsài le.**
Of course. I went to watch the track and field events.
当然，我去看田径比赛了。

A: **Shì zài Niǎocháo ma?**
Were they in the Bird's Nest?
是在鸟巢吗？

B: **Shì. Nǐ ne?**
Yes. How about you?
是。你呢？

A: **Wǒ měitiān zài diànshì shang kàn yóuyǒng bǐsài. Wǒ hěn xǐhuan Fēi'ěrpǔsī.**
I watched swimming events every day on TV. I love Phelps.
我每天在电视上看游泳比赛。我很喜欢菲尔普斯。

B: **Wǒ yě shì. Tā déle bā kuài jīnpái, tài bàng le!**
Me too. He got eight gold medals. That's terrific!
我也是。他得了八块金牌，太棒了！

Àolínpǐkè Yùndònghuì /
奥林匹克运动会 /
Àoyùnhuì
奥运会
    Olympic Games

bǐsài
比赛   *match, event*

Niǎocháo *the Bird's Nest*
鸟 巢 *(Stadium)*

Shuǐlìfāng *the Water*
水 立 方 *Cube (Gym)*

dé
得   *get*

jīnpái
金 牌   *gold medal*

bàng
棒   *terrific*

Notes

jiè 届 *(measurement word) is used for a regular meeting.*

kuài 块 *(measurement word) is used for items that are piece or lump-like.*

yí kuài dàngāo
a piece of cake
一块蛋糕

yí kuài shǒubiǎo
a watch
一块手表

18
锻炼身体

Měi dào zhōumò, wǒmen quán jiā dōu chūqù duànliàn shēntǐ.

Our whole family goes out to do some exercise every weekend.

每到周末，我们全家都出去锻炼身体。

Shàng gè Xīngqītiān xiàwǔ, yéye hé nǎinai qù gōngyuán dǎ tàijíquán.

My grandparents practiced tai chi in the park last Sunday afternoon.

上个星期天下午，爷爷和奶奶去公园打太极拳。

Gēge qù hǎibiān yóuyǒng.

My elder brother went swimming at the seaside.

哥哥去海边游泳。

Wǒ hé tóngxuémen yìqǐ qù pǎobù、pá shān.

I went to run and climb a mountain with my classmates.

我和同学们一起去跑步、爬山。

Bàba、māma、jiějie、mèimei hé dìdi qùle tǐyùguǎn.

My parents, sisters and younger brother went to a gym.

爸爸、妈妈、姐姐、妹妹和弟弟去了体育馆。

Bàba hé māma dǎ pīngpāngqiú.

My parents played table tennis.

爸爸和妈妈打乒乓球。

Jiějie dǎ páiqiú.

My elder sister played volleyball.

姐姐打排球。

Dìdi hé mèimei dǎ yǔmáoqiú.

My younger brother and sister played badminton.

弟弟和妹妹打羽毛球。

Xiàwǔ wǔ diǎn zuǒyòu, wǒmen huídào jiā.

We came back home about five o'clock.

下午五点左右，我们回到家。

Dàjiā dōu hěn yúkuài.

We had a good time.

大家都很愉快。

zhōumò 周 末	*weekend*	
quán jiā 全 家	*the whole family*	
duànliàn 锻 炼	*do exercise*	
shēntǐ 身 体	*body, health*	
tàijíquán 太 极 拳	tai chi	
hǎibiān 海 边	*seaside*	
tǐyùguǎn 体 育 馆	*gym*	
tǐyù 体育	*sports*	

 **Form**

lái 来 and qù 去

(See "Grammar Outline", P216)

18
锻炼身体

	In Chinese	In English
Indicates direction	*Verb (+ location object) +* **lái** 来/**qù** 去 **chū (mén) lái/qù** 出 （门） 来／去 **jìn (wū) lái/qù** 进 （屋） 来／去 **shàng (shān) lái/qù** 上 （山） 来／去 **xià (lóu) lái/qù** 下 （楼） 来／去	*Come/Go + preposition + noun* *come/go out of the door* *come/go into the room* *come/go up the mountain/hill* *come/go down the stairs*
Indicates purpose	**lái**来/**qù**去 *(+ noun) + verb / verbal phrase* **Wǒ qù hǎibiān yóuyǒng.** 我 去 海边 游 泳。 **Tāmen lái kàn zúqiú bǐsài.** 他 们 来 看 足球 比赛。	*Come/Go + to-infinitive or –ing form* *I'm going swimming at the seaside.* *They're coming to watch a football match.*

Indicates means	*Verbal phrase +* **lái**来/**qù** 去 *+ noun*
	
	Wǒ měi tiān zuò gōnggòng
	我 每天 坐 公 共
	qìchē qù xuéxiào.
	汽车 去 学校。
	
	Qiáoyī zuótiān chéng fēijī
	乔 伊 昨天 乘 飞机
	lái Zhōngguó.
	来 中 国。
		1. *Verbal phrase + come/go + noun*
		  I take bus to go to school every day.
		  Joy took the plane to come to China yesterday.
		
		2. *Come/Go + by + transportation*
		  I go to school by bus every day.
		  Joy came to China by plane yesterday.

Two or more verbs (verbal phrases) in a sentence

In Chinese	In English
In time sequence **Tā shàngwǔ ná qián qù (yóujú) jì** 他　上　午　拿　钱　去（邮局）寄 **bāoguǒ.** 包　裹。 **Tā xǐle zǎo shàng chuáng shuìjiào.** 他　洗了澡　上　床　　睡　觉。 **Wǒ měi tiān kāi chē qù mǎi dōngxi.** 我　每　天　开　车　去　买　东西。	*Use to-infinitive pattern or conjunction "and", "and then"…* *He took some money to go (to the post office) to send a parcel in the morning.* *He had a bath and then went to bed.* *I drive the car to go shopping every day.*

⟲ Exercises

⟲ 1. Translate into English.

(1)	dǎ 打	lánqiú 篮　球	_____
		yǔmáoqiú 羽　毛　球	_____
		diànhuà 电　话	_____
		wǎngqiú 网　球	_____
(2)	kàn 看	shū 书	_____
		bǐsài 比　赛	_____
		péngyou 朋　友	_____
		yīshēng 医　生	_____

(3) kāi
开

mén
门 _____

chē
车 _____

xué
学 _____

huì
会 _____

(4) shàng/xià
上 / 下

fēijī
飞机 _____

chuáng
床 _____

bān
班 _____

shān
山 _____

2. **Answer the questions after listening.** 🎧

(1) Dì-èrshíjiǔ jiè Àolínpǐkè Yùndònghuì shì zài nǎr kāi de?

_____

(2) Yóuyǒng bǐsài shì zài nǎr? _____

(3) Wǒ zuì xǐhuan de yùndòngyuán shì shéi?

_____

(4) Tā déle jǐ kuài jīnpái? _____

3. **Fill in the blanks after listening.** 🎧

(1) Zǎochen wǒmen _____ qù xuéxiào.

(2) Shàngwǔ wǒ kāi chē _____ jiē shū.

(3) Míngnián chūntiān tāmen yào qù Běijīng _____.

(4) Zuótiān tā _____ mǎile yì shuāng xié.

(5) Míngtiān dàjiā dōu _____ hē chá ba.

(6) Wǎnshang wǒ xǐle zǎo _____.

(7) Wǎnfàn hòu tā _____ sànbù.

(8) Xīngqītiān tóngxuémen qù hǎibiān _____ ma?

4. **Put the words in the correct order.**

(1) Tā mǎi liǎng běn shū xiǎng dào shūdiàn.

_____.

(2) Xiǎo Lǐ kàn bào le qù shūfáng.

_____.

(3) Wǒmen chī wǔfàn qù fàndiàn.

_____.

(4) Nǐ néng mǎi liǎng jīn píngguǒ bāng wǒ ma?

_____?

(5) Wǒmen dōu dǎ lánqiú xǐhuan.

_____.

(6) Zhōumò wǒ mǎile yóupiào sān zhāng qù yóujú.

_____.

(7) Zǎochen qī diǎn wǒ qù shàngbān yīyuàn qí (zìxíng)chē.

_____.

(8) Shàng gè yuè wǒ qù Chángchéng yóulǎn le Běijīng.

_____.

5. Fill in the blanks after listening. 🎧

Jīntiān shì _____, Wǒmen dōu yǒu shìr. Líndá qù kàn _____, Mǎlìyà qù _____ mǎi _____, Jiǎn hé Qiáoyī _____ qù _____, wǒ hé Jiékè、Piáo Jīnzhé _____ qù _____ mǎi shū. Wǒmen mǎile 《_____》 hé jǐ běn Zhōngwén _____. Zhèxiē shū néng _____ wǒmen xué hǎo Zhōngwén.

6. Speaking: What did you do last weekend?

⊃ Cultural tip

Physical exercise in early mornings and evenings

*All people expect to be healthier and live longer. You can see Chinese people, especially the elderly doing exercise in the early morning or after dinner in the evening. They practice tai chi, do yangge dance (**niǔ yāngge** 扭秧歌) or fan dance (**shànwǔ** 扇舞), play a waist drum (**dǎ yāogǔ** 打腰鼓) and so on. Parks and public squares are often the venues.*

There is various body-building equipment installed in parks of residential areas and small squares which is free to use.

*The eighth of August every year in China is named as "National Health Day" (**Quánmín jiànshēn rì** 全民健身日).*

19

Qǐng màn yòng!

Take your time to enjoy the meal please!

请慢用！

Key points

Express the degree of extreme

➲ Start here

Listen and repeat. 🎧

⤸ Match the words with the pictures

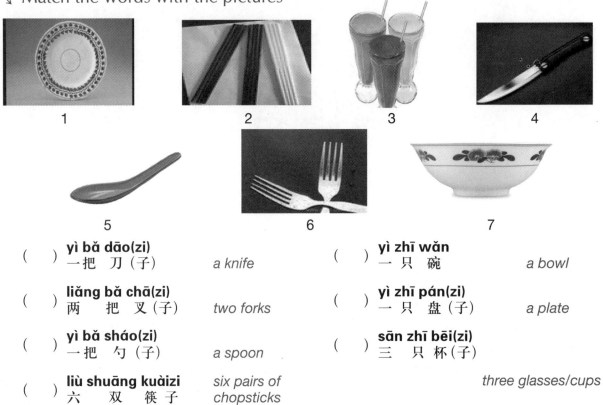

1

2

3

4

5

6

7

( ) **yì bǎ dāo(zi)**
　　一把 刀（子）　　*a knife*

( ) **yì zhī wǎn**
　　一只 碗　　*a bowl*

( ) **liǎng bǎ chā(zi)**
　　两　把 叉（子）　　*two forks*

( ) **yì zhī pán(zi)**
　　一只 盘（子）　　*a plate*

( ) **yì bǎ sháo(zi)**
　　一把　勺（子）　　*a spoon*

( ) **sān zhī bēi(zi)**
　　三　只 杯（子）

( ) **liù shuāng kuàizi**
　　六　双　筷 子　　*six pairs of chopsticks*

three glasses/cups

⤸ Names of things that can be borrowed as measurement words

bēi　　**yì bēi chá**
杯　　一 杯 茶　　*a cup of tea*

wǎn　　**yì wǎn mǐfàn**
碗　　一 碗 米饭　　*a bowl of boiled rice*

pán　　**yì pán shuǐguǒ**
盘　　一 盘 水 果　　*a plate of fruit*

sháo　　**yì sháo tāng**
勺　　一 勺 汤　　*a spoon of soup*

píng　　**yì píng jiǔ**
瓶　　一 瓶 酒　　*a bottle of wine*

(See "Grammar Outline", P219)

168

↘ Dishes, beverages and tastes

càidān 菜 单	*Menu*	**zhǔshí** 主 食	*Staple food*
qīngzhēngyú 清 蒸 鱼	*steamed fish*	**mǐfàn** 米 饭	*(boiled) rice*
hóngshāoròu 红 烧 肉	*pork braised in brown sauce*	**mántou** 馒 头	*mantou*
báizhǎnjī 白 斩 鸡	*tender boiled chicken*	**miàntiáo** 面 条	*noodles*
kǎoyā 烤 鸭	*roast duck*	**cōngyóubǐng** 葱 油 饼	*green onion pancake*
málà dòufu 麻辣 豆 腐	*spicy hot tofu*	**jiǎozi** 饺 子	*Chinese dumpling*
chǎodòujiǎo 炒 豆 角	*stir-fried kidney beans*	**húntun** 馄 饨	*wonton*
xīhóngshì jīdàn tāng 西 红 柿 鸡蛋 汤	*tomato and egg soup*	**xiǎolóngbāo** 小 笼 包	*steamed small meat bun*

yǐnliào 饮 料			*Beverage*
xīguāzhī 西 瓜 汁	*watermelon juice*	**suānnǎi** 酸 奶	*yogurt*
píngguǒzhī 苹 果 汁	*apple juice*	**báijiǔ** 白 酒	*liquor*
pútaozhī 葡 萄 汁	*grape juice*	**huángjiǔ** 黄 酒	*yellow rice wine*
chéngzhī 橙 汁	*orange juice*	**pútaojiǔ** 葡 萄 酒	*grape wine*
niúnǎi 牛 奶	*milk*	**píjiǔ** 啤酒	*beer*

wèidào 味 道			*Taste*
tián 甜	*sweet*	**là** 辣	*spicy*
suān 酸	*sour*	**xián** 咸	*salty*
kǔ 苦	*bitter*	**dàn** 淡	*light*

19
请慢用！

169

1

A: **Qǐng zhè biān zuò··· Zhè shì càidān, qǐng diǎn cài.**
Take a seat here, please... Here is the menu. May I take your order?
请这边坐……这是菜单，请点菜。

B: **Yǒu shénme hǎochī de cài?**
What delicious dishes do you have?
有什么好吃的菜？

A: **Hěn duō. Kǎoyā、hóngshāoròu、qīngzhēngyú··· Dōu hǎochī. Zuì hǎochī de shì málà dòufu.**
Plenty. Roast duck, pork braised in brown sauce, steamed fish... All are delicious. The best is the spicy hot tofu.
很多。烤鸭、红烧肉、清蒸鱼……都好吃。最好吃的是麻辣豆腐。

B: **Wǒ bù xǐhuan tài là de wèidào, yào yì pán qīngzhēngyú、yì pán chǎodòujiǎo hé yì wǎn xīhóngshì jīdàn tāng ba.**
I don't like a too spicy taste. I want a plate of steamed fish, the stir-fried kidney beans and a bowl of tomato and egg soup.
我不喜欢太辣的味道，要一盘清蒸鱼、一盘炒豆角和一碗西红柿鸡蛋汤吧。

A: **Hǎo. Hē diǎnr shénme? Píjiǔ、pútaojiǔ、huángjiǔ háishi báijiǔ?**
OK. Anything to drink? Beer, grape wine, yellow rice wine or liquor?
好。喝点儿什么？啤酒、葡萄酒、黄酒还是白酒？

B: **Yì píng hóngpútaojiǔ, yào zuì hǎo de.**
A bottle of the best red grape wine, please.
一瓶红葡萄酒，要最好的。

A: **Yào shénme zhǔshí? Mǐfàn、mántou、jiǎozi、cōngyóubǐng···**
What staple food do you want? Boiled rice, mantou, dumpling, green onion pancake...
要什么主食？米饭、馒头、饺子、葱油饼……

B: **Yì wǎn mǐfàn. Qǐng kuài diǎnr, wǒ è jí le.**
I'd like a bowl of boiled rice, as soon as possible, please. I'm extremely hungry!
一碗米饭。请快点儿，我饿极了。

A: **Qǐng shāo děng, mǎshàng lái.**
One moment, please. They will be served soon.
请稍等，马上来。

---

diǎn cài
点 菜　　*order dishes*

cài 菜　*vegetable, dish*

hǎochī
好 吃　　*delicious*

(**nánchī**
难 吃　　*tasteless*)

dòufu
豆 腐　　*tofu, bean curd*

dòujiǎo
豆 角　　*kidney beans*

tāng
汤　　*soup*

kuài
快　　*fast, quick*

(**màn**
慢　　*slow*)

è
饿　　*hungry*

(**bǎo**
饱　　*full*)

màn yòng
慢 用
take your time to enjoy the meal **yòng** 用／**xiǎngyòng** 享用 *enjoy*

1

......

A: **Lái le! Qǐng màn yòng!**
Here you are. Take your time to enjoy the meal, please!
来了！请慢用！

2

A: **Nín hǎo, Lántiān Fàndiàn.**
Hello, Lantian Restaurant.
您好，蓝天饭店。

B: **Nín hǎo, wǒ xiǎng dìng zuò.**
Hello, I'd like to book a table.
您好，我想订座。

A: **Jǐ wèi?**
For how many people, please?
几位？

B: **Wǔ wèi.**
Five.
五位。

A: **Shénme shíhou?**
What time, please?
什么时候？

B: **Jīntiān wǎnshang qī diǎn. Yǒu bāojiān ma?**
7 o'clock tonight. Do you have a private room?
今天晚上七点。有包间吗？

A: **Yǒu.**
Yes, we do.
有。

B: **Kǎoyā xūyào yùdìng ma?**
Do I need to make an order now if I want a roast duck?
烤鸭需要预订吗？

A: **Yào de.**
Yes.
要的。

B: **Hǎo, wǒ dìng gè bāojiān, dìng yì zhī kǎoyā.**
OK, I want to book a private room and one roast duck, please.
好，我订个包间，订一只烤鸭。

dìng zuò		
订 座	*book a table, book a seat*	
bāojiān		
包 间	*private room (in a restaurant)*	
yùdìng		
预 订	*book, reserve*	

Notes

wèi 位 *(measurement word)* is used instead of " **gè**个" as a measurement word for people to show respect.

sān wèi lǎoshī
three teachers
三位老师

yí wèi xiānsheng
one gentleman
一位先生

3

A: **Qǐng guòlái rùzuò.**
Please come here and take a seat.
请过来入座。

B: **Zhème duō cài! Nín tài xīnkǔ le.**
So many dishes! Thank you very much.
这么多菜！您太辛苦了。

A: **Nǎlǐ, nǎlǐ, jiācháng-biànfàn. Qǐng zìjǐ dòngshǒu.**
Not really. It is just a homely meal. Please help yourself.
哪里，哪里，家常便饭。请自己动手。

B: **Zhè cài wèidào zhēn hǎo!**
This dish is really delicious!
这菜味道真好！

A: **Xièxie kuājiǎng. Chángchang zhè pán cài, bié kèqi.**
Thanks for your praise. Try this one please. Make yourself at home.
谢谢夸奖。尝尝这盘菜，别客气。

B: **Búcuò, hǎochī.**
Very nice.
不错，好吃。

A: **Zài gěi nín tiān diǎnr fàn ba?**
Would you like to have some more boiled rice?
再给您添点儿饭吧？

B: **Bú yào le, wǒ chī bǎo le. Xièxie.**
No, thanks. I'm full.
不要了，我吃饱了。谢谢。

guòlái 过来	come on	
rùzuò 入座	take a seat	
xīnkǔ 辛苦	work hard	
nǎlǐ, nǎlǐ 哪里，哪里	*(the meaning is "not really")*	
jiācháng-biànfàn 家常便饭	*homely meal*	
zìjǐ dòngshǒu 自己动手	*help yourself*	
kuājiǎng 夸奖	praise	
cháng 尝	taste	
bié kèqi 别客气	*(the meaning is "make yourself at home")*	
tiān 添	add, increase	

Form

Expressing the degree of extreme
(See "Grammar Outline", P225)

In Chinese	In English
zuì最 + *adjective* + **de**的 (*+ noun*)	*Use the superlative adjective*
zuì gānjìng de yīfu 最 干 净 的衣服	*the cleanest clothes*
zuì piàoliang de gōngyuán 最 漂 亮 的 公 园	*the most beautiful park*
tài太 + *adjective* + **le**了	*Use adverb before adjective*
Tài lěng le! 太 冷 了！	*Too cold!*
Tài hǎo le! 太 好 了！	*Very nice!*
Tài gāoxìng le! 太 高 兴 了！	*So happy!*
Adjective + complement of degree	*Usually use adverb before adjective*
jí le / sǐ le 极了／死了	
Guì jí/sǐ le! 贵 极／死了！	*Extremely expensive!*
È jí/sǐ le! 饿极／死了！	*Extremely hungry!*
Zāng jí/sǐ le! 脏 极／死了！	*Extremely dirty!*
sǐ 死 *die When being used after an adjective, it is an expression to mean that someone can no longer put up with something.*	

173

➲ Exercises

◁ 1. Substitution reading. 🎧

zuì 最	piānyi 便宜	de 的	diànshìjī 电视机
	měilì 美丽		guójiā 国家
	xǐhuan 喜欢		shū 书
	hǎochī 好吃		shuǐguǒ 水果
	dà 大		fēijīchǎng 飞机场
	kuài 快		qìchē 汽车

Zhè shuāng xié 这双鞋	guì 贵	jí le. 极了。
Yīfu 衣服	piàoliang 漂亮	
Zuò qìchē 坐汽车	kuài 快	
Xuéxiào 学校	yuǎn 远	
Xīběifēng 西北风	dà 大	
Jiàoshì 教室	gānjìng 干净	

Mǎlà dòufu 麻辣豆腐	tài 太	là 辣	le. 了。
Jīntiān tiānqì 今天天气		lěng 冷	
Háizimen 孩子们		gāoxìng 高兴	
Zhèxiē huār 这些花儿		měi 美	
Cèsuǒ 厕所		zāng 脏	
Chāoshì li rén 超市里人		duō 多	

◁ 2. Fill in the blanks with the following words after listening. 🎧

hóng 红	dà 大	hǎo 好	yúkuài 愉快	shūfu 舒服
xīnxiān 新鲜	zāng 脏	rè 热		

(1) Zhè fēijīchǎng _____ jí le !

(2) Zhè huángguā hǎo _____ !

(3) Nà jiàn yīfu tài _____ le!

(4) Tā yào hē zuì _____ de pútaojiǔ.

(5) Zuótiān qìwēn sānshíwǔ dù, _____ sǐ le!

(6) Jīntiān qù lǚyóu, háizimen _____ jí le.

(7) Zuò zài shāfā shang hē chá hǎo _____ !

(8) Zhè tiáo qúnzi yánsè tài _____ le.

◁ 3. Speaking.

(1) *Book a table in a restaurant.*

(2) *Use polite speech to praise someone's treat.*

(3) *If you are a host, what do you say?*

—*When guests praise you*
—*When you have finished the meal, but the guests have not*
—*When guests want to leave*

◁ 4. Write a menu with Pinyin, then describe it.
(You should have a look at some menus from Chinese restaurants first.)

Table manners

Chinese dining tables are normally round. Usually the main host's seat faces the serving door, the main guest's seat is at the main host's right, the second most important guest's seat is at the main host's left or at the main guest's right, and the second most important host takes the seat near the door .

Chinese use chopsticks when having meals. When dishes are served on the dining table, usually the main guest is the first to help himself/herself. There are certain table manners to follow when using chopsticks: do not pick too much at a time; do not use them to make a gesture when chatting with someone; do not use them to search through the food.

20 Kàn yīshēng
See a doctor
看医生

Key points

1 Verb reduplication
2 Common ways of describing symptoms

Start here

Listen and repeat. 🎧

↘ Main parts of the body

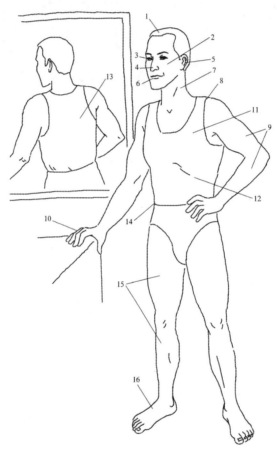

1. **tóu / nǎodai** 头 ／脑袋	*head*		6. **zuǐ** 嘴	*mouth*	
2. **liǎn** 脸	*face*		**yá(chǐ)** 牙（齿）	*tooth*	
3. **yǎn(jing)** 眼（睛）	*eye*		**shétou** 舌头	*tongue*	
4. **bízi** 鼻子	*nose*		**hóulong / sǎngzi** 喉咙 ／嗓子	*throat*	
5. **ěrduo** 耳朵	*ear*		7. **jǐng / bózi** 颈 ／脖子	*neck*	

8. **jiān(bǎng)**
肩 （膀） *shoulder*

9. **bì / gēbo**
臂／胳膊 *arm*

10. **shǒu**
手 *hand*

11. **xiōng**
胸 *chest*

xīn(zàng)
心 （脏） *heart*

12. **fù / dùzi**
腹／肚子 *abdomen*

wèi
胃 *stomach*

13. **bèi**
背 *back*

14. **yāo**
腰 *waist*

15. **tuǐ**
腿 *leg*

16. **jiǎo**
脚 *foot*

↙ Useful expressions of seeing a doctor

bìng
病 *illness, fall ill*

kàn yīshēng / kànbìng
看 医 生 ／ 看 病 *see a doctor*

gǎnmào
感 冒 *catch cold*

fāshāo
发 烧 *have a fever*

tóuténg
头 疼 *have a headache*

tóuyūn
头 晕 *dizzy*

késou
咳 嗽 *cough*

liú bítì
流 鼻 涕 *have a runny nose*

bítì
鼻 涕 *snot*

sǎngzi téng
嗓 子 疼 *have a sore throat*

liú (yǎn)lèi
流 （眼） 泪 *shed tears*

yǎnlèi
眼 泪 *tears*

Name a part of your body and point to that part following the example.

e.g. **yǎnjing**
眼 睛 *eye*

Dialogues

1

A: **Nǐ zěnme le?**
What's the matter?
你怎么了？

B: **Wǒ yǒudiǎnr fāshāo, sǎngzi téng.**
I have a fever and a sore throat.
我有点儿发烧，嗓子疼。

A: **Wǒ gěi nǐ liángliang tǐwēn, kànkan nǐ de sǎngzi. Késou ma?**
Let me take your temperature and have a look at your throat. Do you cough?
我给你量量体温，看看你的嗓子。咳嗽吗？

B: **Késou, hái liú yǎnlèi, liú bítì…**
Yes, I cough, shed tears and have a runny nose…
咳嗽，还流眼泪，流鼻涕……

A: **Ō, sānshíqī dù jiǔ, tǐwēn yǒudiǎnr gāo. Nǐ gǎnmào le.**
Oh, 37.9 degrees Celsius. Your temperature is a little high. You have a cold.
噢，三十七度九，体温有点儿高。你感冒了。

B: **Yào zhùyuàn ma?**
Do I need to stay in hospital?
要住院吗？

A: **Bú yòng.**
No, you don't need to stay in hospital.
不用。

B: **Yào bu yào dǎzhēn?**
Do I need an injection?
要不要打针？

A: **Yě bú yòng, chī diǎnr yào, duō hē kāishuǐ, duō xiūxi, jiù huì hǎo de.**
No, you don't need that either. Just take some medicine, drink more water and have a rest, then you'll be fine.
也不用，吃点儿药，多喝开水，多休息，就会好的。

téng / tòng 疼 ／ 痛	*pain, ache*	
liáng tǐwēn 量 体温	*take sb's temperature*	
liáng 量 *measure*, **tǐwēn** 体温 *(body) temperature*		
zhùyuàn 住 院	*stay in hospital*	
dǎzhēn 打 针	*give an injection*	
yào 药	*medicine*	
kāishuǐ 开 水	*boiled water*	

A: **Yīshēng, wǒ gǎnjué bù shūfu. Zuótiān yèli dào xiànzài yòu lā dùzi yòu tù.**
Doctor, I don't feel well. I had an upset stomach and vomited from last night to now.
医生，我感觉不舒服。昨天夜里到现在又拉肚子又吐。

B: **Ràng wǒ kànkan nǐ de shétou, hàohao nǐ de mài.**
Show me your tongue please and let me feel your pulse.
让我看看你的舌头，号号你的脉。

Nǐ chī shénme le?
What did you eat?
你吃什么了？

A: **Zuótiān qù fàndiàn chī wǎnfàn, hēle yìdiǎnr jiǔ. Jīntiān méi chī dōngxi.**
Yesterday I had dinner at a restaurant and drank a little wine, but today I've had nothing.
昨天去饭店吃晚饭，喝了一点儿酒。今天没吃东西。

B: **Kěnéng shì chángyán.**
I'm afraid you are suffering from enteritis.
可能是肠炎。

Wǒ xiān gěi nǐ zhēnjiǔ, kěyǐ zhǐ tù. Zài gěi nǐ kāi yí gè zhōngyào yàofāng. Nǐ qù yàofáng qǔ yào.
First I'll do some acupuncture for you. It can stop the vomiting. Then I'm going to prescribe some Chinese medicine for you. Get the medicine from the pharmacy.
我先给你针灸，可以止吐。再给你开一个中药药方。你去药房取药。

A: **Qǐngwèn, yàofáng zài nǎr?**
Excuse me, where is the pharmacy?
请问，药房在哪儿？

B: **Zài èr lóu. Nǐ kěyǐ chéng diàntī shàngqù.**
On the second floor. You can take the lift to go there.
在二楼。你可以乘电梯上去。

shūfu 舒服	*be well*	
yòu…yòu… 又……又……	*…and…*	
lā dùzi 拉肚子	*have diarrhoea, have an upset stomach*	
tù / ǒutù 吐 / 呕吐	*vomit*	
hào mài 号脉	*feel sb's pulse*	
dōngxi 东西	*thing*	
kěnéng 可能	*probably*	
chángyán 肠炎	*enteritis*	
zhēnjiǔ 针灸	*acupuncture and moxibustion*	
zhǐ 止	*stop*	
kāi yàofāng 开药方	*prescribe*	
yàofāng 药方	*prescription*	
zhōngyào 中药	*Chinese medicine*	
yàofáng 药房	*pharmacy*	
lóu(céng) 楼（层）	*floor*	
diàntī 电梯	*lift*	

A: **Zhè shì nǐ de yàopiàn.**
These are your tablets.
这是你的药片。

B: **Zěnme chī? Yì tiān chī jǐ cì, yí cì chī duōshao?**
How do I take them? How many times a day and how many tablets do I take each time?
怎么吃？一天吃几次，一次吃多少？

A: **Yì tiān sān cì, yí cì liǎng piàn.**
Three times a day, two tablets a time.
一天三次，一次两片。

B: **Fàn qián chī háishi fàn hòu chī?**
Before meals or after meals?
饭前吃还是饭后吃？

A: **Fàn hòu chī. Duō hē kāishuǐ, bú yào hē jiǔ.**
After meals. You should drink more boiled water and don't drink any wine.
饭后吃。多喝开水，不要喝酒。

B: **Xièxie.**
Thanks.
谢谢。

yàopiàn
药　片　　*tablet*

Notes

piàn 片 *(measurement word) is used for flat items or slices.*

yí piàn miànbāo
a slice of bread
一片面包

liǎng piàn yào
two tablets
两片药

Form

Verb reduplication
(See "Grammar Outline", P217)

*In Chinese, some verbs can be reduplicated to indicate the shortness or the attempting of an action. The form is "verb (+ **yī** 一) + identical verb".*

cháng (yi) cháng 尝　（一）尝	**kàn (yi) kàn** 看　（一）看
liáng (yi) liáng 量　（一）量	**shì (yi) shì** 试　（一）试

Common ways of describing symptoms

In Chinese	In English
Subject + symptom **Wǒ wèi téng.** 我 胃 疼。	*Subject + have + a + symptom* *I have a stomachache.*
Tā fāshāo. 他 发 烧。	*He has a fever.*
Tā liú bítì. 她 流 鼻涕。	*She has a runny nose.*

⊃ Exercises

◁ 1. Read dialogue 1, then answer the questions.

(1) *What's wrong with the patient?*

(2) *What are his/her symptoms?*

    A. tóuténg   C. sǎngzi téng   E. yǒudiǎnr fāshāo

    B. tǐwēn bù gāo   D. bù késou   F. liú yǎnlèi、bítì

(3) *What is the doctor's advice?*

    A. búyòng zhùyuàn   C. yào dǎzhēn   E. chī diǎnr yào

    B. duō hē shuǐ   D. duō xiūxi   F. duō gōngzuò

◁ 2. Read dialogue 2, then answer the questions.

(1) *What are the patient's symptoms?*

    A. lā dùzi   C. fāshāo   E. ǒutù

    B. tóuténg   D. tóuyūn

(2) *How is the doctor going to treat the patient?*

    A. dǎzhēn   B. zhēnjiǔ   C. chī yào

◁ 3. Read dialogue 3, then answer the questions.

(1) *How many times a day to take the tablets?*

    A. yí cì   B. liǎng cì   C. sān cì

(2) *How many tablets each time?*

    A. yí piàn   B. liǎng piàn   C. sān piàn

(3) *Before meals or after meals?*

    A. fàn qián   B. fàn hòu   C. dōu kěyǐ

◁ 4. Choose the right answers after listening. 🎧

(1) Zuótiān wǒ qù yīyuàn _____.

A. kàn péngyou   B. kānbìng   C. mǎi yào

(2) Zuótiān wǒ _____.

A. tóuténg   B. dùzi téng   C. yá téng

(3) Zuótiān wǒ de tǐwēn _____.

A. hěn gāo   B. yǒudiǎnr gāo   C. bù gāo

(4) Zuótiān wǒ _____.

A. dǎle yì zhēn   B. méiyǒu dǎzhēn   C. dǎle liǎng zhēn

(5) Yīshēng gěile wǒ liǎng zhǒng yào, _____.

A. bái yàopiàn fàn hòu chī, huáng yàopiàn fàn qián chī

B. bái yàopiàn fàn hòu chī, huáng yàopiàn shuìjiào qián chī

C. bái yàopiàn shuìjiào qián chī, huáng yàopiàn fàn hòu chī

(6) Huáng yàopiàn _____.

A. yì tiān chī sān cì, yí cì chī yí piàn

B. yì tiān chī yí cì, yí cì chī yí piàn

C. yì tiān chī yí cì, yí cì chī sān piàn

⊃ Cultural tip

Going to see a doctor

In China, patients can usually go to a hospital without having to make an appointment. There is no "General Practitioner" system. There are clinics everywhere, in communities, factories, universities, etc.

There are certain procedures to follow when going to see a doctor: firstly you go to register; secondly you see the doctor and have your illness treated; thirdly you go to pay the bill and finally you go to the pharmacy which is within the hospital and get the prescription filled. If you need emergency treatment, you can go right to the emergency room of the hospital.

*Today there are outpatient departments of Chinese medicine and Western medicine in many hospitals. Traditional Chinese medicine is a complete medical system that combines herbs (**zhōngcǎoyào** 中草药), cupping (**bá huǒguàn** 拔火罐), acupuncture and moxibustion (**zhēnjiǔ** 针灸), massage (**tuīná** 推拿), qigong (**qìgōng** 气功), etc. Herbs, cupping, acupuncture and moxibustion, and massage typically focus on treatment for sickness, but qigong usually focuses on maintaining good health.*

Cíyǔ suǒyǐn

VOCABULARY INDEX

词语索引

ài 爱	3	bàotíng 报 亭	10	cái 才	11
bā 八	5	bēi(zi) 杯（子）	19	cài 菜	19
Bāyuè 八 月	9	běi(bian) 北 （边）	10	càidān 菜 单	19
bǎ 把	7	bèi 背	20	cānguān 参 观	16
bàba 爸爸	3	běn 本	4	cānjiā 参 加	9
ba 吧	5	bítì 鼻 涕	20	cǎo 草	15
bái(sè) 白（色）	14	bízi 鼻 子	20	cèsuǒ 厕 所	10
báicài 白 菜	13	bǐ 比	14	chā(zi) 叉（子）	19
báijiǔ 白 酒	19	bǐsài 比 赛	18	chá 茶	6
báitiān 白 天	3	bǐ 笔	4	chájī 茶 几	7
báizhǎnjī 白 斩 鸡	19	bì／gēbo 臂／胳 膊	20	chà 差	8
bǎi 百	5	bié kèqi 别 客气	19	cháng 长	14
bàn 半	8	bīnguǎn／lǚguǎn 宾 馆／旅馆	10	chángduǎn／dàxiǎo 长 短／大 小	14
bāng(zhù) 帮 （助）	11	bìng 病	20	chángshòu 长 寿	9
bàng 棒	18	bōcài 菠 菜	13	chángshòumiàn 长 寿 面	9
bāoguǒ 包 裹	12	bózi／jǐng 脖子／颈	20	chángyán 肠 炎	20
bāoguǒdān 包 裹 单	12	búcuò 不 错	14	cháng 尝	19
bāojiān 包 间	19	bú kèqi 不 客气	1	cháng／jīngcháng 常 ／经 常	17
bǎo 饱	19	bú shì 不 是	2	chàng (gē) 唱 （歌）	9
bào(zhǐ) 报 （纸）	4	bú yòng／bù xūyào 不 用／不 需要	10	chāoshì／chāojí shìchǎng 超 市／超 级 市 场	
		bù 不	1		10
bàoshè 报 社	6			cháoshī 潮 湿	17

词语索引

读拼音学汉语

词语索引

189

huā(r) 花（儿）	7	jí 级	17	jiǎo 脚	20
huáxuě 滑雪	15	jí 极	16	jiào 叫	1
huà 画	4	jǐ / duōshao 几／多少	5	jiàoshī / lǎoshī 教师／老师	2
huà(r) 画（儿）	4	jìzhě 记者	6	jiějie 姐姐	3
huài 坏	1	jì(jié) 季(节)	15	jièshào 介绍	2
huānyíng 欢迎	9	jì / yóujì 寄／邮寄	12	jiè 届	18
huàn / duìhuàn 换／兑换	12	jiā 加	6	jīn 斤	13
huáng(sè) 黄（色）	14	jiākè 夹克	14	jīnnián 今年	9
huángguā 黄瓜	13	jiā 家	3	jīntiān 今天	9
huángjiǔ 黄酒	19	jiācháng-biànfàn 家常便饭	19	jīnpái 金牌	18
huí 回	10	jiāxiāng 家乡	16	jìn / jìnlái 进／进来	2
huílái 回来	4	jià(qián) 价（钱）	14	jìn 近	10
huìlǜ 汇率	12	jià(rì) 假(日)	15	jīngcháng / cháng 经常／常	17
huì 会	11	jiàqī 假期	16	jǐng / bózi 颈／脖子	20
húntun 馄饨	19	jiān(bǎng) 肩（膀）	20	jiǔ 九	5
huó 活	13	jiǎnjià 减价	14	Jiǔyuè 九月	9
huǒchē 火车	10	jiàn 见	1	jiǔ 酒	9
huǒchēzhàn 火车站	10	jiàn 件	7	jiù 旧	14
jīpiào 机票	15	jiāo 教	11	jiù 就	9
jī(ròu) 鸡(肉)	13	jiǎo / máo 角／毛	12	jùhuì 聚会	9
jīdàn 鸡蛋	13	jiǎozi 饺子	19	kāfēi 咖啡	6

191

luòdìchuāng 落地窗	7	mén 门	8	nán(bian) 南（边）	10
luòdìdēng 落地灯	7	men 们	1	nánchī 难吃	19
māma 妈妈	3	mǐ 米	7	nánkàn 难看	14
málà dòufu 麻辣豆腐	19	mǐfàn 米饭	19	nánshòu 难受	16
ma 吗	1	miànbāo 面包	10	nǎodai / tóu 脑袋 / 头	20
mǎi 买	9	miànbāodiàn 面包店	10	ne 呢	2
mài 卖	9	miàntiáo 面条	19	néng 能	11
mántou 馒头	19	miǎo 秒	8	nǐ 你	1
màn shān 漫山	15	míngzi 名字	1	nǐ hǎo 你好	1
màn 慢	19	míngbai 明白	16	nǐmen 你们	1
màn yòng 慢用	19	míngnián 明年	9	nián 年	9
màn zǒu 慢走	6	míngtiān 明天	9	niánlì 年历	7
máng 忙	15	nǎ 哪	2	nín 您	1
māo 猫	7	nǎr / nǎlǐ 哪儿/哪里	5	niúnǎi 牛奶	19
máo / jiǎo 毛 / 角	12	nǎlǐ, nǎlǐ 哪里,哪里	19	niúròu 牛肉	13
méi(yǒu) 没（有）	3	nà 那	4	niúzǎikù 牛仔裤	14
méi guānxi 没关系	6	nàr / nàlǐ 那儿/ 那里	15	nǚ 女	1
měi 每	8	nàxiē 那些	4	nǚ'ér 女儿	3
měi tiān 每天	8	nǎinai 奶奶	3	nǚháir 女孩儿	7
měi(lì) 美（丽）	15	nán 男	1	nǚshì 女士	1
mèimei 妹妹	3	nánháir 男孩儿	7	nuǎnhuo / wēnnuǎn 暖和 / 温暖	17

sǎn / yǔsǎn 伞 / 雨伞	7,17	shétou 舌头	20	shōufā 收发	4
sànbù 散步	8	shéi / shuí 谁	2	shōuhuò 收获	15
sǎngzi / hóulong 嗓子／喉咙	20	shéi de 谁的	4	shǒu 手	7
sǎngzi téng 嗓子疼	20	shēnqǐng 申请	12	shǒubiǎo 手表	7
shāfā 沙发	7	shēntǐ 身体	18	shǒujī 手机	5
shān 山	15	shénme 什么	1	shòu 瘦	13
shāngdiàn / diàn 商店／店	10	shēng / chūshēng 生／出生	9	shòu(xiǎo) 瘦（小）	14
shàng 上	8	shēngrì 生日	9	shū 书	4
shàng(bian) 上（边）	7	Shèngdànkǎ 圣诞卡	12	shūchú 书橱	7
shàngbān 上班	3	shí 十	5	shūdiàn 书店	10
shàngwǎng 上网	4	Shí'èryuè 十二月	9	shūfáng 书房	4
shàngwǔ 上午	8	Shíyīyuè 十一月	9	shūzhuō 书桌	7
shàng (gè) xīngqī / 上（个）星期／	15	Shíyuè 十月	9	shūfu 舒服	16,20
shàng zhōu 上周		shízì lùkǒu 十字路口	10	shūcài 蔬菜	13
shàngxué 上学	3	shíhou / shíjiān 时候／时间	8	shǔjià 暑假	17
shàngyī 上衣	7	shìjiè 世界	4	shù 树	15
shàng (gè) yuè 上（个）月	9	shìyàng / yàngshì 式样／样式	14	(shù)yè （树）叶	15
shāo(wēi) 稍（微）	14	shì(qing) 事（情）	8	shuā 刷	8
shāo děng 稍等	5	shì 试	14	shuā yá 刷牙	8
shāo(zi) 勺（子）	19	shì 是	2	shuāng 双	7
shǎo 少	4	shōu 收	4	shuǐ 水	6

wǎngqiú 网 球	18	wǔ 五	5	xià xuě 下 雪	17
wǎng 往	10	Wǔyuè 五 月	9	xià yǔ 下 雨	17
wǎng / xiàng 往 ／ 向	10	wǔfàn 午 饭	6	xià (gè) yuè 下 (个) 月	9
wèi 喂	5	wǔtīng 舞 厅	8	xià (tiān) 夏 (天)	15
wèi 为	9			xiān 先	5
wèishénme 为 什 么	15	xī(bian) 西 (边)	10	xiānsheng 先 生	1
wèi 位	19	xīguā 西 瓜	6	xiān…zài… 先 …… 再 ……	17
wèidào 味 道	19	xīguāzhī 西 瓜 汁	19	xiānhuā 鲜 花	7
wèi 胃	20	xīhóngshì / fānqié 西 红 柿／番 茄	13	xián 咸	19
wēndù 温 度	17	xīhóngshì jīdàn tāng 西 红 柿鸡蛋 汤	19	xiànzài 现 在	15
wēnnuǎn / nuǎnhuo 温 暖 ／ 暖 和	17	xīyān 吸 烟	11	xiāngxìn / xìn 相 信 ／ 信	14
wèn 问	1	xǐ 洗	8	xiāngjiāo 香 蕉	6
wènhòu 问 候	1	xǐ liǎn 洗 脸	8	xiǎngyòng / yòng 享 用 ／ 用	19
wèntí 问 题	11	xǐzǎo 洗 澡	8	xiǎng 想	12
wǒ 我	1	xǐhuan 喜 欢	4	xiàng / wǎng 向 ／ 往	10
wǒmen 我 们	1	xiā 虾	13	xiàng 像	17
wò 卧	7	xià 下	8	xiǎo 小	1,7
wòpù 卧 铺	16	xià(bian) 下 (边)	7	xiǎochī 小 吃	16
wòshì 卧 室	7	xiàbān 下 班	3	xiǎolóngbāo 小 笼 包	19
wū (zi) 屋 (子)	7	xià (yí) cì 下 (一) 次	11	xiǎoshí 小 时	8
wúyānqū 无 烟 区	11	xiàwǔ 下 午	8	xiào 笑	11
		xià (gè) xīngqī / xià zhōu 下 (个) 星 期／下 周	15		

Zhuānmíng

专名

Proper Nouns

Yǔfǎ

GRAMMAR OUTLINE

语法

Common interrogative sentence forms

1. Interrogative particles **ma** 吗 and **ne** 呢

Declarative sentence + **ma** 吗?

Nǐ shì xuésheng ma?
Are you a student?
你是学生吗?

Tā yǒu dìdi ma?
Does he have any younger brothers?
他有弟弟吗?

Nǐ chī píngguǒ ma?
Would you like to eat an apple?
你吃苹果吗?

Nǐ xiǎng qù gōngyuán ma?
Would you like to go to the park?
你想去公园吗?

Jīntiān shì Jiǔyuè shíqī rì ma?
Is today the 17th of September?
今天是九月十七日吗?

Nǐ néng bāng wǒ ma?
Can you help me?
你能帮我吗?

Nǐ yào qù yóujú mǎi yóupiào ma?
Do you want to go to the post office to buy some stamps?
你要去邮局买邮票吗?

Nàxiē shū guì ma?
Are those books expensive?
那些书贵吗?

Nà gè fángjiān gānjìng ma?
Is that room clean?
那个房间干净吗?

Declarative sentence + **hǎo ma** 好吗?

Wǒmen liǎ yìqǐ qù Xiǎo Zhōu jiā, hǎo ma?
Shall we go to Xiao Zhou's home together?
我们俩一起去小周家,好吗?

Xiàwǔ qù tǐyùguǎn dǎ pīngpāngqiú, hǎo ma?
Let's go to the gym to play table tennis this afternoon. Is that ok?
下午去体育馆打乒乓球,好吗?

ne 呢 (interrogative particle)

It is used after a noun or a pronoun in a question.
When the context is clear, we can omit the predicate of the previous sentence. Even the subject can be omitted when a demonstrative pronoun precedes the subject.

Wǒ shì xuésheng, nǐ ne?   我是学生,你呢?
(**=Wǒ shì xuésheng, nǐ shì xuésheng ma?** 我是学生,你是学生吗?)
I'm a student. How about you?

Wǒ yào chī píngguǒ, nǐ ne?   我要吃苹果,你呢?
(**=Wǒ yào chī píngguǒ, nǐ yào chī píngguǒ ma?** 我要吃苹果,你要吃苹果吗?)
I'd like to eat an apple. How about you?

Nàxiē shū guì, zhèxiē ne?   那些书贵,这些呢?
(**=Nàxiē shū guì, zhèxiē shū guì ma?**   那些书贵,这些书贵吗?)
Those books are expensive. How about these?

2. Orders of verbs

⊿ Positive verb + negative verb

Nǐ shì bu shì xuésheng?
Are you a student? / Are you a student or not?
你是不是学生？

Tā yǒu méiyǒu dìdi?
Does he have any younger brothers? / Does he have any younger brothers or not?
他有没有弟弟？

Nǐ chī bu chī píngguǒ?
Would you like to eat an apple? / Would you like to eat an apple or not?
你吃不吃苹果？

Nǐ qù bu qù gōngyuán ?
Would you like to go to the park? / Would you like to go to the park or not?
你去不去公园？

Jīntiān shì bu shì Jiǔyuè shíqī rì?
Is today the 17th of September or not?
今天是不是九月十七日？

⊿ Positive modal verb + negative modal verb

Nǐ néng bu néng bāng wǒ?
Can you help me?
你能不能帮我？

Nǐ yào bu yào qù yóujú mǎi yóupiào?
Do you want to go to the post office to buy some stamps?
你要不要去邮局买邮票？

⊿ Positive adjective + negative adjective

Nàxiē shū guì bu guì ?
Are those books expensive? / Are those books expensive or not?
那些书贵不贵？

Nà gè fángjiān gānjìng bu gānjìng?
Is that room clean? / Is that room clean or not?
那个房间干净不干净？

⊿ Declarative sentence + **hǎo bu hǎo** 好不好?

Wǒmen liǎ yìqǐ qù Xiǎo Zhōu jiā, hǎo bu hǎo?
Shall we go to Xiao Zhou's home together?
我们俩一起去小周家，好不好？

Xiàwǔ qù tǐyùguǎn dǎ pīngpāngqiú, hǎo bu hǎo?
Let's go to the gym to play table tennis this afternoon. Is that ok?
下午去体育馆打乒乓球，好不好？

3. Conjunction **háishi** 还是

It is used in alternative questions.

Nǐ xué Zhōngwén háishi (xué) Yīngwén?
Would you like to learn Chinese or English?
你学中文还是(学)英文？

Nǐ hē chá háishi (hē) kāfēi?
Would you like to drink tea or coffee?
你喝茶还是(喝)咖啡？

4. Interrogative pronouns

shénme 什 么	what	**Tā xìng shénme?** *What is his surname?* 他姓什么？ **Zhè shì shénme?** *What is this?* 这是什么？
nǎ 哪	which what	**Nǎ běn shū shì nǐ de?** *Which book is yours?* 哪本书是你的？ **Nǐ zuò nǎ cì chē?** *What/Which train do you take?* 你坐哪次车？
shéi 谁	who	**Nà gè rén shì shéi?** *Who is that person?* 那个人是谁？ **Shéi shì lǎoshī?** *Who is the teacher?* 谁是老师？

shéi de 谁 的	*whose*	**Zhè shì shéi de shū?** *Whose book is this?* 这是谁的书？ **Zhè jiàn yīfu shì shéi de?** *To whom do the clothes belong?* 这件衣服是谁的？
shénme 什 么 **shíhou** 时 候	*when*	**Nǐ shénme shíhou qù Běijīng?** *When are you going to Beijing?* 你什么时候去北京？ **Tā shénme shíhou lái?** *When is he coming?* 他什么时候来？
nǎ nián / 哪 年/ **nǎ yuè /** 哪 月/ **nǎ tiān** 哪 天	*which year /* *which month /* *which day*	**Nǐ nǎ nián chūshēng?** *In which year were you born? /* *When were you born?* 你哪年出生？ **Nǐ nǎ tiān lái wǒ jiā?** *On which day are you going to my home?* 你哪天来我家？
jǐ diǎn 几 点	*what time*	**Túshūguǎn jǐ diǎn kāimén?** *What time does the library open?* 图书馆几点开门？ **Nǐ jǐ diǎn xiàbān?** *What time do you finish working?* 你几点下班？
shénme **dìfang / nǎr /** **nǎlǐ** 什么地方/哪 儿/哪里	*where*	**Nǐ jiā zài shénme dìfang?** *Where is your home?* 你家在什么地方？ **Nǐ qù nǎr?** *Where are you going?* 你去哪儿？ **Yínháng zài nǎlǐ?** *Where is the bank?* 银行在哪里？

読拼音学汉语

duōshao (+ measure- ment word) 多 少 （+量词）	*how many* *how much* *what's the number*	**Nǐ mǎile duōshao?** *How many did you buy?* 你买了多少? **Duōshao qián yì jīn?** *How much is it for half a kilo?* 多少钱一斤? **Diànhuà hàomǎ shì duōshao?** *What's the telephone number?* 电话号码是多少?
jǐ +measure- ment word 几+量词		**Tā yǒu jǐ gè háizi ?** *How many children has she got?* 她有几个孩子? **Nǐ mǎile jǐ jīn?** *How many half kilos did you buy?* 你买了几斤?
duō jiǔ 多 久	*how long*	**Nǐ qù duō jiǔ?** *How long are you going for?* 你去多久? **Tā zài Běijīng zhùle duō jiǔ?** *How long did he stay in Beijing?* 他在北京住了多久?
zěnme 怎 么	*how*	**Qù yínháng zěnme zǒu?** *How can I get to the bank?* 去银行怎么走? **Jiǎozi zěnme zuò?** *How do you make dumplings?* 饺子怎么做?
zěnmeyàng 怎 么 样	*What is/are...like* *How is/are*	**Jīntiān tiānqì zěnmeyàng?** *What's the weather like today?* 今天天气怎么样? **Nǐ de bàba māma zěnmeyàng?** *How are your parents?* 你的爸爸妈妈怎么样?

206

wèishénme 为 什 么	*why*	**Tā wèishénme méi lái shàngbān?** *Why didn't he come to work?* 他为什么没来上班? **Túshūguǎn wèishénme bù kāimén?** *Why is the library closed?* 图书馆为什么不开门?

In Chinese, the interrogative pronouns are usually positioned in the question in a way that tells where the answer is to be placed in the reply, unlike English which put all interrogatives at the beginning of the sentences, e.g.

Túshūguǎn jǐ diǎn kāimén?
What time does the library open?
图书馆几点开门?

Túshūguǎn bā diǎn kāimén.
The library opens at 8 a.m.
图书馆八点开门。

Nǐ de diànhuà hàomǎ shì duōshao?
What's your telephone number?
你的电话号码是多少?

Wǒ de diànhuà hàomǎ shì sān bā èr yāo wǔ liù qī jiǔ.
My telephone number is 38215679.
我的电话号码是三八二么五六七九。

Shéi shì lǎoshī?
Who is the teacher?
谁是老师?

Wáng xiānsheng shì lǎoshī.
Mr. Wang is a teacher.
王先生是老师。

⊃ Common pronouns and possessive words

Singular		Plural	
Personal pronouns **wǒ** 我	*I/me*	*Personal pronouns* **wǒmen** 我 们	*we/us*
nǐ 你	*you/you*	**nǐmen** 你 们	*you/you*
tā 他、她、它	*he, she, it/ him, her, it*	**tāmen** 他们、她们、它们	*they/them*

In Chinese, the form remains the same for both subject and object.

Possessive words			Possessive words		
wǒ de 我 的		*my/mine*	**wǒmen de** 我 们 的		*our/ours*
nǐ de 你 的		*your/yours*	**nǐmen de** 你 们 的		*your/yours*
tā de 他 的、她的、它 的		*his, her, its/* *his, hers, ×*	**tāmen de** 他 们 的、她们的、它 们 的		*their/theirs*
lǎoshī de 老 师 的		*teacher's*	**lǎoshīmen de** 老 师 们 的		*teachers'*

In Chinese, the form remains the same for both modifier and object.

Demonstrative pronouns			Demonstrative pronouns		
zhè 这		*this*	**zhèxiē** 这 些		*these*
nà 那		*that*	**nàxiē** 那 些		*those*

↰ **de** 的 (particle)

(1) (structural particle) It is used after a noun or a pronoun to indicate the possessive relation.

wǒ de jiā 我 的 家	*my home*	**Běijīng de chūntiān** 北 京 的 春 天	*the spring of Beijing*

de 的 *can usually be omitted when there is close personal relationship between the possessive pronoun and the noun.*

wǒ (de) māma 我 （的）妈 妈	*my mother*

It is also used after an adjective or adjectival phrase to indicate a modifier.

xīnxiān de huángguā 新 鲜 的 黄 瓜	*fresh cucumber*	**xiǎo diǎnr de xié** 小 点儿 的 鞋	*smaller shoes*

When the context is clear, the noun can be omitted. (See Unit 14 Form, P129)

xīnxiān de
新 鲜 的　　　　　　　　　*fresh*

xiǎo diǎnr de
小　点儿 的　　　　　　　*smaller*

(2) (modal particle) It is used at the end of a declarative sentence to express a tone of affirmation.

Hǎo de.
好 的　　　　　　　　　　*OK.*

Wǒ huì lái de.
我　会 来 的　　　　　*I will come here.*

⟳ There are no changes in verbs' forms

Unlike English, there are no changes in verbs' forms in Chinese sentences. Verbs neither change their forms when following different nouns or pronouns, nor do they change with different times. How to express the time of action?

⟨ Verb **shì** 是 and its negative **bú shì** 不是

In Chinese	In English
Wǒ shì / guòqù shì / jiāng shì··· 我　是 / 过 去 是 / 将　是······	*I am / was / will be...*
Wǒmen shì / guòqù shì / jiāng shì··· 我 们 是 / 过 去 是/　将　是······	*We are / were / will be...*
Nǐ shì / guòqù shì / jiāng shì··· 你 是/ 过 去 是/ 将　是······	*You are / were / will be...*
Nǐmen shì / guòqù shì / jiāng shì··· 你 们 是/ 过 去 是/　将　是······	*You are / were / will be...*
Tā shì / guòqù shì / jiāng shì··· 他 是/ 过 去 是/ 将　是······	*He is / was / will be...*
Tāmen shì / guòqù shì / jiāng shì··· 他 们 是 / 过 去 是/ 将　是······	*They are / were / will be...*

⟨ Verb **yǒu** 有 (have)

*It is used to express possession, and **yǒu** 有 (there is/are) expresses existence. The negative is **méi(yǒu)** 没(有) (haven't, there isn't/aren't).*

209

↖ The words or phrases of time

The words or phrases of time are used before verbs to express the time. It is different from English.

Expressing the time of actions	
In Chinese	In English
The words or phrases of time are usually placed before the verbs or at the beginning of the sentences. **Tā míngnián shàng dàxué.** 他 明 年 上 大学。 **Wǒ měi tiān qī diǎn qǐchuáng.** 我 每 天 七 点 起 床。 **Shàng xīngqī tā qùle Měiguó.** 上 星 期他 去了 美 国。	*The words or prepositional phrases of time are usually placed at the end of the sentences.* *He is going to the university next year.* *I get up at 7 o'clock every day.* *He went to the U.S.A. last week.*
Before and after	
zǎochen qī diǎn yǐqián 早 晨 七 点 以 前 **wǎnshang jiǔ diǎn yǐhòu** 晚 上 九 点 以 后	*before 7 o'clock in the morning* *after 9 o'clock in the evening*

↖ Tense auxiliaries are used

"Verb + **zhe** 着/ **le** 了/ **guo** 过*", the verbal phrases express different tenses*

(1) Form"verb + **zhe** 着*"is used to express continuity of an action or state. It is similar to present (past) continuous in English, e.g.*

Wǒmen hēzhe chá liáotiānr.
We're drinking tea and chatting.
我们喝着茶聊天儿。

Tā tīngzhe yīnyuè kāi chē.
She's listening to the music and driving the car.
她听着音乐开车。

We can also put the word "**zhèng** 正 / **zhèngzài** 正在" before the verb to emphasize that the action is in progress.

Wǒ zhèngzài hē chá. 我正在喝茶。(/ **Wǒ zhèng hēzhe chá.** 我正喝着茶。)
I'm drinking tea.

Tā zhèngzài tīng yīnyuè. 她正在听音乐。(/ **Tā zhèng tīngzhe yīnyuè.** 她正听着音乐。)
She's listening to the music.

But there aren't equivalent forms between Chinese and English in some sentences, e.g.

Wǒ zài chēzhàn děng huǒchē, huǒchē 我 在 车 站 等 火 车，火 车 **kuài lái le.** 快 来 了。 (*not* **Wǒ zài chēzhàn děngzhe huǒchē···**) （我 在 车 站 等 着 火 车······）	*I'm at the station. I'm waiting for the train. Oh, it's coming now.*
Zuótiān, wǒmen zuò zài chuán shang, 昨 天，我 们 坐 在 船 上， **hēzhe chá, tīngzhe yīnyuè liáotiānr.** 喝 着 茶，听 着 音 乐 聊 天 儿。	*We drank some tea, listened to the music and chatted while we were sitting on the boat yesterday.*

(2) Form "*verb / verbal phrase* + **le** 了" is used to express the action is done. The form is used for any complete action. We don't consider what time the action was completed, e.g.

Wǒ hēle chá. 我 喝了茶。	*I drank tea.*
Shàngwǔ wǒ hēle chá. 上 午我 喝了茶。	*I drank tea in the morning.*
Tā tīngle yīnyuè. 她 听了音乐。	*She listened to the music.*
Zuótiān tā tīngle yīnyuè. 昨 天 她 听了音乐。	*She listened to the music yesterday.*
Negative: **Wǒ méi hē chá.** 我 没喝茶。	*Negative:* *I didn't drink tea.*
Shàngwǔ wǒ méi hē chá. 上 午我 没喝茶。	*I didn't drink tea in the morning.*
Tā méi tīng yīnyuè. 她 没听音乐。	*She didn't listen to the music.*
Zuótiān tā méi tīng yīnyuè. 昨 天 她 没听音乐。	*She didn't listen to the music yesterday.*

*(3) Form "verb + **guo** 过" is used to express the action is past and to emphasize the past experience, e.g.*

Wǒ hēguo chá. 我 喝 过 茶。	*I've drunk tea.*
Tā tīngguo yīnyuè. 她 听 过 音乐。	*She has listened to the music.*
Negative: **Wǒ méi hēguo chá.** 我 没 喝 过 茶。	*Negative:* *I haven't drunk tea.*
Tā méi tīngguo yīnyuè. 她 没 听 过 音乐。	*She hasn't listened to the music.*

*We can also put "**le** 了" at the end of a sentence to emphasize the action is past, e.g.*

Shàngwǔ wǒ hēguo chá le. 上 午我 喝 过 茶 了。	*I've drunk tea in the morning.*
Zuótiān tā tīngguo yīnyuè le. 昨 天 她 听 过 音 乐 了。	*She has listened to the music yesterday.*

↳ **le** 了 (modal particle)

It is placed at the end of the sentence to emphasize something that has already changed or the emergence of a new state.

Xià yǔ le. 下 雨 了。	*It starts raining.*	**Nǐ pàng le.** 你 胖 了。	*You've put on weight.*
Tiān hēi le. 天 黑 了。	*It has been dark.*	**Chūntiān lái le, huā kāi le.** *Spring is coming. The flowers are blooming.* 春天来了，花开了。	

*After the adjective in the sentence, "**le** 了" is a common adjunct of hyperbole.*

Wǒ kě sǐ le. 我 渴 死了。	*I am extremely thirsty.*	**Měilì jí le!** 美 丽极了!	*So beautiful!*
Tài rè le. 太 热 了。	*Too hot.*		

↳ **guò** 过 (verb)

(1) To cross, to pass

guò mǎlù 过 马路	*cross the road*	**Guòle shízì lùkǒu jiù shì tǐyùchǎng.** *Pass through the crossroads, then you will see the stadium.* 过了十字路口就是体育场。	
guò hé 过 河	*cross the river*		

(2) The meaning is similar to celebrate

读拼音学汉语

guò shēngrì 过　生　日　　*celebrate a birthday*	**guò jié** 过　节　　*celebrate a festival*
guò nián 过　年　　*celebrate the New Year*	

⊃ Modal verbs

1. huì 会，néng 能 and kěyǐ 可以

They are similar to "can" in English and are used to express that someone has the ability or the possibility to do something. We can't strictly distinguish their meanings, but there are slight differences. What are the differences among them?

↳ For expressing abilities

huì 会 *and* **néng** 能 *are used to express that someone has the ability to do something. The tone is strong.* **kěyǐ** 可以 *means someone can do something but with difficulty. The tone is weak.*

Wǒ huì/néng shuō pǔtōnghuà.
我　会／能　　说　普　通　话。

Wǒ kěyǐ shuō pǔtōnghuà.
我　可　以　说　普　通　话。

↳ For expressing possibilities

(1) **néng** 能 *and* **kěyǐ** 可以 *emphasize objectivity.* **huì** 会 *emphasizes subjectivity.*
　　Question:

Xià gè yuè wǒmen qù Shànghǎi lǚyóu, nǐ qù ma?
We are going to travel in Shanghai next month. Will you go with us?
下个月我们去上海旅游，你去吗？

　　Answers:

Wǒ bù néng / bù kěyǐ qù.
I can't.
我不能／不可以去。

Both emphasize an objective condition which does not allow someone to go somewhere or do something.

Wǒ bú huì qù.
I won't.
我不会去。

It emphasizes the subjectivity. The meaning is similar to "I wouldn't like to go there."

213

(2) If we can see or feel that something is certain to happen in the future, we use
huì 会.

Tiān yīn le, xiàwǔ huì xià yǔ.
It is cloudy. It's going to rain in the afternoon.
天阴了，下午会下雨。

(3) If something is certain to happen in the future following a rule, we also use **huì** 会.

Háizi huì zhǎngdà, huì lǎo.
Children will grow up, then get older.
孩子会长大，会老。

2. **yào** 要 and **xiǎng** 想

They are modal verbs, which have meanings similar to "want", "will", "would", etc. in English. We use modal verbs **yào** 要 *or* **xiǎng** 想 *to express needs, demand or wishes when we place them before the first verb in the sentence.*

Wǒ xiǎng chàng gēr.
I'd like to sing songs.
我想唱歌儿。

Wǒ yào xué tàijíquán.
I'd like to learn tai chi.
我要学太极拳。

Wǒ yào chéng fēijī dào Zhōngguó qù.
I'll go to China by plane.
我要乘飞机到中国去。

Wǒ xiǎng xǐle zǎo shàng lóu shuìjiào.
I want to have a bath and then go upstairs to bed.
我想洗了澡上楼睡觉。

⤹ **yào** 要

It has another meaning which is similar to "must", "have to".

Chéng gōngjiāochē yào mǎi piào.
Everybody has to buy a ticket to take the bus.
乘公交车要买票。

Xīngqīyī yào shàngbān.
You must go to work on Monday.
星期一要上班。

⤹ They can also be a verb

Wǒ yào liǎng zhāng yóupiào.
I want two stamps .
我要两张邮票。

Wǒ xiǎng wǒ de péngyou.
I miss my friends.
我想我的朋友。

⤷ lái 来 and qù 去

1. lái 来 and qù 去 as directional verbs

lái 来 *indicates the direction toward the speaker and* **qù** 去 *the direction away from the speaker.*

(1) They are simple direction indicators, e.g.

Yéye lái le.
Grandpa is coming.
爷爷来了。

Nǎinai qù Zhōngguó le.
Grandma has gone to China.
奶奶去中国了。

Mèimei qù xuéxiào le.
My younger sister has gone to school.
妹妹去学校了。

(2) **lái** 来 *and* **qù** 去 *can be combined with a set of directional verbs to indicate more precise directions.*

		lái 来 towards	**qù** 去 away from
shàng *(verb)* 上	*up (preposition)*	**shànglái** 上 来	**shàngqù** 上 去
xià *(verb)* 下	*down (preposition)*	**xiàlái** 下 来	**xiàqù** 下 去
jìn *(verb)* 进	*in/into (preposition)*	**jìnlái** 进 来	**jìnqù** 进 去
chū *(verb)* 出	*out (of) (preposition)*	**chūlái** 出 来	**chūqù** 出 去
guò *(verb)* 过	*across/over (preposition)*	**guòlái** 过 来	**guòqù** 过 去
huí *(verb)* 回	*back (verb)*	**huílái** 回 来	**huíqù** 回 去
qǐ *(verb)* 起	*upward (adverb)*	**qǐlái** 起来	

语
法

The location object is placed between the two directional verbs.

shàng shān lái 上　山　来	*come up the mountain*	**chū mén qù** 出　门　去	*go out of the door*
xià lóu qù 下　楼　去	*go down the stairs*	**guò qiáo lái** 过　桥　来	*come over the bridge*
jìn wū lái 进 屋 来	*come into the room*	**huí Měiguó qù** 回　美 国　去	*go back to the U.S.A.*

       shàng lái shān
Not: 上　来 山

(3) **dào** 到 *can be combined with* **lái** 来 *or* **qù** 去 *in a sentence to indicate the direction. The form is* "**dào** 到 + *location object* + **lái** 来 / **qù** 去".

dào yóujú qù 到　邮局去	*go to the post office*	**dào yīyuàn qù** 到 医 院 去	*go to the hospital*
dào wǒ jiā lái 到　我 家 来	*come to my home*	**dào fàndiàn lái** 到　饭 店 来	*come to the restaurant*

       dào qù yóujú
Not: 到　去 邮 局

2. **lái** 来/**qù** 去 (+ location object) + verb / verbal phrase

The second verb or verbal phrase indicates the purpose of **lái** 来 *or* **qù** 去. *In English, to-infinitive or -ing form is used to indicate the purpose.*

qù jì bāoguǒ 去寄包裹	*go to send a parcel*	**qù yóujú jì bāoguǒ** 去 邮局 寄 包 裹	*go to the post office to send a parcel*
lái kàn shū 来 看 书	*come to read books*	**lái túshūguǎn kàn shū** 来 图 书 馆 看 书	*come to the library to read books*
qù yóuyǒng 去 游 泳	*go swimming*	**qù hǎibiān yóuyǒng** 去 海 边 游 泳	*go swimming at the seaside*

3. Verb + transportation + **lái** 来/**qù** 去 (+ location object)

The first verbal phrase indicates the means of **lái** 来 *or* **qù** 去. *In English, we can use the prepositional phrase "by + transportation" at the end of the sentence to indicate the means.*

zuò gōnggòng qìchē qù xuéxiào *go to school by bus* 坐公共汽车去学校	**chéng fēijī lái Zhōngguó** *come to China by plane* 乘飞机来中国

When there are two or more verbs or verbal phrases in a sentence, the order is similar to English.

In Chinese	In English
One after another in time sequence.	*Use to-infinitive pattern or conjunction "and", "and then"...*
Shàngwǔ tā ná qián qù (yóujú) jì bāoguǒ. 上　午他拿钱去（邮局）寄包裹。	*He took some money to go (to the post office) to send a parcel in the morning.*
Tā xǐle zǎo shàng chuáng shuìjiào. 他洗了澡　上　床　睡　觉。	*He had a bath and then went to bed.*
Wǒ měi tiān kāi chē qù mǎi dōngxi. 我　每天开车去买　东西。	*I drive the car to go shopping every day.*

Verb reduplication form

When the monosyllabic verb is reduplicated, the form is:

*Verb (A) (+**yi** 一)+verb (A) →A (**yi**) A*

liáng 量	→	**liáng (yi) liáng** 量　（一）量	**shì** 试	→	**shì (yi) shì** 试　（一）试
kàn 看	→	**kàn (yi) kàn** 看　（一）看	**bāng** 帮	→	**bāng (yi) bāng** 帮　（一）帮

When the disyllabic verb is reduplicated, the form is:

Verb (A B)+verb (A B) →A B A B

xiūxi 休息	→	**xiūxi xiūxi** 休息 休息	**cānguān** 参　观	→	**cānguān cānguān** 参　观　参　观
xuéxí 学习	→	**xuéxí xuéxí** 学习　学习	**bāngzhù** 帮　助	→	**bāngzhù bāngzhù** 帮　助 帮　助

217

Numbers and measurement words

1. Cardinal numbers and ordinal numbers

(1) Digits of number

gè 个	*1*	**qiān** 千	*1,000*
shí 十	*10*	**wàn** 万	*10,000*
bǎi 百	*100*	**yì** 亿	*100,000,000*

(2) The way of reading numbers of over ten

shí'èr 十 二	12	**qīshíbā** 七十 八	78
yìbǎi wǔshísān 一百 五 十 三	153	**yìbǎi liù(shí)** 一百 六（十）	160
sānqiān sì(bǎi) 三 千 四（百）	3,400		

When **líng** 零 is placed between numbers (1-9) , we read it as **líng** 零. When **líng** 零 is at the end of the number, we read out the digit.

sìbǎi líng bā 四百 零 八	408	**sānwàn líng sìbǎi** 三 万 零 四百	30,400
yìqiān líng liùshí 一 千 零 六十	1,060		

(3) The way of reading **yī** 一 *and* **èr** 二

yī 一 and **yāo** 幺

"1" is usually read as **yī** 一. But when it is within a number, such as phone number, house number, we read it as **yāo** 幺. Read the numbers below.

Telephone Directory, call the number :114	Fire service, call the number:119
To report a burglary, call the number :110	Ambulance, call the number :120

èr 二 and **liǎng** 两

"2" is usually read as **èr** 二. But when it is followed by a measurement word and within 1-10, we read it as **liǎng** 两.

liǎng gè rén 两 个 人	*two people*	**liǎng běn shū** 两 本 书	*two books*

When the number is over three digits, we also read it as **liǎng** 两.

liǎngqiān liǎngbǎi èrshí'èr   *2,222*
两　千　两　百　二 十 二

(4) Ordinal numbers

Ordinals in Chinese are formed simply by adding the prefix **dì** 第 *to cardinal numbers, e.g.*

yī 一	*one*	**dì–yī** 第 一	*first*
shí'èr 十 二	*twelve*	**dì–shí'èr** 第 十 二	*twelfth*

Other examples are:

dì–èr gè háizi 第 二 个 孩子	*the second child*	**dì–shí'èr yè** 第 十 二 页	*page 12*

But **dì** 第 *will normally be omitted in some phrases, e. g.*

sān lóu 三　楼	*the third floor*	*not*	**dì–sān lóu** 第 三 楼
jiǔ lù chē 九 路 车	*Bus Route 9*	*not*	**dì–jiǔ lù chē** 第 九 路 车
yī děng cāng 一　等　舱	*first class (on a ship or plane)*	*not*	**dì–yī děng cāng** 第 一 等 舱

2. Measurement words

(1) Numerals usually cannot be put immediately in front of the nouns in Chinese. The measurement words must be put between the numerals and the nouns. The form is: number + measurement word + noun, e.g.

yí gè nánháir 一 个 男 孩儿	*one boy*	**sì běn shū** 四 本 书	*four books*
liǎng wèi xiānsheng 两　位　先　生	*two gentlemen*	**wǔ bǎ sǎn** 五 把 伞	*five umbrellas*
sān zhāng zhǐ 三　张　纸	*three pieces of paper*	**liù shuāng kuàizi** 六　双　筷 子	*six pairs of chopsticks*

Some names of things can be borrowed as measurement words, e.g.

bēi — yì bēi chá 杯　一 杯 茶	*a cup of tea*	**wǎn — yì wǎn mǐfàn** 碗　一　碗　米饭	*a bowl of boiled rice*

píng — yì píng jiǔ		**zhuōzi — yì zhuōzi cài**	
瓶　一瓶酒	*a bottle of wine*	桌子　一桌子菜	*a table of dishes*
chuán — yì chuán rén		**wūzi — yì wūzi shū**	
船　一船人	*a boat load of people*	屋子　一屋子书	*a room of books*

(2) Measurement word reduplication

Many measurement words can be repeated to modify the nouns. Usually the form is: (yī 一) + AA (measurement words) + noun.

yí gègè nǚháir	**yí chuànchuàn dēnglong**
一个个 女孩儿	一串串 灯笼
yì bēibēi jiǔ	**yì pánpán cài**
一杯杯酒	一盘盘菜

The meaning is "every one".

Yí gègè nǚháir dōu hěn piàoliang.	**Yí chuànchuàn dēnglong dōu shì hóng de.**
Every girl is beautiful.	*Every string of lanterns is red.*
一个个女孩儿都很漂亮。	一串串灯笼都是红的。

Another meaning is "not only one".

Chuán shang guàzhe yí chuànchuàn hóng dēnglong.
There are strings of red lanterns hung on the boat.
船上挂着一串串红灯笼。

Tiānshang piāozhe yì duǒduǒ bái yún.
The white clouds are floating in the sky.
天上飘着一朵朵白云。

⤵ Location and direction

1. Common specific position words

shàng		**xià**	
上	*on*	下	*under*
lǐ		**wài**	
里	*inside*	外	*outside*
qián		**hòu**	
前	*front*	后	*behind*

zuǒ 左	*left*	**yòu** 右	*right*
dōng 东	*east*	**xī** 西	*west*
nán 南	*south*	**běi** 北	*north*
pángbiān 旁 边	*next to*	**zhōngjiān** 中 间	*between*
duìmiàn 对 面	*opposite*	**fùjìn** 附近	*nearby*

2. Specific positional phrase is used to point out the location

Wū li yǒu yì zhāng zhuōzi.
There is a table inside the room.
屋里有一张桌子。

Zhuōzi shang yǒu yì píng huā.
There is a vase with flowers in it on the table.
桌子上有一瓶花。

Zhuōzi xià wòzhe yì zhī gǒu.
A dog is lying under the table.
桌子下卧着一只狗。

Qiáng shang guàzhe yì běn niánlì.
A calendar is hanging on the wall.
墙上挂着一本年历。

Wū wài yǒu liǎng gè rén.
There are two people outside the room.
屋外有两个人。

Wū hòu yǒu yí gè xiǎo gōngyuán.
There is a small park behind the house.
屋后有一个小公园。

Fángzi de pángbiān shì shūdiàn.
A bookshop is next to the house.
房子的旁边是书店。

Shūdiàn de duìmiàn shì xuéxiào.
A school is opposite the bookshop.
书店的对面是学校。

Gōngyuán de zuǒbian shì yīyuàn.
A hospital is on the left side of the park.
公园的左边是医院。

Gōngyuán de yòubian yǒu yí gè qìchēzhàn.
There is a bus stop on the right side of the park.
公园的右边有一个汽车站。

As we have seen, in Chinese, location expressions are at the beginning of the sentences, as "somewhere has something"; in English, as "(there is) something somewhere".

3. Preposition "zài 在" and specific position word are used to point out the location

zài shàngbian
在 上 边

zài zhōngjiān
在 中 间

zài pángbiān
在 旁 边

zài fùjìn
在 附近

(1) The prepositional phrase can be before or after the verb, and **zài** 在 *usually cannot be omitted,e.g.*

Tāmen zài shù xià liáotiānr.
他 们 在 树 下 聊 天 儿。

They're chatting under the tree.

Nǎinai zuò zài yǐzi shang.
奶 奶 坐 在 椅子 上。

Grandma is sitting on the chair.

Wǒmen zhù zài xuéxiào de dōngbian.
我 们 住 在 学 校 的 东 边。

We live to the east of the school.

(2) **zài** 在 *can be a verb in the sentence,e.g.*

Shūdiàn zài yínháng duìmiàn.
书 店 在 银 行 对 面。

The bookshop is opposite the bank.

Huǒchēzhàn zài tǐyùchǎng hé lǚguǎn
火 车 站 在 体育 场 和 旅 馆

zhōngjiān.
中 间。

The train station is between the stadium and the hotel.

4. Preposition and position word are used to point out the direction

xiàng qián zǒu
向 前 走   *go ahead*

wǎng zuǒ guǎi
往 左 拐   *turn left*

⮕ Predicate

1. Nominal predicate

In Chinese, nouns, noun phrases, quantifiers, etc. can directly follow the subject in the sentences. They are often used to express nationality, age, time, date, weather, price, etc. In English, similar sentences must have the verb "be", e.g.

Tā Běijīngrén, shíbā suì.
He is eighteen years old and from Beijing.
他北京人，十八岁。

Zuótiān Èryuè shí'èr hào, Xīngqīsān.
It was the twelfth of February, Wednesday, yesterday.
昨天二月十二号，星期三。

Xiànzài bā diǎn.
It is eight o'clock now.
现在八点。

Jīntiān qíngtiān.
It is sunny today.
今天晴天。

Zhè běn shū wǔ kuài bā.
This book is ¥ 5.8.
这本书五块八。

2. Adjectival predicate

Some adjectives can directly follow the subject in the sentences. They are usually used to describe someone or something. In English, similar sentences must have the verb "be".

Tiān qíng le.
It is clear now.
天晴了。

Háizi dà le.
The child is grown up.
孩子大了。

(1) *Adjectives are always modified by an adverb of degree or are followed by a complement of degree.*

Wǒ de chábēi hěn gānjìng.
My teacup is very clean.
我的茶杯很干净。

Nà liàng zìxíngchē piányi de hěn.
That bicycle is too cheap.
那辆自行车便宜得很。

Zhè shuāng xié tài xiǎo.
This pair of shoes is too small.
这双鞋太小。

(2) **duō 多**

A. *(adverb) It can be used before adjective in the exclamatory sentence to indicate extreme degree, e.g.*

Duō piányi ya!
How cheap it is!
多便宜呀！

When it is used after adjective to show a high degree with comparison, the meaning is "much", e.g.

Gānjìng duō le.
It is much cleaner.
干净多了。

B. *(interrogative pronoun) It can be used before adjective to ask about degree, e.g.*

Xuéxiào yǒu duō yuǎn?
How far is the school from here?
学校有多远？

Guǎngzhōu yǒu duō rè?
How hot is it in Guangzhou?
广州有多热？

(3) *Some adjectives can also be reduplicated to express a pleasant feeling.When the monosyllabic adjective is reduplicated, the form is:*

adjective (A) + adjective (A) + de 的 → *A A* **de**

dà 大	→	dàdà de 大 大 的	hóng 红	→	hónghóng de 红 红 的
cháng 长	→	chángcháng de 长 长 的	tián 甜	→	tiántián de 甜 甜 的

When the disyllabic adjective is reduplicated, the form is:

adjective (A B) + adjective (A B) → AABB

gānjìng 干 净	→	gāngānjìngjìng 干 干 净 净	gāoxìng 高 兴	→	gāogāoxìngxìng 高 高 兴 兴
piàoliang 漂 亮	→	piàopiàoliangliang 漂 漂 亮 亮	shūfu 舒 服	→	shūshūfufu 舒 舒 服 服

⊃ Comparative sentences

To compare one thing with the other, we use the word **bǐ** 比 *between the two things. The form is: A +* **bǐ** 比 *+ B + adjective.*

Tā bǐ tā de dìdi gāo.
He is taller than his younger brother.
他比他的弟弟高。

Some words are often used to indicate the degree of differences between the objects. The form is: A + **bǐ** 比 *+ B (+ adverb) + adjective (+ complement).*

Tā bǐ tā de dìdi gāo yìdiǎnr.
He is a little taller than his younger brother.
他比他的弟弟高一点儿。

Tā bǐ tā de dìdi shāo(wēi) gāo yìdiǎnr.
He is slightly taller than his younger brother.
他比他的弟弟稍(微)高一点儿。

Tā bǐ tā de dìdi gèng gāo.
He is even taller than his younger brother.
他比他的弟弟更高。

Tā bǐ tā de dìdi gāo de duō (/ duō le).
He is much taller than his younger brother.
他比他的弟弟高得多(/多了)。

读拼音学汉语

When two or more things are the same, the pattern is:

A + **hé** 和 + *B* + **yíyàng** 一样 + *adjective*

Tā hé tā de dìdi yíyàng gāo.
He is as tall as his younger brother.
他和他的弟弟一样高。

⊃ Expressing the degree of extreme

1. Usage of **zuì** 最

The adverb of degree **zuì** 最 can be used before the adjective to express the highest degree. The form is like superlative adjective (-est, most) in English.

zuì dà de 最 大 的	*the biggest*	**zuì gāo de** 最 高 的	*the highest*
zuì piàoliang de 最 漂 亮 的	*the most beautiful*		

2. Usage of other adverbs of degree

There are other adverbs that can be used before adjectives to express the extreme degree, e.g. **tài** 太, **hěn** 很, **fēicháng** 非常, **hǎo** 好, **zhēn** 真, etc. These adverbs have similar meanings.

tài guì le 太 贵 了	*too expensive*	**hǎo xīnxiān** 好 新 鲜	*very fresh*
hěn gānjìng 很 干 净	*very clean*	**zhēn měi** 真 美	*really beautiful*
fēicháng dà 非 常 大	*very big*		

3. The complement of degree after the adjective

Kūnmíng měi jí le! *Kunming is extremely beautiful!* 昆明美极了!	**Wǒ è sǐ le!** *I'm extremely hungry!* 我饿死了!

4. Other usage of **hǎo** 好

(1) It is used in greeting each other.

Nǐ hǎo! *How are you?* 你好!	**Zǎoshang hǎo!** *Good morning!* 早上好!

语法

(2) Being put before a noun or a verb, the meaning of it is "good".

hǎo rén
好　人　　　　　　　*a good person*

hǎo xuésheng
好　学　生　　　　　*a good student*

hǎokàn
好　看　　　　　　　*good-looking*

hǎochī
好　吃　　　　　　　*delicious*

(3) Being put after a verb, it indicates the action is completed to perfect.

jì hǎo
系好　　　　　　　　*fasten*

zǒuhǎo
走　好　　　　　　　*the meaning is "be careful on the way"*

Liànxí dá'àn hé tīnglì wénběn

KEYS AND AUDIO SCRIPTS OF EXERCISES

练习答案和听力文本

Unit 1

读拼音学汉语

1. Fill in the blanks after listening. 🎧

A: Qǐngwèn, nín guìxìng?
请 问， 您 贵 姓？

B: Wǒ xìng Liú.
我 姓 刘。

A: Nín jiào shénme ?
您 叫 什 么？

B: Wǒ jiào Liú Hǎi.
我 叫 刘 海。

A: Tā jiào shénme míngzi?
他 叫 什 么 名 字？

B: Tā jiào Zhāng Jūn. Xiānsheng, nín guìxìng?
他 叫 张 军。先 生， 您 贵 姓？

A: Xìng Lǐ.
姓 李。

B: Jiào shénme míngzi?
叫 什 么 名 字？

A: Lǐ Jiànguó.
李 建 国。

2. Put the words in the correct order.

(1) Wǒ xìng Zhāng.

(2) Huáng xiānsheng nín hǎo!

(3) Lǐ xiānsheng nín jiào shénme míngzi?

(4) Xiānsheng nín guìxìng?

(5) Wǒ xìng Wáng jiào Zhìqiáng.

3. Put the sentences in the correct order after listening. 🎧

(2) Lǎo Liú, hǎojiǔ bú jiàn!
老 刘， 好 久 不 见！

(4) Hǎojiǔ bú jiàn, Lǎo Zhào. Nǐ hǎo ma?
好 久 不 见，老 赵。你 好 吗？

(3) Hǎo. Nǐ de péngyou Xiǎo Wú hǎo ma?
好。你 的 朋 友 小 吴 好 吗？

(1) Tā hěn hǎo. Xièxie! Zàijiàn!
他 很 好。谢 谢！再 见！

(5) Zàijiàn!
再 见！

4. Circle the right answers after listening. 🎧

(1) Wǒ de hǎo péngyou xìng Niú.
我 的 好 朋 友 姓 牛。

(2) Lǐ nǚshì jiào Lǐ Yíngchūn.
李 女 士 叫 李 迎 春。

228

(3) Zǎoshang hǎo, <u>Huáng</u> xiānsheng!
　　早　上　好，　黄　　先　生！

(4) Tā nánpéngyou de míngzi jiào <u>Mǐ Dàshān</u>.
　　她　男　朋　友　的　名 字 叫　米　大　山。

☟ 5. Choose the correct answers.
(1) B　　　(2) C　　　(3) C　　　(4) A

☟ 6. Write questions for the answers provided below.
(1) Nǐ xìng shénme?　　　　　(4) Zhào nǚshì jiào shénme?
(2) Nǐ jiào shénme?　　　　　(5) Liú xiānsheng hǎo ma?
(3) Tā xìng shénme?

Unit 2

☟ 2. Choose the question words which best fit in these sentences.
(1) shéi　　(3) Shéi　　(5) shì bu shì　　(7) nǎ　　(9) ne
(2) shénme　(4) ma　　(6) shénme　　　(8) ma　　(10) shì bu shì

☟ 3. Use suitable words to fill in the blanks, and then practice the dialogue.
A: Nǐ, xuésheng
B: shì
A: shì
B: bú shì
A: Nǐmen, tóngxué
B: shì
A: shì bu shì
B: Bú shì, tāmen
A: ne

☟ 4. Listen to the passage and tell whether the statements are true (√) or false (×). 🎧

　　Liú xiānsheng shì lǎoshī. Tā shì Zhōngguórén. Wǒ shì tā de xuésheng. Líndá(Linda) shì Jiānádàrén. Mǎlìyà(Maria) shì Àodàlìyàrén. Tāmen shì wǒ de tóngxué. Chálǐ(Charlie) shì Yīngguórén. Tā bú shì wǒmen de tóngxué.

　　刘先生是老师。他是中国人。我是他的学生。琳达是加拿大人。玛丽亚是澳大利亚人。她们是我的同学。查理是英国人。他不是我们的同学。

(1) (3) √　　　　　　　　　(2) (4) (5) (6) ×

☟ 5. Answer these questions after listening. 🎧
　　Wáng Qiáng shì xuésheng, Zhōngguórén. Shānběn Yīláng(Yamamoto Ichiro) yě shì xuésheng, Rìběnrén. Xiǎo Wáng shì tā de tóngxué. Tāmen de lǎoshī shì Měiguórén, míngzi jiào Bǎoluó(Paul). Bǎoluó lǎoshī de tóngxué jiào Nínà(Nina), tā shì Yīngguórén.

王强是学生，中国人。山本一郎也是学生，日本人。小王是他的同学。他们的老师是美国人，名字叫保罗。保罗老师的同学叫尼娜，她是英国人。

(1) Wáng Qiáng.　　　(3) Bǎoluó.　　　(5) Bú shì, tā shì Měiguórén.
(2) Rìběnrén.　　　　(4) Bú shì.

≤ 6. Introduce yourself.

　e.g. (1) Wǒ jiào Dàwèi (*David*).
　　　 (2) Wǒ shì Yīngguórén.

Unit 3

≤ 2. Look at the picture and write the relationship among the family members after listening. 🎧

(1) A shì B de <u>zhàngfu</u>.
　　A 是 B 的　丈　夫。

(2) A hé B shì C de <u>bàba māma</u>.
　　A 和 B 是 C 的 爸 爸 妈　妈。

(3) D shì C de <u>qīzi</u>.
　　D 是 C 的 妻子。

(4) E hé G shì C hé D de <u>érzi</u>.
　　E 和 G 是 C 和 D 的 儿子。

(5) F hé H shì C hé D de <u>nǚ'ér</u>.
　　F 和 H 是 C 和 D 的　女 儿。

(6) E shì F、G hé H de <u>gēge</u>.
　　E 是 F，G 和 H 的　哥哥。

(7) F shì G hé H de <u>jiějie</u>.
　　F 是 G 和 H 的 姐姐。

(8) G shì E hé F de <u>dìdi</u>.
　　G 是 E 和 F 的 弟弟。

(9) H shì E、F hé G de <u>mèimei</u>.
　　H 是 E，F 和 G 的 妹 妹。

(10) A hé B shì E、F、G hé H de <u>yéye nǎinai</u>.
　　A 和 B 是 E、F，G 和 H 的 爷爷 奶 奶。

(11) E hé G shì A hé B de <u>sūnzi</u>.
　　E 和 G 是 A 和 B 的 孙子。

(12) F hé H shì A hé B de <u>sūnnǚ</u>.
　　F 和 H 是 A 和 B 的 孙 女。

≤ 3. Choose the correct answers after listening. 🎧

(1) Mǎlìyà de gēge shì <u>gōngchéngshī</u>.
　　玛 丽 亚 的 哥 哥 是　工　程　师。

读拼音学汉语

(2) Jiékè yǒu jiějie hé <u>dìdi</u>, méiyǒu gēge hé měimei.
杰 克 有 姐 姐 和 弟 弟，没 有 哥 哥 和 妹 妹。

(3) Wǒ de tóngxué yǒu Yīngguórén、Zhōngguórén hé Xīnxīlánrén.
我 的 同 学 有 英 国 人、 中 国 人 和 新 西 兰 人。

(4) <u>Fāngfang</u> shì tā mèimei.
芳 芳 是 他 妹 妹。

(5) Xiǎo Wáng de bàba shì yīshēng, <u>māma</u> shì lǎoshī, jiějie shì xuésheng.
小 王 的 爸 爸 是 医 生， 妈 妈 是 老 师，姐 姐 是 学 生。

(6) <u>Liú</u> xiānsheng shì wǒmen de lǎoshī.
刘 先 生 是 我 们 的 老 师。

(1) B　　(2) C　　(3) C　　(4) A　　(5) B　　(6) A

Unit 4

↘ 3. Match the questions with the answers.
(1) d　　　(2) c　　　(3) a　　　(4) e　　　(5) f　　　(6) b

↘ 4. Choose the correct words to fill in the blanks after listening. 🎧
(1) Zhè shì yì běn <u>cídiǎn</u>.
这 是 一 本 词 典。

(2) Nàxiē shì <u>Zhōngwén bàozhǐ</u>.
那 些 是 中 文 报 纸。

(3) Nàxiē <u>zhǐ</u> shì <u>lǎoshī</u> de.
那 些 纸 是 老 师 的。

(4) Zhè shì <u>gēge</u> de <u>yuánzhūbǐ</u>.
这 是 哥 哥 的 圆 珠 笔。

(5) Nà běn <u>Měiguó dìtú</u> shì Lùxī de.
那 本 美 国 地 图 是 露 西 的。

(6) Zhè běn <u>zázhì</u> shì <u>yīshēng</u> de.
这 本 杂 志 是 医 生 的。

Unit 5

↘ 2. Write down the Pinyin of numbers after listening. 🎧
(1) Wǒ jiā zhù zài Xīnhuá Lù <u>yìbǎi yīshíwǔ</u> hào.
我 家 住 在 新 华 路 一 百 一 十 五 号。

(2) Dào lǎoshī jiā zuò <u>yāo liù jiǔ</u> lù gōngjiāochē, bú zuò <u>yāo líng jiǔ</u> lù.
到 老 师 家 坐 幺 六 九 路 公 交 车，不 坐 幺 零 九 路。

(3) Zhāng yīshēng yǒu <u>yìqiān líng sìshísì</u> běn Zhōngwén shū, <u>liǎngbǎi qīshísì</u>
张 医 生 有 一 千 零 四 十 四 本 中 文 书，两 百 七 十 四

běn Yīngwén zázhì.
本 英 文 杂 志。

231

(4) Xiǎo Lǐ de diànhuà shì <u>sān wǔ líng bā yāo sì qī yāo</u>.
小 李的 电 话 是 三 五 零 八 幺 四 七 幺。

(5) Wǒ yǒu <u>yí gè</u> gēge, <u>liǎng gè</u> jiějie hé <u>yí gè</u> mèimei.
我 有 一 个 哥哥, 两 个 姐姐 和 一 个 妹妹。

(6) Wǒmen xuéxiào yǒu <u>yìqiān wǔbǎi líng èr</u> gè xuésheng.
我 们 学 校 有 一 千 五 百 零 二 个 学 生。

♬ 3. Listen to the sentences and tell whether the answers are true (√) or false (×). 🎧

(1) Xiǎo Wáng yǒu sì gè jiějie、yí gè mèimei.
小 王 有 四个姐姐、一 个 妹妹。

(2) Lǎo Lǐ yǒu shí gè péngyou.
老 李 有 十 个 朋 友。

(3) Zhōngguó yǒu shísān yì rén. Měiguó yǒu sānyì rén. Rìběn yǒu yíyì èrqiān
中 国 有 十 三 亿人。美 国 有 三 亿人。日 本 有 一 亿二千

qībǎi wàn rén.
七 百 万 人。

(4) Tā de diànhuà hàomǎ shì sān wǔ yāo wǔ jiǔ sì qī bā.
他 的 电 话 号 码 是 三 五 幺 五 九 四 七 八。

(5) Wǒ yǒu hěn duō Yīngwén shū, hái yǒu yì běn 《Yīng-Zhōng Cídiǎn》.
我 有 很 多 英 文 书, 还 有 一 本 《英 中 词 典》。

(6) Wǒmen xuéxiào yǒu yìqiān liùbǎi líng wǔ gè xuésheng.
我 们 学 校 有 一 千 六 百 零 五 个 学 生。

(7) Tā jiā zhù zài Zhōngshān Lù jiǔshíbā hào.
他 家 住 在 中 山 路九 十 八 号。

(8) Wǒ hé Xiǎo Lǐ shì tóngxué, Xiǎo Lǐ shì Shànghǎirén, wǒ shì Běijīngrén.
我 和 小 李 是 同 学, 小 李 是 上 海 人, 我 是 北 京 人。

(9) Tā māma shì yīshēng, zài yīyuàn shàngbān.
他 妈 妈 是 医 生, 在 医 院 上 班。

(10) Xiǎo Chén jiā yǒu qī kǒu rén, nǎinai、bàba、māma、yí gè gēge hé liǎng gè
小 陈 家 有 七 口 人, 奶奶、爸爸、妈妈、一 个 哥哥 和 两 个

mèimei.
妹 妹。

(11) Dàwèi yǒu shíqī běn Zhōngwén shū, qīshí běn Yīngwén shū.
大 卫 有 十 七 本 中 文 书, 七 十 本 英 文 书。

(12) Zǎochen bàba chéng gōngjiāochē qù shàngbān.
早 晨 爸爸 乘 公 交 车 去 上 班。

(1) (6) (8) (10) √　　　　　　　　　　(2) (3) (4) (5) (7) (9) (11) (12) ×

♬ 4. Tell people where you live and what your telephone number is.
e.g. Wǒ jiā zhù zài Dàběi Jiē yìbǎi liùshíjiǔ hào, diànhuà hàomǎ shì yāo sì wǔ bā
liù èr qī sān.

Unit 6

☟2. Match the questions with the answers. (Every answer will be used twice.)

(1) (3) A   (2) (4) B   (5) (7) C   (6) (8) D

☟3. Choose the right words to fill in the blanks.

(1) shì   (3) hē   (5) shì bu shì   (7) méiyǒu

(2) yǒu méiyǒu   (4) chī   (6) xǐhuan   (8) háishi

☟4. Fill in the blanks after listening , then read the paragraph aloud. 🎧

     Xiǎo Wáng shì <u>diànnǎo gōngchéngshī</u>. Tā de <u>qīzi</u> Huáng Yīng shì <u>bàoshè jìzhě</u>. Xiǎo Wáng wèn Huáng Yīng:"Wǒ de lǎo tóngxué Xiǎo Lǐ yě shì diànnǎo gōngchéngshī. <u>Wǎnshang</u> wǒmen qù tā jiā, hǎo ma?" Huáng Yīng wèn:"Tā jiā zài <u>nǎr</u>?" "<u>Zài</u> Zhōngshān Lù." Huáng Yīng shuō:"Hǎo de, wǒmen yìqǐ <u>zuò gōngjiāochē</u> qù ba."

     Dàole Xiǎo Lǐ jiā, Xiǎo Lǐ <u>hěn gāoxìng</u>. Xiǎo Lǐ wèn tāmen xǐhuan <u>hē</u> shénme, chá、kāfēi、<u>háishi</u> guǒzhī. Xiǎo Wáng xǐhuan hē <u>chá</u>, Huáng Yīng xǐhuan hē <u>bù jiā táng</u> de <u>kāfēi</u>. Xiǎo Lǐ <u>qǐng</u> tāmen <u>chī shuǐguǒ</u>, yǒu píngguǒ、lí、chéngzi, <u>hái yǒu</u> pútao. Xiǎo Wáng ài chī <u>pútao</u>, Huáng Yīng ài chī <u>chéngzi</u>. Xiǎo Wáng wèn Xiǎo Lǐ:"Nǐ de <u>érzi</u> hé <u>nǚ'ér</u> zài jiā ma?" Xiǎo Lǐ shuō:"Tāmen dōu zài shūfáng xuéxí. Nǚ'ér xǐhuan <u>dúshū</u>. Érzi xǐhuan <u>shàngwǎng</u>." Xiǎo Wáng shuō:"Tā liǎ dōu shì <u>hǎo xuésheng</u>."

     小王是电脑工程师。他的妻子黄英是报社记者。小王问黄英:"我的老同学小李也是电脑工程师。晚上我们去他家,好吗?"黄英问:"他家在哪儿?""在中山路。"黄英说:"好的,我们一起坐公交车去吧。"

     到了小李家,小李很高兴。小李问他们喜欢喝什么,茶、咖啡,还是果汁。小王喜欢喝茶,黄英喜欢喝不加糖的咖啡。小李请他们吃水果,有苹果、梨、橙子,还有葡萄。小王爱吃葡萄,黄英爱吃橙子。小王问小李:"你的儿子和女儿在家吗?"小李说:"他们都在书房学习。女儿喜欢读书。儿子喜欢上网。"小王说:"他俩都是好学生。"

☟5. Draw pictures of the fruit after listening. 🎧

(1) Xiǎo Wáng jiā yǒu xiāngjiāo.
     小 王 家 有 香 蕉。

(2) Jiékè gěile wǒ yí gè píngguǒ.
     杰克 给了 我 一 个 苹 果。

(3) Líndá bù hē chá, tā chī lí.
     琳 达 不 喝 茶,她 吃 梨。

(4) Bàba xǐhuan chī pútao.
     爸爸 喜欢 吃 葡萄。

(5) Wǒmen yìqǐ chī xīguā ba!
     我 们 一 起 吃 西 瓜 吧!

(6) Nǐ jiā yǒu chéngzi ma?
     你 家 有 橙 子 吗?

☟6. What will you say?

e.g. (1) Qǐng jìn! Nǐ hǎo!

    (2) Qǐng zuò!

    (3) Hē diǎnr shénme? Xǐhuan hē chá háishi kāfēi?

    (4) Qǐng hē chá/kāfēi/guǒzhī.

    (5) Qǐngwèn, nǐ de qīzi/zhàngfu xìng shénme?

(6) Màn zǒu! Zàijiàn!

Unit 7

◁ 2. **Describe the picture.**

Zhè shì wòshì. Wū li yǒu yì zhāng zhuōzi、yì zhāng chuáng、yì bǎ yǐzi. Qiáng shang yǒu yì zhāng zhàopiàn. Zhuō shang yǒu shū hé bàozhǐ, hái yǒu yí gè diànshìjī. Chuáng shang yǒu sān jiàn yīfu. Chuáng xià yǒu yì shuāng xié. Chuāng wài yǒu yí gè rén.

这是卧室。屋里有一张桌子、一张床、一把椅子。墙上有一张照片。桌上有书和报纸，还有一个电视机。床上有三件衣服。床下有一双鞋。窗外有一个人。

◁ 3. **Describe your study.**

e.g. Zhè shì wǒ de shūfáng. Lǐbian yǒu yì zhāng dà <u>shūzhuō</u> hé liǎng bǎ <u>yǐzi</u>. Shūzhuō shang yǒu yì zhǎn <u>dēng</u> hé liǎng běn <u>shū</u>, hái yǒu yì zhī <u>qiānbǐ</u>、liǎng gè <u>píngguǒ</u> hé yì bǎ xiǎo <u>dāozi</u>. Yǐzi shang yǒu wǒ de yí jiàn <u>yīfu</u>. Wǒ xǐhuan zài zhèlǐ dúshū.

◁ 4. **Listen and fill in the blanks.** 🎧

(1) Jiàoshì li yǒu <u>sānshí zhāng</u> zhuōzi、<u>sānshí'èr</u> bǎ yǐzi、<u>yí gè</u> dà diànshì.
教 室 里 有 三 十 张 桌子、三 十 二 把 椅子、一 个 大 电 视。

(2) Qiáng shang yǒu <u>liǎng zhāng dìtú</u>, <u>yì zhāng</u> shì shìjiè dìtú, <u>yì zhāng</u> shì
墙 上 有 两 张 地图，一 张 是 世 界 地 图，一 张 是

Zhōngguó dìtú.
中 国 地 图。

(3) Zhuōzi shang yǒu <u>wǔ běn</u> shū、<u>yì běn</u> cídiǎn、<u>sān zhāng</u> bàozhǐ、<u>liǎng zhī</u>
桌 子 上 有 五 本 书、一 本 词 典、 三 张 报 纸、 两 支

yuánzhūbǐ.
圆 珠 笔。

(4) Yǐzi shang yǒu <u>yí jiàn</u> shàngyī, yǐzi xià yǒu <u>yì zhī</u> māo.
椅子 上 有 一 件 上 衣，椅子 下 有 一 只 猫。

◁ 5. **Make questions with "jǐ 几"or "duōshao 多少".**

(1) Xiǎo Zhāng zhù zài jǐ hào?

(2) Qù lǎoshī jiā zuò jǐ lù gōnggòng qìchē?

(3) Jiějie de shǒujī hàomǎ shì duōshao?

(4) Nǐmen bān yǒu duōshao xuésheng?

Unit 8

◁ 1. **Match the words in line A with the times in line B after listening.** 🎧

(1) zǎochen liù diǎn yí kè
早 晨 六 点 一 刻

(2) shàngwǔ shí diǎn
上 午 十 点

234

（3）zhōngwǔ shí'èr diǎn líng wǔ fēn
中 午 十 二 点 零 五 分

（4）xiàwǔ chà wǔ fēn sān diǎn
下 午 差 五 分 三 点

（5）wǎnshang jiǔ diǎn bàn
晚 上 九 点 半

（6）yèli yī diǎn sān kè
夜 里 一 点 三 刻

（1）6:15　　（2）10:00　　（3）12:05　　（4）2:55　　（5）9:30　　（6）1:45

⊿ 3. Put the words below into the proper boxes.
chī —— shuǐguǒ　wǎnfàn　fàn　lí
hē —— kāfēi　chá　shuǐ　guǒzhī
xǐ —— shuǐguǒ　chē　liǎn　lí　yīfu　pánzi
kàn —— dìtú　diànshì　bàozhǐ　huàr

⊿ 4. Look at the pictures, tell the time and talk about what the boy is doing.
（1）Tā zǎochen liù diǎn bàn qǐchuáng.
（2）Tā zǎochen bā diǎn yí kè chī zǎofàn.
（3）Tā shàngwǔ bā diǎn sìshíwǔ qù shàngxué.
（4）Tā xiàwǔ sì diǎn huíjiā.
（5）Tā wǎnshang jiǔ diǎn èrshí xǐzǎo.
（6）Wǎnshang shí diǎn zhěng, tā shàng chuáng shuìjiào.

Unit 9

⊿ 1. Read the dates. 🎧
yī bā sì líng nián Liùyuè sān rì
一 八 四 零 年 六 月 三 日

yī bā jiǔ sì nián Jiǔyuè shíqī rì
一 八 九 四 年 九 月 十 七 日

yī jiǔ líng líng nián Bāyuè shíliù rì
一 九 零 零 年 八 月 十 六 日

yī jiǔ yī yī nián Shíyuè shí rì
一 九 一 一 年 十 月 十 日

yī jiǔ yī jiǔ nián Wǔyuè sì rì
一 九 一 九 年 五 月 四 日

yī jiǔ sān yī nián Jiǔyuè shíbā rì
一 九 三 一 年 九 月 十 八 日

yī jiǔ sān qī nián Qīyuè qī rì
一 九 三 七 年 七 月 七 日

yī jiǔ sì wǔ nián Bāyuè shíwǔ rì
一 九 四 五 年 八 月 十 五 日

yī jiǔ sì jiǔ nián Shíyuè yī rì
一 九 四 九　年 十 月 一日

yī jiǔ qī yī nián Shíyuè èrshíwǔ rì
一 九 七 一　年 十 月 二 十 五 日

èr líng líng bā nián Bāyuè bā rì
二 零 零 八 年 八 月 八 日

èr líng yī líng nián Wǔyuè yī rì
二 零 一 零 年 五 月 一日

↙ 3. Tell whether the following sentences are right (√) or wrong (×).
(1) (3) (5) ×　　　　(2) (4) (6) √

↙ 5. Fill in the blanks and repeat the sentences after listening. 🎧
(1) <u>Èr líng yī èr</u> nián <u>Wǔyuè shísì</u> rì shì Xiǎo Mǎ de shēngrì.
二 零 一 二 年 五 月 十 四 日 是 小 马 的　生 日。

(2) Tā qǐng péngyoumen cānjiā tā de <u>shēngrì jùhuì</u>.
他 请 朋 友 们　参 加 他 的　生 日聚会。

(3) Péngyoumen sòng gěi tā hěn duō <u>lǐwù</u>.
朋　友 们　送 给 他 很 多 礼物。

(4) Dàwèi <u>mǎi dàngāo</u>, Nínà <u>mǎi xiānhuā</u>, Yīláng <u>mǎi jiǔ</u>, Xiǎo Wáng <u>mǎi</u>
大 卫 买　蛋 糕, 尼 娜 买 鲜 花, 一 郎　买 酒, 小　王 买

<u>shuǐguǒ</u>.
水　果。

(5) Dàjiā yìqǐ <u>chàng shēngrìgē</u>, hé Xiǎo Mǎ <u>gānbēi</u>, zhù tā shēngrì <u>kuàilè</u>.
大 家 一起　唱　生 日歌, 和 小 马 干 杯, 祝 他　生 日 快乐。

Unit 10

↙ 1. Look at the map on page 93. Suppose you're at the point marked "You are here", match the questions and answers after listening. 🎧
(1) Dàhuá Fàndiàn zài nǎr?
大 华 饭 店 在 哪儿?

Zài Zhōngshān Běilù. Qiánbian shízì lùkǒu zuǒ guǎi, zuǒbian dì-yī jiā jiù shì.
在　中 山 北路。前 边 十 字 路 口 左　拐, 左 边 第 一 家 就 是。

(2) Huǒchēzhàn zài nǎr?
火　车 站 在 哪儿?

Zài Zhōngshān Dōnglù hé Zhōngshān Nánlù de shízì lùkǒu.
在　中 山　东 路 和 中　山　南 路 的 十 字 路口。

(3) Qù tǐyùchǎng zěnme zǒu?
去 体 育 场　怎 么　走?

Wǎng huí zǒu, guòle shízì lùkǒu, jiù kànjiàn le.
往　回 走, 过 了 十 字 路口, 就 看 见 了。

(4) Qù qìchēzhàn zěnme zǒu?
去 汽 车 站 怎 么 走?

Wǎng qián zǒu, yòu guǎi, zài guò yí gè shízì lùkǒu, zuǒbian jiù shì.
往 前 走,右 拐,再 过 一 个 十 字 路 口,左 边 就 是。

2. Look at the map again. Listen to the recording and fill in the blanks. 🎧

(1) Qǐngwèn, chāoshì zài nǎr?
请 问,超 市 在 哪儿?

Zài Zhōngshān <u>Běilù</u>, diànyǐngyuàn hé shūdiàn <u>zhōngjiān</u>.
在 中 山 北路,电 影 院 和 书 店 中 间。

(2) Qǐngwèn, nǎr yǒu lǚguǎn?
请 问,哪儿 有 旅 馆?

Zhōngshān <u>Dōnglù</u> yǒu, zài xuéxiào <u>nánbian</u>.
中 山 东 路 有,在 学 校 南 边。

(3) Qǐngwèn, túshūguǎn zài nǎr?
请 问,图 书 馆 在 哪儿?

Zài Zhōngshān <u>Nánlù</u>, gōngyuán <u>pángbiān</u>.
在 中 山 南 路,公 园 旁 边。

(4) Qǐngwèn, yīyuàn zài nǎr?
请 问,医 院 在 哪儿?

Zài Zhōngshān <u>Xīlù</u>, gōngyuán <u>duìmiàn</u>.
在 中 山 西 路,公 园 对 面。

3. Look at the map again and answer the questions.

(1) Wǎng qián zǒu, dào shízì lùkǒu yòu guǎi, yìzhí zǒudào dì-èr gè shízì lùkǒu, zuǒbian jiù shì.

(2) Wǎng huí zǒu, dào shízì lùkǒu wǎng zuǒ guǎi, zài guò yí gè shízì lùkǒu, yòubian jiù shì.

(3) Wǎng nán zǒu, zuǒbian jiù shì.

(4) Qiánbian shízì lùkǒu yòu guǎi, dào dì-èr gè shízì lùkǒu zài yòu guǎi, guòle shūdiàn jiù shì.

(5) Wǎng huí zǒu, dào lùkǒu zuǒ guǎi, dì-èr gè lùkǒu zài zuǒ guǎi, túshūguǎn qiánbian jiù shì.

4. Listen to the recording and draw a picture. 🎧

Wǒ jiā zhù zài Zhōngshān Xīlù. Fùjìn yǒu gè xiǎo gōngyuán. Gōngyuán lǐbian huār hěn duō, rén hěn shǎo. Wǒ jiā mén qián yǒu tiáo lù, duìmiàn shì gè dà shāngdiàn, pángbiān yǒu gè kāfēiguǎn. Wǒ hé péngyou cháng zài nǎr hē kāfēi.

我家住在中山西路。附近有个小公园。公园里边花儿很多,人很少。我家门前有条路,对面是个大商店,旁边有个咖啡馆。我和朋友常在那儿喝咖啡。

237

Unit 11

📝 2. Transform the declarative sentences to interrogative sentences.

(1) Chē shang kěyǐ xīyān ma?

Chē shang kě(yǐ) bu kěyǐ xīyān?

(2) Hǎilún néng kàn Zhōngwén zázhì ma?

Hǎilún néng bu néng kàn Zhōngwén zázhì?

(3) Tā de qīzi huì zuò dàngāo ma?

Tā de qīzi huì bu huì zuò dàngāo?

(4) Xiǎo Zhāng huì tiàowǔ ma?

Xiǎo Zhāng huì bu huì tiàowǔ?

🎧 3. Listen to the passage and tell whether the statements are true (√) or false (×). 🎧

Wǒ jiào Lǐ Nà. Wǒ bàba shì gāngqín lǎoshī. Wǒ huì tán gāngqín. Zhāng Lì shì wǒ de péngyou. Tā māma shì Yīngguórén. Tā huì shuō Yīngyǔ. Zhāng Lì kěyǐ jiāo wǒ shuō Yīngyǔ. Wǒ kěyǐ jiāo Zhāng Lì xué tán qín. Wǒ hé tā dōu xǐhuan chàng gē. Wǒmen zài yìqǐ hěn kuàilè.

我叫李娜。我爸爸是钢琴老师。我会弹钢琴。张丽是我的朋友。她妈妈是英国人。她会说英语。张丽可以教我说英语。我可以教张丽学弹琴。我和她都喜欢唱歌。我们在一起很快乐。

(1) (3) (6) (8) √   (2) (4) (5) (7) ×

📝 4. Read the explanation of "**huì**会", "**néng**能" and "**kěyǐ**可以" in "Grammar Outline" (P213), then fill in the blanks with them.

(1) huì   huì   (4) néng/kěyǐ   néng/kěyǐ

(2) kěyǐ/néng   (5) néng   kěyǐ/néng

(3) huì   néng/kěyǐ   (6) kěyǐ

Unit 12

🎧 2. Choose the correct answers after listening. 🎧

(1) Xiǎo Wáng jīntiān shōudàole yì fēng xìn, tā hěn gāoxìng.
小　王　今天　收　到　了一　封　信，他　很　高　兴。

(2) Chálǐ wèn, jīntiān Ōuyuán duìhuàn Rénmínbì de huìlǜ shì duōshao?
查　理　问，今天　欧　元　兑　换　人　民　币　的　汇率　是　多　少？

(3) Xiàwǔ tā qù yínhāng qǔ qián le.
下　午　他　去　银　行　取　钱　了。

(4) Zǎochen wǒ gěi Dàhuá Bīnguǎn dǎle gè diànhuà.
早　晨　我　给　大　华　宾　馆　打　了个　电　话。

(5) Lǐ Míng yòng sìbǎi Měiyuán duìhuànle liǎngqiān wǔbǎi èrshísì yuán
李　明　用　四　百　美　元　兑　换　了　两　千　五　百　二　十　四　元

Rénmínbì.
人　民　币。

(1) C (2) C (3) A (4) B (5) C

⊿ 3. Match A. with B. (Every A. verbal phrase will be used more than once.)

A. (1) ——B. (1)(5)(7)(8)   A. (3) ——B. (2)(6)(9)(12)

A. (2) ——B. (3)(4)(10)(11)

Unit 13

⊿ 2. Read dialogue 1 on pages 118-119, then make a shopping list and answer the questions.

(1) Huángguā、xīhóngshì、tǔdòu、dàbáicài、cōng.

(2) Huángguā yí kuài bā, xīhóngshì liǎng kuài yī, tǔdòu yí kuài èr, dàbáicài liǎng kuài sì, cōng liǎng kuài.

(3) Jiǔ kuài wǔ.

(4) Shí kuài.

(5) Wǔ máo.

B's shopping list		
Name	How many	How much
huángguā	2 gēn	¥ 1.8
xīhóngshì	1 jīn	¥ 2.1
tǔdòu	1 jīn	¥ 1.2
dàbáicài	4 jīn	¥ 2.4
cōng	1 bǎ	¥ 2
		Total: ¥ 9.5

⊿ 4. Fill in the blanks after listening. 🎧

Jīntiān <u>shuǐguǒ</u> hěn piányi. Píngguǒ yí kuài liù yì jīn, wǒ mǎile <u>liǎng jīn</u>, huāle <u>sān kuài èr</u> . Chéngzi wǔ kuài qián sān jīn, wǒ mǎile <u>sān jīn</u>, huāle <u>wǔ kuài</u> qián. Dìnà xǐhuan chī xiāngjiāo, tā mǎile <u>wǔ gè</u>, <u>sì kuài bā</u>. Tā gěile <u>wǔ kuài</u> qián, zhǎole tā <u>liǎng máo</u>.

今天水果很便宜。苹果一块六一斤，我买了两斤，花了三块二。橙子五块钱三斤，我买了三斤，花了五块钱。蒂娜喜欢吃香蕉，她买了五个，四块八。她给了五块钱，找了她两毛。

Unit 14

⊿ 2. Choose the right words to fill in the blanks from the box below.

(1) xiǎo de duō   (3) yíyàng gānjìng   (5) xīnxiān yìdiǎnr

(2) shāowēi duō yìdiǎnr   (4) gèng guì

✑ 4. Complete the sentences, using the words in the box below.

(1) hóng de huáng de lán de bái de　　(3) jiù de xīn de

(2) Piányi de guì de　　　　　　　　　(4) Nǚ de nán de

Unit 15

✑ 1. Look at the calendar of October and fill in the blanks.

(2) Míngtiān　　　(5) Xīngqīyī　　　(8) xià gè yuè

(3) Xīngqīwǔ　　　(6) qī　　　　　　(9) Qùnián

(4) shíwǔ rì　　　(7) Xià zhōu　　　(10) Míngnián

✑ 2. Choose the right answers after listening. 🎧

(1) A: Jīntiān Yīyuè 31 hào, shì Mǎlì de shēngrì ma?
　　　今 天 1 月 31 号，是 玛丽 的　生 日 吗？

　　B: Bù, míngtiān shì Mǎlì de shēngrì.
　　　不，明 天 是 玛丽 的　生 日。

(2) A: Xiǎo Wáng yào qù Jiānádà, tā zǒule ma?
　　　小　　 王　要 去 加拿大，他 走 了 吗？

　　B: Zǒule, jīnnián Sìyuè zǒu de.
　　　走 了，今 年 四 月 走 的。

(3) A: Wǒmen shì jīntiān jùhuì ma?
　　　我 们 是 今 天 聚会 吗？

　　B: Bù, jīntiān shì Xīngqīwǔ, wǒmen Lǐbàitiān jùhuì.
　　　不，今 天 是　星 期 五，我 们 礼 拜 天 聚会。

(4) A: Wǒmen shénme shíhou qù Shànghǎi lǚyóu?
　　　我 们　什 么 时 候 去　上　海 旅游？

　　B: Xià Xīngqīwǔ.
　　　下　星 期 五。

(5) A: Nǐ xǐhuan Běijīng de nǎ jǐ gè jìjié?
　　　你 喜 欢　北 京 的 哪 几 个 季节？

　　B: Wǒ xǐhuan Běijīng de xiàtiān、qiūtiān hé dōngtiān.
　　　我 喜 欢　北 京 的 夏天、　秋 天 和　冬 天。

(1) B　　　(2) C　　　(3) B　　　(4) C　　　(5) A

✑ 3. Read dialogue 3 on page 138, then answer the questions.

(1) Shànghǎi.　　　　　　　　　　　(4) Xiàwǔ sān diǎn bàn qǐfēi.

(2) Shíyuè èrshíwǔ rì de jīpiào.　　　(5) Xiàwǔ wǔ diǎn èrshí fēn dào.

(3) Liǎng zhāng.　　　　　　　　　　(6) Yí gè xiǎoshí wǔshí fēnzhōng.

✑ 4. What do you say?

(1) Zhù nǐ shēngrì kuàilè!　　　　　(3) Xīnnián hǎo!

(2) Zhù nǐ yílù-píng'ān!　　　　　 (4) Shèngdàn kuàilè!

Unit 16

☞ 1. Match the words.
  (1) A—d B—b C—a D—c   (3) A—a B—c C—d D—b
  (2) A—c B—a C—d D—b

☞ 2. Put the words "**zhe**着", "**le**了" and "**guo**过" into the correct places.
  (1) A   (2) C   (3) B   (4) B   (5) C   (6) C

☞ 3. Fill in the blanks with "**zhe**着", "**le**了" or "**guo**过" after listening. 🎧

    Tuōní méi qù<u>guo</u> Xiǎo Lǐ jiā. Xīngqīliù xiàwǔ, wǒmen liǎ qù<u>le</u> Xiǎo Lǐ jiā. Mén zhèng kāi<u>zhe</u>. Xiǎo Lǐ jiàn<u>le</u> wǒmen hěn gāoxìng. Tā qǐng wǒmen jìn wū zuòxià, xiào<u>zhe</u> wèn: "Hē<u>guo</u> Lóngjǐng chá ma?" Wǒmen shuō: "Méi hē-<u>guo</u>." Tā qǐng wǒmen hē. Wǒmen hē<u>zhe</u> chá liáotiānr. Zuò dào hěn wǎn, wǒmen cái zǒu.

    托尼没去过小李家。星期六下午，我们俩去<u>了</u>小李家。门正开着。小李见<u>了</u>我们很高兴。他请我们进屋坐下，笑<u>着</u>问："喝<u>过</u>龙井茶吗？"我们说："没喝<u>过</u>。"他请我们喝。我们喝<u>着</u>茶聊天儿。坐到很晚，我们才走。

☞ 4. Speaking.
 e.g. (1) Wǒ xǐhuan zài jiàqī li qù Zhōngguó, yīnwèi Zhōngguó hěn dà, fēngjǐng hěn měi, yǒu hěn duō kěyǐ yóulǎn de dìfāng.
    (2) Wǒ qùguo Hángzhōu. Nàlǐ yǒu shān yǒu shuǐ, fēngjǐng měilì. Zuò yóuchuán yóu Xī Hú, shūfu jí le.
    (3) Wǒ xiǎng qù Běijīng, liǎng tiān shíjiān kěyǐ yóulǎn Chángchéng、Yíhé Yuán.

Unit 17

☞ 2. Correct the sentences.
  (1) Wǒ de yīfu zāng, nǐ de yīfu hěn gānjìng.
  (2) Zhè běnr shū hěn guì, nà běnr shū hěn piányi.
  (3) Chūntiān bù lěng, qiūtiān bú rè.
  (4) Túshūguǎn hěn dà, shū hěn duō.
  (5) Shàngwǔ qíngtiān, xiàwǔ xià yǔ.
  (6) Nǐ lěng bu lěng? Wǒ yǒudiǎnr lěng.

☞ 5. Fill in the blanks and read the weather forecast aloud after listening. 🎧
Tiānqì yùbào:
    Qīyuè shísān rì, Xīngqīsì. Shàngwǔ <u>duōyún</u>, xiàwǔ <u>yīn</u>, yèli yǒu <u>xiǎo yǔ</u>. Zuì gāo <u>wēndù</u> èrshíbā dù, zuì dī wēndù <u>èrshí'èr dù</u>.
    Qīyuè shísì rì, Xīngqīwǔ. <u>Qíng</u>. Zuì gāo wēndù <u>sānshí dù</u>, zuì dī <u>wēndù</u>

ērshísì dù.

天气预报：

七月十三日，星期四。上午多云，下午阴，夜里有小雨。最高温度28℃，最低温度22℃。

七月十四日，星期五。晴。最高温度30℃，最低温度24℃。

Unit 18

◁ 1. Translate into English.

(1) *play basketball*　　　*play badminton*　　　*make a phone call*　*play tennis*

(2) *read a book*　　　　　*watch a match*　　　　*visit a friend*　　　*see a doctor*

(3) *open the door*　　　　*drive the car*　　　　　*school opens*
have a meeting

(4) *board a plane, alight from a plane*
go to bed, get out of bed
go to work, get off work
climb the mountain, go down the mountain

◁ 2. Answer the questions after listening. 🎧

Dì-èrshíjiǔ jiè Àolínpǐkè Yùndònghuì shì zài Běijīng kāi de. Wǒ xǐhuan yóuyǒng. Wǒ qù Shuǐlìfāng kànle yóuyǒng bǐsài. Fēi'ěrpǔsī déle bā kuài jīnpái. Tā shì wǒ zuì xǐhuan de yùndòngyuán.

第二十九届奥林匹克运动会是在北京开的。我喜欢游泳。我去水立方看了游泳比赛。菲尔普斯得了八块金牌。他是我最喜欢的运动员。

(1) Běijīng.　　　(2) Shuǐlìfāng.　　　(3) Fēi'ěrpǔsī.　　　(4) Bā kuài jīnpái.

◁ 3. Fill in the blanks after listening. 🎧

(1) Zǎochen wǒmen <u>zuò gōngjiāochē</u> qù xuéxiào.
早　晨　我们　坐　公　交　车　去　学　校。

(2) Shàngwǔ wǒ kāi chē <u>qù túshūguǎn</u> jiè shū.
上　　午　我　开　车　去　图　书　馆　借　书。

(3) Míngnián chūntiān tāmen yào qù Běijīng <u>xué Zhōngwén</u>.
明　年　春　天　他　们　要　去　北　京　学　中　文。

(4) Zuótiān tā <u>qù shāngdiàn</u> mǎile yì shuāng xié.
昨　天　他　去　商　店　买　了　一　双　鞋。

(5) Míngtiān dàjiā dōu <u>lái wǒ jiā</u> hē chá ba.
明　天　大　家　都　来　我　家　喝　茶　吧。

(6) Wǎnshang wǒ xǐle zǎo <u>shuìjiào</u>.
晚　上　我　洗　了　澡　睡　觉。

(7) Wǎnfàn hòu tā <u>dào gōngyuán</u> sànbù.
晚　饭　后　他　到　公　园　散　步。

(8) Xīngqītiān tóngxuémen qù hǎibiān <u>yóuyǒng</u> ma?
星　期　天　同　学　们　去　海　边　游　泳　吗?

读拼音学汉语

⊾4. Put the words in the correct order.
(1) Tā xiǎng dào shūdiàn mǎi liǎng běn shū.
(2) Xiǎo Lǐ qù shūfáng kàn bào le.
(3) Wǒmen qù fàndiàn chī wǔfàn.
(4) Nǐ néng bāng wǒ mǎi liǎng jīn píngguǒ ma?
(5) Wǒmen dōu xǐhuan dǎ lánqiú.
(6) Zhōumò wǒ qù yóujú mǎile sān zhāng yóupiào.
(7) Zǎochen qī diǎn wǒ qí (zìxíng)chē qù yīyuàn shàngbān.
(8) Shàng gè yuè wǒ qù Běijīng yóulǎnle Chángchéng.

⊾5. Fill in the blanks after listening. 🎧
    Jīntiān shì Lǐbàitiān, wǒmen dōu yǒu shìr. Líndá qù kàn péngyou, Mǎlìyà qù shāngdiàn mǎi yīfu, Jiǎn hé Qiáoyī kāi chē qù lǚyóu, wǒ hé Jiékè、Piáo Jīnzhé yìqǐ qù shūdiàn mǎi shū. Wǒmen mǎile «Zhōng-Yīng Cídiǎn» hé jǐ běn Zhōngwén zázhì. Zhèxiē shū néng bāngzhù wǒmen xué hǎo Zhōngwén.
    今天是礼拜天，我们都有事儿。琳达去看朋友，玛丽亚去商店买衣服，简和乔伊开车去旅游，我和杰克、朴金哲一起去书店买书。我们买了《中英词典》和几本中文杂志。这些书能帮助我们学好中文。

Unit 19

⊾2. Fill in the blanks with the following words after listening. 🎧
(1) Zhè fēijīchǎng dà jí le!
    这 飞机 场 大 极了！

(2) Zhè huángguā hǎo xīnxiān!
    这 黄 瓜 好 新鲜！

(3) Nà jiàn yīfu tài zāng le!
    那 件 衣服 太 脏 了！

(4) Tā yào hē zuì hǎo de pútaojiǔ.
    他 要 喝 最 好 的 葡萄酒。

(5) Zuótiān qìwēn sānshíwǔ dù, rè sǐ le!
    昨 天 气温 三 十 五 度，热 死了！

(6) Jīntiān qù lǚyóu , háizimen yúkuài jí le.
    今 天 去 旅游，孩子们 愉 快 了。

(7) Zuò zài shāfā shang hē chá hǎo shūfu!
    坐 在 沙发 上 喝 茶 好 舒服！

(8) Zhè tiáo qúnzi yánsè tài hóng le.
    这 条 裙子 颜色 太 红 了。

⊾3. Speaking.
e.g. (1) Qǐngwèn, wǒ xiǎng dìng zhōngwǔ shí'èr diǎn de liù rén zuò, kěyǐ ma?
     (2) Zhème duō cài! / Zhèxiē cài zhēn hǎochī! /
        Cài de yánsè hǎo, wèidào gèng hǎo! / Xīnkǔ nín le!

练习答案和听力文本

(3) ——Nǎlǐ, nǎlǐ, jiāchǎng-biànfàn. /
　　　Xièxie kuājiǎng.

　　——Qǐng màn yòng! /
　　　Zài tiān diǎnr shénme? Bié kèqi.

　　——Qǐng màn zǒu! /
　　　Zǒu hǎo, zàijiàn!

Unit 20

◁ 1. Read dialogue 1, then answer the questions.

(1) Gǎnmào.　　　　(2) C E F　　　　(3) A B D E

◁ 2. Read dialogue 2, then answer the questions.

(1) A E　　　　(2) B C

◁ 3. Read dialogue 3, then answer the questions.

(1) C　　　　(2) B　　　　(3) B

◁ 4. Choose the right answers after listening. 🎧

　Zuótiān, wǒ qù yīyuàn kànbìng. Yīshēng wèn wǒ nǎlǐ bù shūfu, wǒ shuō yá téng. Liángguo tǐwēn yǐhòu, yīshēng shuō: "Sānshíqī dù sì, tǐwēn bù gāo, bú yòng dǎzhēn." Gěile wǒ liǎng zhǒng yào, báisè de fàn hòu chī, yì tiān sān cì, yí cì yí piàn; huángsè de shuìjiào qián chī, yì tiān yí cì, yí cì sān piàn. Wǒ chīle yào, shuìle yí yè, jīntiān jiù hǎo le.

　昨天，我去医院看病。医生问我哪里不舒服，我说牙疼。量过体温以后，医生说："三十七度四，体温不高，不用打针。"给了我两种药，白色的饭后吃，一天三次，一次一片；黄色的睡觉前吃，一天一次，一次三片。我吃了药，睡了一夜，今天就好了。

(1) B　　(2) C　　(3) C　　(4) B　　(5) B　　(6) C

Xiǎocídiǎn

MINI–DICTIONARY

小词典

Entries in the MINI—DICTIONARY
Xiǎocídiǎn tiáomù
小 词 典　条 目

读拼音学汉语

小词典

A Dress yī 衣

A1 *Clothing* fúzhuāng 服装

apron	wéiqún 围裙
attire of traditional Chinese style	
	tángzhuāng 唐装
bathrobe	yùyī 浴衣
bikini	bǐjīní yǒngyī 比基尼泳衣
bra	rǔzhào 乳罩，xiōngzhào 胸罩
briefs	sānjiǎokù 三角裤
cardigan	kāijīn máoyī 开襟毛衣
cashmere sweater, cashmere cardigan	
	yángróngshān 羊绒衫
cheongsam	qípáo 旗袍
clothes	yīfu 衣服
overcoat	wàitào 外套
corset	jǐnshēn nèiyī 紧身内衣
woman's suit	tàoqún 套裙
one-piece dress	liányīqún 连衣裙
down wear	yǔróngfú 羽绒服
coarse wool coat	cū máo wàiyī 粗毛外衣
windbreaker	fēngyī 风衣
everyday suit	biànfú 便服
fur coat	máopí dàyī 毛皮大衣
jacket	duǎnshàngyī 短上衣，jiākè 夹克
jeans	niúzǎikù 牛仔裤
mandarin jacket	mǎguà 马褂
Chinese tunic suit	zhōngshānzhuāng 中山装
overcoat	dàyī 大衣
pocket	yīdài 衣袋
collar T-shirt	yǒu lǐng T xù 有领T恤
business suit	zhíyèzhuāng 职业装
pyjamas	shuìyī 睡衣
raincoat	yǔyī 雨衣
shirt	chènshān 衬衫

short skirt	duǎnqún 短裙
shorts	duǎnkù 短裤
skirt	qúnzi 裙子
sportswear	yùndòngfú 运动服
Western suit	xīzhuāng 西装
sweater	máoyī 毛衣
sweater, jumper, pullover	
	tàotóu máoyī 套头毛衣
cotton sweatshirt	miánmáoshān 棉毛衫
swimsuit	yǒngyī 泳衣
tights	jǐnshēnyī 紧身衣，
	jǐnshēnkù 紧身裤
Chinese-style clothing	
	zhōngshì fúzhuāng 中式服装
trousers, pants	chángkù 长裤，kùzi 裤子
T-shirt	T xùshān T恤衫
underpants, panties	kùchǎ 裤衩
undershirt	hànshān 汗衫
underskirt	chènqún 衬裙
underwear	nèiyī 内衣
uniform	zhìfú 制服
vest, singlet	bèixīn 背心
waistcoat	mǎjiǎ 马甲，bèixīn 背心

A2 *Footwear* xié wà 鞋袜
Hat màozi 帽子

boots	xuēzi 靴子
clogs	mùjī 木屐 (*shoes made entirely of wood or with a wooden sole*)
cloth shoes	bùxié 布鞋
cotton-padded shoes	miánxié 棉鞋
embroidered shoes	xiùhuāxié 绣花鞋 (*embroidered flowers on the upper or instep*)

high heels	gāogēnxié 高跟鞋		headcloth	tóujīn 头巾
climbing boots	dēngshānxié 登山鞋		necklace	xiàngliàn 项链
skate	huábīngxié 滑冰鞋		purse	qiánbāo 钱包
leather shoes	píxié 皮鞋		earring	ěrhuán 耳环
rain boots	yǔxié 雨鞋		ring	jièzhi 戒指
sandals	liángxié 凉鞋		scarf	wéijīn 围巾
slippers	tuōxié 拖鞋		tie	lǐngdài 领带
socks	duǎnwà 短袜		wallet	píjiā 皮夹
sports shoes	yùndòngxié 运动鞋		zipper	lāliàn 拉链
stockings	chángtǒngwà 长筒袜			
straw sandals	cǎoxié 草鞋			
tights	liánkùwà 连裤袜			
walking shoes	lǚyóuxié 旅游鞋			

A4 *Material* zhìliào 质料
Color yánsè 颜色

gumboots, wellingtons			agate	mǎnǎo 玛瑙
	chángtǒng yǔxuē 长筒雨靴		artificial fibre	rénzào xiānwéi 人造纤维
fur hat	pímào 皮帽		imitation jewel	rénzào bǎoshí 人造宝石
helmet	tóukuī 头盔		artificial pearl	rénzào zhēnzhū 人造珍珠
peaked cap	yāshémào 鸭舌帽		artificial wool	rénzàomáo 人造毛
straw hat	cǎomào 草帽,		cotton	mián 棉
	zhēyángmào 遮阳帽		crystal	shuǐjīng 水晶
woollen hat	yángmáomào 羊毛帽		diamond	zuànshí 钻石
			flax	yàmá 亚麻
			gauze	shā 纱
			gold	jīn 金

A3 *Jewelry and accessories* shǒushì
hé shìpǐn 首饰和饰品

bow tie	lǐngjié 领结		jade	yù 玉, fěicuì 翡翠
bracelet	shǒuzhuó 手镯		jewelry	zhūbǎo 珠宝
brooch	xiōngzhēn 胸针		leather	pígé 皮革
button	kòuzi 扣子, niǔkòu 纽扣		leatherette	rénzàogé 人造革
cape, shawl	pījiān 披肩		pearl	zhēnzhū 珍珠
gauze kerchief	shājīn 纱巾		plastic	sùliào 塑料
girdle, belt	yāodài 腰带, pídài 皮带		platinum	báijīn 白金
gloves	shǒutào 手套		precious stone	bǎoshí 宝石
hairpin	fàqiǎ 发卡		rayon	rénzàosī 人造丝
handbag	shǒutíbāo 手提包		rubber	xiàngjiāo 橡胶
handkerchief	shǒupà 手帕, shǒujuàn 手绢		silk	sīchóu 丝绸
			silver	yín 银

小词典

staple rayon	rénzàomián 人造棉
timber	mùliào 木料
woollens	máoliào 毛料
black	hēi(sè) 黑(色)
blue	lán(sè) 蓝(色)
brown	zōng(sè) 棕(色)
colorful	wǔyán-liùsè 五颜六色
grey	huī(sè) 灰(色)
green	lǜ(sè) 绿(色)
orange	chéng(sè) 橙(色)
purple	zǐ(sè) 紫(色)
red	hóng(sè) 红(色)
white	bái(sè) 白(色)
yellow	huáng(sè) 黄(色)

A5 Describing clothing
fúzhuāng miáoshù 服装描述

beautiful, good looking	hǎokàn 好看，piàoliang 漂亮，
	měi(lì) 美(丽)
ugly	nánkàn 难看
clean	gānjìng 干净
dirty	zāng 脏
fashionable	shímáo 时髦，shíshàng 时尚
unfashionable	guòshí 过时
flowery	huálì 华丽
plain	pǔsù 朴素
long	cháng 长
short	duǎn 短
loose	féi(dà) 肥(大)
tight	shòu(xiǎo) 瘦(小)
new	xīn 新
old, used, worn	jiù 旧
normal, common	píngcháng 平常，yìbān 一般
strange	qítè 奇特，xīnqí 新奇
suitable	héshì 合适
unsuitable	bù héshì 不合适

B Eating shí 食

B1 Grain liángshi 粮食

black bean	hēidòu 黑豆
black rice	hēimǐ 黑米
broad bean	cándòu 蚕豆
buckwheat	qiáomài 荞麦，qiáomàifěn 荞麦粉
corn	yùmǐ 玉米
cornmeal	yùmǐmiàn 玉米面
flour	miànfěn 面粉
glutinous rice	nuòmǐ 糯米
haricot bean	biǎndòu 扁豆
millet	xiǎomǐ 小米
millet flour	xiǎomǐmiàn 小米面
mung bean	lǜdòu 绿豆
oats	yànmài 燕麦，màipiàn 麦片
pea	wāndòu 豌豆

red bean	chìdòu 赤豆
rice	mǐ 米，dàmǐ 大米
soya bean	huángdòu 黄豆
wheat	xiǎomài 小麦

B2 Fish yú 鱼，Meat ròu 肉，Poultry qín 禽，Egg dàn 蛋

carp	lǐyú 鲤鱼
catfish	niányú 鲇鱼
crab	xiè 蟹
cuttlefish	mòyú 墨鱼，wūzéi 乌贼
dried fish	yúgān 鱼干
dried shrimp	xiāmi 虾米
frog	tiánjī 田鸡，qīngwā 青蛙
grass carp	cǎoyú 草鱼

herring	qīngyú 青鱼	black fungus	hēimù'ěr 黑木耳
lobster	lóngxiā 龙虾	broccoli	xīlánhuā 西兰花
octopus	zhāngyú 章鱼	cabbage	juǎnxīncài 卷心菜
prawn	dàxiā 大虾	carrot	húluóbo 胡萝卜
salmon	guīyú 鲑鱼, dàmǎhāyú 大马哈鱼	cauliflower	huācài 花菜
sea cucumber	hǎishēn 海参	celery	qíncài 芹菜
seafood	hǎixiān 海鲜	chilli	làjiāo 辣椒
shark	shāyú 鲨鱼	Chinese cabbage	(dà)báicài （大)白菜
shrimp	xiā 虾	coriander	xiāngcài 香菜, yánsuī 芫荽
soft-shelled turtle	jiǎyú 甲鱼 (*Lives in the fresh water. Its shell hasn't any clear decorative pattern, unlike turtle in the sea.*)	cucumber	huángguā 黄瓜
		eggplant	qiézi 茄子
		fuzzy melon	sīguā 丝瓜
squid	yóuyú 鱿鱼, qiāngwūzéi 枪乌贼	garlic	suàn 蒜
trout	zūnyú 鳟鱼	garlic stem	suànmiáo 蒜苗
yellow croaker	huángyú 黄鱼	ginger	jiāng 姜
bacon	xiánròu 咸肉	gourd	húlu 葫芦
beef	niúròu 牛肉	green soybean	máodòu 毛豆
chicken	jī(ròu) 鸡(肉)	in season	shílìng shūcài 时令蔬菜
duck	yā(ròu) 鸭(肉)	leek	jiǔcài 韭菜
fresh meat	xiānròu 鲜肉	leek shoot	jiǔhuáng 韭黄
game	yěwèi 野味 (*wild animals or birds for food*)	lettuce	wōjù 莴苣, shēngcài 生菜
		lotus root	ǒu 藕
ham	huǒtuǐ 火腿	marrow	xīhúlu 西葫芦
lamb	yángròu 羊肉	mushroom	mógu 蘑菇
mince	ròuxiànr 肉馅儿	mustard leaf	jiècài 芥菜
pork	zhūròu 猪肉	onion	yángcōng 洋葱
sausage	xiāngcháng 香肠	pimento	tiánjiāo 甜椒,
duck egg	yādàn 鸭蛋		dēnglongjiāo 灯笼椒
egg	dàn 蛋, jīdàn 鸡蛋	potato	tǔdòu 土豆, mǎlíngshǔ 马铃薯
		pumpkin	nánguā 南瓜

B3 *Vegetables* shūcài 蔬菜

asparagus	lúsǔn 芦笋	radish	luóbo 萝卜
bamboo shoot	sǔn 笋	spinach	bōcài 菠菜
bean sprouts	dòuyá 豆芽	spring onion	cōng 葱
fresh bean	dòujiǎo 豆角	straw mushroom	cǎogū 草菇
bitter melon	kǔguā 苦瓜	sweet potato	hóngshǔ 红薯, gānshǔ 甘薯, dìguā 地瓜

taro	yùnǎi 芋艿，yùtou 芋头
tomato	xīhóngshì 西红柿，fānqié 番茄
white fungus	yín'ěr 银耳
white gourd	dōngguā 冬瓜
water bamboo	jiāobái 茭白
yam	shānyào 山药

B4 *Fruit* shuǐguǒ 水果
Nut jiānguǒ 坚果

apricot	xìng 杏
apple	píngguǒ 苹果
banana	xiāngjiāo 香蕉
black date	hēizǎo 黑枣
cherry	yīngtao 樱桃
coconut	yēzi 椰子
date palm	yēzǎo 椰枣
date	zǎo 枣
durian	liúlián 榴莲
fig	wúhuāguǒ 无花果
grape	pútao 葡萄
grapefruit	yòuzi 柚子
lemon	níngméng 柠檬
litchi	lìzhī 荔枝
longan	lóngyǎn 龙眼，guìyuán 桂圆
loquat	pípa 枇杷
tangerine	júzi 橘子
mango	mángguǒ 芒果
melon	guā 瓜，xiāngguā 香瓜
mulberry	sāngshèn 桑葚
orange	chéngzi 橙子
pawpaw	mùguā 木瓜
peach	táozi 桃子
pear	lí 梨
persimmon	shìzi 柿子
pineapple	bōluó 菠萝，fènglí 凤梨
plum	lǐzi 李子

pomegranate	shíliu 石榴
strawberry	cǎoméi 草莓
sugarcane	gānzhe 甘蔗
watermelon	xīguā 西瓜
almond, apricot seed	xìngrén 杏仁
cashew	yāoguǒ 腰果
chestnut	lìzi 栗子
hazelnut	zhēnzi 榛子
lotus seed	liánzǐ 莲子
melon seed	guāzǐ 瓜子
nut	jiānguǒ 坚果，guǒrén 果仁
peanut	huāshēng 花生
pine nut	sōngrén 松仁，sōngzǐ 松子
pumpkin seed	nánguāzǐ 南瓜子，báiguāzǐ 白瓜子
sesame	zhīma 芝麻
sunflower seed	kuíhuāzǐ 葵花子
walnut	hétao 核桃
watermelon seed	xīguāzǐ 西瓜子，hēiguāzǐ 黑瓜子

B5 *Drink* yǐnliào 饮料

boiling water	kāishuǐ 开水
cold water	lěngshuǐ 冷水
hot water	rèshuǐ 热水
iced water	bīngshuǐ 冰水
mineral water	kuàngquánshuǐ 矿泉水
soft drink	qìshuǐ 汽水
water	shuǐ 水
chrysanthemum tea	júhuāchá 菊花茶
green tea	lùchá 绿茶
jasmine tea	mòlìhuāchá 茉莉花茶
red tea	hóngchá 红茶
tea	chá 茶
apple juice	píngguǒzhī 苹果汁
grape juice	pútaozhī 葡萄汁
juice	guǒzhī 果汁

orange juice	chéngzhī 橙汁
watermelon juice	xīguāzhī 西瓜汁
coffee	kāfēi 咖啡
milk	niúnǎi 牛奶
soya milk	dòujiāng 豆浆
yogurt	suānnǎi 酸奶
beer	píjiǔ 啤酒
Cognac	báilándì 白兰地
wine	pútaojiǔ 葡萄酒
red wine	hóngpútaojiǔ 红葡萄酒
rice wine	mǐjiǔ 米酒
champagne	xiāngbīn 香槟
white wine	báipútaojiǔ 白葡萄酒
white spirit	báijiǔ 白酒
wine, liquor	jiǔ 酒
yellow rice wine	huángjiǔ 黄酒

B6 Seasoning   tiáowèipǐn 调味品

aniseed	huíxiāng 茴香
cassia bark	guìpí 桂皮
corn oil	yùmǐyóu 玉米油
dried chilli	gān làjiāo 干辣椒
jam	jiàng 酱
monosodium glutamate (MSG)	
	wèijīng 味精
mustard	jièmo 芥末
oil	yóu 油
olive oil	gǎnlǎnyóu 橄榄油
oyster sauce	háoyóu 蚝油
peanut oil	huāshēngyóu 花生油
pepper	hújiāo 胡椒
salt	yán 盐
sesame oil	máyóu 麻油, xiāngyóu 香油
soy sauce	jiàngyóu 酱油
soya oil	dòuyóu 豆油
sugar	táng 糖

tea oil	cháyóu 茶油
vegetable oil	càiyóu 菜油
vinegar	cù 醋
wild pepper	huājiāo 花椒

B7 Cooking   pēngrèn 烹饪

boil	zhǔ 煮
(of food) cold and dressed with sauce	
	liáng bàn 凉拌
deep-fry, French-fry	yóu zhá 油炸
fry	jiān 煎
pickle	yān 腌
smoke	xūn 熏
steam	zhēng 蒸
soak	jìn 浸, pào 泡
stew, braise	dùn 炖, mèn 焖
stir-fry	chǎo 炒
toast, bake, grill, broil	kǎo 烤

B8 Tableware   cānjù 餐具

bowl	wǎn 碗
chopsticks	kuàizi 筷子
cup, glass	bēi(zi) 杯(子)
dish	dié(zi) 碟(子)
fork	chā(zi) 叉(子)
goblet	gāojiǎobēi 高脚杯
knife	dāo(zi) 刀(子)
plate	pán(zi) 盘(子)
soup spoon, ladle	tāngsháo 汤勺,
	chángbǐngsháo 长柄勺
spoon	sháo(zi) 勺(子), chí 匙
teacup glass	chábēi 茶杯
teapot	cháhú 茶壶
wine glass	jiǔbēi 酒杯
wine pot	jiǔhú 酒壶

B9 *Restaurant* cānguǎn 餐馆
Bar jiǔbā 酒吧

bar	jiǔbā 酒吧
cafeteria	zìzhù cāntīng 自助餐厅
coffee house	kāfēiwū 咖啡屋
snack bar	xiǎochīdiàn 小吃店
snack	xiǎochī 小吃
takeaway	wàimàidiàn 外卖店
tearoom, teahouse	cháshì 茶室，cháguǎn 茶馆
have a meal, dine	chīfàn 吃饭，jìncān 进餐
Western-style restaurant	
	xīcāntīng 西餐厅

B10 *Chinese food* Zhōngcān 中餐
Western food Xīcān 西餐

tender boiled chicken	báizhǎnjī 白斩鸡
(boiled) rice	mǐfàn 米饭
mutton shish kebab	kǎoyángròuchuànr 烤羊肉串儿
bean-starch jelly	liángfěn 凉粉
cooked food, dish	càiyáo 菜肴
deep-fried twisted two dough sticks	
	yóutiáo 油条
deep-fried dough cake	
	yóubǐng 油饼
dumpling	jiǎozi 饺子
pancake	làobǐng 烙饼
fried dumpling	guōtiē 锅贴
fried noodles	chǎomiàn 炒面
fried rice	chǎofàn 炒饭
green onion pie	cōngyóubǐng 葱油饼
jellied bean curd	dòufunǎor 豆腐脑儿
steamed fish	qīngzhēngyú 清蒸鱼
pie	xiànrbǐng 馅儿饼
millet porridge	xiǎomǐzhōu 小米粥
New Year cake	niángāo 年糕
noodles	miàntiáo 面条

pancake	jiānbing 煎饼
porridge	zhōu 粥
preserved egg	pídàn 皮蛋，sōnghuādàn 松花蛋
rice porridge	dàmǐzhōu 大米粥
rice dumpling, rice ball	
	tāngyuán 汤圆，yuánxiāo 元宵
rice noodles	mǐfěn 米粉，mǐxiàn 米线
roast duck	kǎoyā 烤鸭
salted duck egg	xiányādàn 咸鸭蛋
salted egg	xiánjīdàn 咸鸡蛋
sesame seed cake	shāobing 烧饼
soup	tāng 汤
spicy hot tofu	málà dòufu 麻辣豆腐
spring roll	chūnjuǎnr 春卷儿
staple food	zhǔshí 主食
steamed roll	huājuǎnr 花卷儿
mantou	mántou 馒头
steamed small meat bun	
	xiǎolóngbāo 小笼包
pork braised in brown sauce	
	hóngshāoròu 红烧肉
stir-fried kidney beans	
	chǎodòujiǎo 炒豆角
tea egg	cháyèdàn 茶叶蛋
tofu, been curd	dòufu 豆腐
tomato and egg soup	xīhóngshì jīdàn tāng
	西红柿鸡蛋汤
wonton, dumpling soup	
	húntun 馄饨
bread	miànbāo 面包
butter	huángyóu 黄油，nǎiyóu 奶油
cake	dàngāo 蛋糕
cheese	nǎilào 奶酪
French fries	zháshǔtiáo 炸薯条
hamburger	hànbǎobāo 汉堡包
ice cream	bīngqílín 冰淇淋

读拼音学汉语

macaroni	tōngxīnfěn 通心粉
margarine	rénzào huángyóu 人造黄油
pasta	Yìdàlìmiàn 意大利面
pizza	bǐsàbǐng 比萨饼
salad	shālā 沙拉，sèlā 色拉
sandwich	sānmíngzhì 三明治
toast	tǔsī 土司

B11 Entertaining guests qǐngkè 请客

bill	zhàngdān 账单
book a table	dìng zuò 订座
book	yùdìng 预订
compartment	bāojiān 包间
serve the dishes	shàng cài 上菜
feast	yànhuì 宴会，jiǔxí 酒席
menu	càidān 菜单
order dishes	diǎn cài 点菜
pay bill	fùzhàng 付账，mǎidān 买单
receipt	fāpiào 发票，shōujù 收据
drinking more	duō hē diǎnr 多喝点儿
eating more	duō chī diǎnr 多吃点儿
help yourself	zìjǐ dòngshǒu 自己动手
home cooked meal, plain home cooking	
	jiācháng-biànfàn 家常便饭
lowly fare	cūchá-dànfàn 粗茶淡饭
make yourself at home	
	bié kèqi 别客气，qǐng biàn 请便
not any more	bú yào le 不要了
pass the…please	qǐng bǎ……dì gěi wǒ
	请把……递给我
please take your time to enjoy it	
	qǐng mànyòng 请慢用
some more	tiān diǎnr 添点儿，

	zài lái diǎnr 再来点儿
take a seat	rù zuò 入座，qǐng zuò 请坐
taste please	qǐng pǐncháng 请品尝
thank you for your hospitality and generosity	
	ràng nín pòfèi le 让您破费了
the color, smell and taste are all good	
	sè-xiāng-wèi jù quán 色香味俱全

B12 Feeling gǎnjué 感觉
Taste wèidào 味道

drunk	zuì 醉
full	bǎo 饱
hungry	è 饿
thirsty	kě 渴
bitter	kǔ 苦
salty	xián 咸
sour	suān 酸
spicy, hot	là 辣
sweet	tián 甜
taste	wèidào 味道
delicious	hǎochī 好吃
horrible	bù hǎochī 不好吃，nánchī 难吃
fat	féi 肥
lean	shòu 瘦
fresh	xīnxiān 新鲜
stale	bù xīnxiān 不新鲜
greasy	yóunì 油腻
light, weak	qīngdàn 清淡
mouth-watering	hǎo xiāng 好香
tasteless	dàn ér wúwèi 淡而无味
soft	sōngruǎn 松软
stiff	tài yìng 太硬，
	yǎo bu dòng 咬不动

C   *Living* zhù 住

C1 *House*   fángzi 房子，fángwū 房屋
Apartment   gōngyù 公寓

ceiling	tiānhuābǎn 天花板
chimney	yāncōng 烟囱
corridor	zǒuláng 走廊，guòdào 过道
door	mén 门
floor	dìbǎn 地板，lóucéng 楼层
French window	luòdìchuāng 落地窗
hall	dàtīng 大厅
passageway	lóudào 楼道
roof	wūdǐng 屋顶
room	fángjiān 房间，wū(zi) 屋(子)
stairs	lóutī 楼梯
wall	qiáng(bì) 墙(壁)
window	chuāng(hu) 窗(户)
air-conditioner	kōngtiáo 空调
alarm	bàojǐngqì 报警器
electric door bell	diànménlíng 电门铃
electricity meter	diànbiǎo 电表
furniture	jiājù 家具
key	yàoshi 钥匙
elevator	diàntī 电梯
lock	suǒ 锁
security door	fángdàomén 防盗门
security window	fángdàochuāng 防盗窗
switch	kāiguān 开关
water meter	shuǐbiǎo 水表

C2 *Bedroom*   wòshì 卧室

air purifier	kōngqì qīngjiéjī 空气清洁机
alarm clock	nàozhōng 闹钟
bed	chuáng 床
bedside	chuángtóuguì 床头柜

chest of drawers	wǔdǒuchú 五斗橱
double bed	shuāngrénchuáng 双人床
dressing table	shūzhuāngtái 梳妆台
massage chair	ànmóyǐ 按摩椅
mattress	chuángdiàn 床垫
single bed	dānrénchuáng 单人床
wardrobe	yīguì 衣柜
bedding	bèirù 被褥
bedspread	chuángzhào 床罩
blanket	tǎnzi 毯子
cotton blanket	miántǎn 棉毯
duvet inner quilt	yǔróngbèi 羽绒被
electric blanket	diànrètǎn 电热毯
pillow	zhěntou 枕头
pillowcase	zhěntào 枕套
quilt with cotton wadding	miánbèi 棉被
sheet	chuángdān 床单
pillow towel	zhěnjīn 枕巾
wool inner quilt	yángmáobèi 羊毛被
woollen blanket	máotǎn 毛毯

C3 *Sitting room*   kètīng 客厅
Balcony   yángtái 阳台

answering machine	diànhuà dálùjī 电话答录机
calendar	niánlì 年历
cassette	héshì cídài 盒式磁带
ceiling light	diàodēng 吊灯
chair	yǐzi 椅子
clock	zhōng 钟
curtain	chuānglián 窗帘
disc, record	chàngpiàn 唱片
electric fan	diànfēngshàn 电风扇

floor lamp	luòdìdēng 落地灯
heater, radiator, central heating	
	qǔnuǎnqì 取暖器
lamp, light	dēng 灯
microphone	huàtǒng 话筒, màikèfēng 麦克风
projector	tóuyǐngyí 投影仪,
	fàngyìngjī 放映机
radio	shōuyīnjī 收音机
recorder	lùyīnjī 录音机
remote control unit	yáokòngqì 遥控器
screen	píngmù 屏幕
sofa	shāfā 沙发
sound box	yīnxiāng 音箱
stool	dèngzi 凳子
tape	lùyīndài 录音带, cídài 磁带
tea table	chájī 茶几
telephone	diànhuà 电话
television	diànshì 电视
TV cabinet	diànshìjīguì 电视机柜
vase	huāpíng 花瓶
video disk	diépiàn 碟片
video player	fàngxiàngjī 放像机
video recorder	lùxiàngjī 录像机
video tape	lùxiàngdài 录像带
wall light	bìdēng 壁灯
wine cabinet	jiǔguì 酒柜
cupboard	bìchú 壁橱, bìguì 壁柜
clothes-horse	liàngyījià 晾衣架
flower pot	huāpén 花盆
plant pot holder	huāpénjià 花盆架

C4 Kitchen chúfáng 厨房
Dining room cāntīng 餐厅

disinfecting cabinet (for tableware)	
	cānjù xiāodúguì 餐具消毒柜
dish cabinet	wǎnchú 碗橱, wǎnguì 碗柜

dining table, table	fànzhuō 饭桌, zhuō(zi) 桌(子)
dish drainer	wǎnjià 碗架
dishwasher	xǐwǎnjī 洗碗机
sink	shuǐchí 水池
pantry	shípǐnguì 食品柜
refrigerator	(diàn)bīngxiāng （电)冰箱
tap	shuǐlóngtóu 水龙头
water purifier	jìngshuǐqì 净水器
clay pot	shāguō 砂锅
electric stove	diànlú 电炉
food steamer	zhēnglóng 蒸笼
frying pan	chǎocàiguō 炒菜锅
gas stove	méiqìzào 煤气灶
induction cooker	diàncílú 电磁炉
microwave	wēibōlú 微波炉
non-stick pan	bùzhānguō 不粘锅
pan	píngdǐguō 平底锅
rice cooker	diànfànguō 电饭锅
soya-milk machine	dòujiāngjī 豆浆机
steamer	zhēngguō 蒸锅
stove	lúzào 炉灶
wok	guō 锅
bottle	píngzi 瓶子
bottle opener	kāipíngqì 开瓶器
can opener	kāiguànqì 开罐器
chopping board	càibǎn 菜板
dish-washing liquid	xǐjiéjīng 洗洁精
funnel	lòudǒu 漏斗
grater	cǎzi 礤子
kettle	diànrèhú 电热壶
lid	guōgài 锅盖
cleaver	càidāo 菜刀
napkin	cānjīnzhǐ 餐巾纸
peeler	xiāopíqì 削皮器
sieve	shāizi 筛子
slice	guōchǎn 锅铲

strainer	zhàoli 笊篱
tablecloth	táibù 台布，zhuōbù 桌布
breakfast	zǎofàn 早饭
dinner	wǎnfàn 晚饭
lunch	wǔfàn 午饭
meal	fàn 饭

C5 Study shūfáng 书房

bookcase	shūchú 书橱，shūguì 书柜
bookshelf	shūjià 书架
computer, desktop	diànnǎo 电脑
laptop, notebook	shǒutí diànnǎo 手提电脑，bǐjìběn diànnǎo 笔记本电脑
computer desk	diànnǎozhuō 电脑桌
desk	shūzhuō 书桌
desk lamp	táidēng 台灯
high-back chair	diànnǎoyǐ 电脑椅
fax machine	chuánzhēnjī 传真机
headset phones	ěrjī 耳机
keyboard	jiànpán 键盘
mouse	shǔbiāo 鼠标
printer	dǎyìnjī 打印机
USB memory stick	U pán U盘
web cam	shèxiàngtóu 摄像头
book	shū 书
dictionary	cídiǎn 词典
document, file	wénjiàn 文件
document pouch	wénjiàndài 文件袋
folder	wénjiànjiā 文件夹
information	zīliào 资料
magazine	zázhì 杂志
map	dìtú 地图
newspaper	bàozhǐ 报纸
picture	túpiàn 图片
ballpoint pen	yuánzhūbǐ 圆珠笔
Chinese ink	mò 墨

inkstone	yàntai 砚台
drawing pin	túdīng 图钉
ink box	mòhé 墨盒
ink-pen	qiānzìbǐ 签字笔
ink	mòshuǐ 墨水
lead (in a pencil)	qiānbǐxīn 铅笔芯
paper	zhǐ 纸
pen container	bǐtǒng 笔筒
pen rack	bǐjià 笔架
pen	bǐ 笔，gāngbǐ 钢笔
pencil sharpener	juǎnbǐdāo 卷笔刀
pencil	qiānbǐ 铅笔
pencil case	qiānbǐhé 铅笔盒
pencil sharpener	qiānbǐdāo 铅笔刀
prepared Chinese ink	mòzhī 墨汁
rubber	xiàngpí 橡皮
staple	dìngshūdīng 订书钉
stapler	dìngshūjī 订书机

C6 Bathroom yùshì 浴室
Washroom xǐshǒujiān 洗手间
Toilet cèsuǒ 厕所

comb	shūzi 梳子
electric shaver	diàndòng tìxūdāo 电动剃须刀
face cleaner	xǐmiànnǎi 洗面奶
face cream	miànshuāng 面霜
hair clipper	tuīzi 推子
hair conditioner	hùfàsù 护发素，hùfàyè 护发液
hair dryer	diànchuīfēng 电吹风
hair gel	dìngxíngjiāo 定型胶
liquid hand wash	xǐshǒuyè 洗手液
mirror	jìngzi 镜子
perfumed soap	xiāngzào 香皂
perfume	xiāngshuǐ 香水
shampoo	xǐfàyè 洗发液
toothbrush	yáshuā 牙刷

toothpaste	yágāo 牙膏	dustpan	bòji 簸箕，běnji 畚箕
towel rail	máojīnjià 毛巾架	energy-saving bulb	jiénéng dēngpào 节能灯泡
towel	máojīn 毛巾，shǒujīn 手巾	glue	jiāoshuǐ 胶水
vanity case	huàzhuānghé 化妆盒	hammer	chuízi 锤子，lángtou 榔头
wash basin	xǐliǎnchí 洗脸池	hot-water bottle	rèshuǐdài 热水袋
bath towel	yùjīn 浴巾	pesticide	shāchóngjì 杀虫剂
bathrobe	yùyī 浴衣	lantern	dēnglong 灯笼
bathtub	yùgāng 浴缸，yùpén 浴盆	lighter	dǎhuǒjī 打火机
shower	línyùqì 淋浴器	match	huǒchái 火柴
soap	féizào 肥皂	mobile phone	shǒujī 手机
water heater	rèshuǐqì 热水器	mop	tuōbǎ 拖把
solar water heater	tàiyángnéng rèshuǐqì	terminal block	jiēxiànbǎn 接线板
	太阳能热水器	nail	dīngzi 钉子
detergent	xǐdíjì 洗涤剂	nail clippers	zhǐjiadāo 指甲刀
electric iron	diànyùndǒu 电熨斗	needle	zhēn 针
ironing board	yùnyībǎn 熨衣板	plug	chātóu 插头
laundry powder	xǐyīfěn 洗衣粉	rechargeable battery	chōngdiàn diànchí 充电电池
liquid laundry detergent		ruler	chǐ 尺
	xǐyīyè 洗衣液	scissors	jiǎndāo 剪刀
washing machine	xǐyījī 洗衣机	sewing machine	féngrènjī 缝纫机
nightstool	mǎtǒng 马桶	socket	chāzuò 插座
toilet tissue	cèzhǐ 厕纸，shǒuzhǐ 手纸	sponge	hǎimián 海绵
		tape measure	juǎnchǐ 卷尺
		thermos	rèshuǐpíng 热水瓶
		thread	xiàn 线

C7 Other daily necessities　qítā rìyòngpǐn 其他日用品

ashtray	yānhuīgāng 烟灰缸	torch	shǒudiàntǒng 手电筒
battery	diànchí 电池	umbrella	sǎn 伞，yǔsǎn 雨伞
broom	sàozhou 扫帚，sàoba 扫把，	watch	shǒubiǎo 手表
	tiáozhou 笤帚		
brush	shuāzi 刷子		

C8 Everyday routines and actions　rìcháng qǐjū hé huódòng 日常起居和活动

bucket	shuǐtǒng 水桶	wake up	xǐnglái 醒来
bulb	dēngpào 灯泡	turn on a light	kāi dēng 开灯
candle	làzhú 蜡烛	get up	qǐchuáng 起床
charger	chōngdiànqì 充电器	put on one's clothes	chuān yīfu 穿衣服
cigarette	xiāngyān 香烟	put on one's shoes	chuān xié 穿鞋
dustbin	lājīxiāng 垃圾箱		

make one's bed	zhěnglǐ chuángpù 整理床铺	walk	zǒu lù 走路，sànbù 散步
brush one's teeth	shuā yá 刷牙	take off one's clothes	tuō yī 脱衣
wash one's hands	xǐ shǒu 洗手	take off one's shoes	tuō xié 脱鞋
wash one's face	xǐ liǎn 洗脸	go to bed, sleep	shàng chuáng 上床，
wash one's hair	xǐ tóu 洗头		shuìjiào 睡觉
take a bath, shower	xǐ zǎo 洗澡	turn off the light	xī dēng 熄灯，guān dēng 关灯
make-up	huàzhuāng 化妆	wash the clothes	xǐ yīfu 洗衣服
comb hair	shū tóu 梳头	dry the clothes in the sun	
have a shave	guā húzi 刮胡子		shài yīfu 晒衣服
eat a meal	chī fàn 吃饭	have a chat	liáotiān 聊天
have breakfast	chī zǎofàn 吃早饭	iron the clothes	yùn yīfu 熨衣服
have lunch	chī wǔfàn 吃午饭	listen to the radio	tīng shōuyīnjī 听收音机
have dinner	chī wǎnfàn 吃晚饭	make a call	dǎ diànhuà 打电话
wear one's hat	dài màozi 戴帽子	answer a call	jiē diànhuà 接电话
close the door	guān mén 关门	mop the floor	tuō dìbǎn 拖地板
close the window	guān chuāng 关窗	put the clothes away	shōu yīfu 收衣服，
lock the door	suǒ mén 锁门		fàng yīfu 放衣服
go out	chūqù 出去	read a book	kàn shū 看书，dú shū 读书
go to school	shàngxué 上学	read the newspaper	kàn bào 看报
go to work	shàngbān 上班	receive E-mails	shōu diànzǐ yóujiàn 收电子邮件
learn	xué(xí) 学(习)	send E-mails	fā diànzǐ yóujiàn 发电子邮件
work	gōngzuò 工作	smoke	xīyān 吸烟
rest	xiūxi 休息	surf the net	shàngwǎng 上网
drink tea	hē chá 喝茶	sweep the floor	sǎo dì 扫地
go to toilet	shàng cèsuǒ 上厕所，	turn on the computer	kāi jī 开机
	jiěshǒu 解手	wash the window	cā chuānghu 擦窗户
after school	fàngxué 放学	watch TV	kàn diànshì 看电视
after work, finish work	xiàbān 下班		
come back, return	huílái 回来		
open the door	kāi mén 开门		

C9 Describing houses　fángwū miáoshù 房屋描述

open the window	kāi chuāng 开窗	bright	míngliàng 明亮
cook a meal	zuò fàn 做饭	dim	yīn'àn 阴暗
cook dishes	chǎo cài 炒菜	bustling with noise	rènao 热闹
clean the pot, wok, pan		lonely	pìjìng 僻静
	shuā guō 刷锅	comfortable	shūshì 舒适
wash the dishes	xǐ wǎn 洗碗	uncomfortable	bù shūshì 不舒适

high	gāo 高	safe	ānquán 安全
low	dī 低	unsafe	bù ānquán 不安全
quiet	ānjìng 安静	neat and tidy	zhěngjié 整洁
noisy	xuānnào 喧闹	untidy	língluàn 凌乱，
roomy	kuānchang 宽敞		bù zhěngqí 不整齐
narrow	xiázhǎi 狭窄		

D *In the city* chéngshì 城市

D1 *Road facilities* jiēmiàn shèshī 街面设施

bridge	qiáo 桥
crossroads	shízì lùkǒu 十字路口
junction, T-shaped	sān chà lùkǒu 三岔路口，
	dīng zì lùkǒu 丁字路口
lane	xiàng 巷，hútòng 胡同
flyover	lìjiāoqiáo 立交桥
overhead walkway	guò jiē tiānqiáo 过街天桥
pedestrian walkway	rénxíngdào 人行道
pedestrian crossing	rénxíng héngdào 人行横道
road	lù 路
street	jiē 街
roundabout	huán xíng jiāochā lùkǒu
	环形交叉路口
traffic lights	jiāotōngdēng 交通灯，
	hónglǜdēng 红绿灯
tunnel	suìdào 隧道
underpass	dìxiàtōngdào 地下通道

D2 *Shop* diànpù 店铺

bakery	miànbāodiàn 面包店
beauty and hair design	
	měiróng měifà diàn 美容美发店
bedding shop	chuáng shang yòngpǐn diàn
	床上用品店
bookshop	shūdiàn 书店
butcher's shop	ròudiàn 肉店

button shop	niǔkòudiàn 纽扣店
café	kāfēidiàn 咖啡店
china shop	táocídiàn 陶瓷店
cobbler stall	xiūxiépù 修鞋铺
confectioner	tángguǒdiàn 糖果店
cooked food shop	shúshídiàn 熟食店
decorative material market	
	zhuāngshì cáiliào shìchǎng
	装饰材料市场
department store	bǎihuò gōngsī 百货公司
dry laundry	gānxǐdiàn 干洗店
fishmonger	yúdiàn 鱼店
florist	huādiàn 花店
fresh food market	càishìchǎng 菜市场
fruit shop	shuǐguǒdiàn 水果店
garage, service station	
	qìchē xiūlǐ chǎng 汽车修理厂
glass goods shop	bōli qìmǐn diàn 玻璃器皿店
glasses shop	yǎnjìngdiàn 眼镜店
grocery shop	záhuòdiàn 杂货店
hardware store	wǔjīndiàn 五金店
leather goods shop	píhuòdiàn 皮货店
market	shìchǎng 市场，jíshì 集市
musical instrument shop	
	yuèqìdiàn 乐器店
news stall	bàotíng 报亭
pharmacy	yàodiàn 药店

261

plastic utensils shop	sùliào qìmǐn diàn 塑料器皿店		feet bathing and massage room	
pub	jiǔbā 酒吧			zúyù ànmó guǎn 足浴按摩馆
bicycle repair stall	zìxíngchē xiūchēpù		garden	huāyuán 花园
	自行车修车铺		gas station	jiāyóuzhàn 加油站
restaurant	fàndiàn 饭店		gym	tǐyùguǎn 体育馆
shop	shāngdiàn 商店		hospital	yīyuàn 医院
sports goods shop	tǐyù yòngpǐn diàn 体育用品店		hotel	bīnguǎn 宾馆，lǚguǎn 旅馆
stationery shop	wénjùdiàn 文具店		library	túshūguǎn 图书馆
supermarket	chāoshì 超市		mahjong and cards room	
tailor stall	cáifengpù 裁缝铺			qípáishì 棋牌室
toy shop	wánjùdiàn 玩具店		middle school	zhōngxué 中学
vegetable shop	shūcàidiàn 蔬菜店		museum	bówùguǎn 博物馆
vegetable stall	càitān 菜摊		newspaper office	bàoshè 报社
watches and clocks	zhōngbiǎodiàn 钟表店		nightclub	yèzǒnghuì 夜总会
white goods	jiāyòng diànqì diàn		park	gōngyuán 公园
	家用电器店		parking	tíngchēchǎng 停车场
			post office	yóujú 邮局

D3 Public places gōnggòng chǎngsuǒ 公共场所

bank	yínháng 银行		primary school	xiǎoxué 小学
botanical garden	zhíwùyuán 植物园		sauna room	sāngnáshì 桑拿室
bus stop	qìchēzhàn 汽车站		school	xuéxiào 学校
cinema	diànyǐngyuàn 电影院		stadium	tǐyùchǎng 体育场
clinic	zhěnsuǒ 诊所		tearoom	cháshì 茶室
club	jùlèbù 俱乐部		telephone box	diànhuàtíng 电话亭
concert hall	yīnyuètīng 音乐厅		theater	jùyuàn 剧院，xìyuàn 戏院
dance hall	wǔtīng 舞厅		train station	huǒchēzhàn 火车站
			university	dàxué 大学
			zoo	dòngwùyuán 动物园

E Business shāngyè 商业

E1 At the shop zài shāngdiàn 在商店

shop assistant	shòuhuòyuán 售货员		counter	guìtái 柜台
cash desk, checkout	fùkuǎntái 付款台，		customer	gùkè 顾客
	fùkuǎnchù 付款处		fitting room	shìyīshì 试衣室
cash register, cash machine			goods	shāngpǐn 商品
	shōuyínjī 收银机		manager	jīnglǐ 经理
			shelf	jiàzi 架子

shopkeeper, boss	diànzhǔ 店主，lǎobǎn 老板	
shopping bag	gòuwùdài 购物袋	
shopping basket	gòuwùlán 购物篮	
storage rack	huòjià 货架	
trolley	gòuwù shǒutuīchē 购物手推车	
auction	pāimài 拍卖	
bargain	tǎojià-huánjià 讨价还价	
brand	shāngbiāo 商标，páizi 牌子	
buy one get one free	mǎiyī-sòngyī 买一送一	
buy	mǎi 买	
change for another	huàn 换	
cheap, low price	piányi 便宜，liánjià 廉价	
convenient	fāngbiàn 方便	
cost	chéngběn 成本	
deliver	sòng huò 送货	
do business	yíngyè 营业	
expensive, high price	guì 贵	
give back, return	tuì huò 退货	
give change	zhǎo (qián) 找（钱）	
best-before date	bǎozhìqī 保质期	
inferior	lièzhìpǐn 劣质品，cìpǐn 次品	
net weight	jìngzhòng 净重	
online shopping	wǎngshang gòuwù 网上购物	
on sale, cut price	jiǎn jià 减价	
pay	fù qián 付钱	
place of production	chǎndì 产地	
price	jiàgé 价格，jiàqian 价钱	
retail	língshòu 零售	
sell	mài 卖	
shopping	gòuwù 购物，mǎi dōngxi 买东西	
spend	huāfèi 花费	
stock	kùcúnpǐn 库存品， jīyā wùzī 积压物资	
superior	yōuzhìpǐn 优质品， shàngděngpǐn 上等品	
wholesale	pīfā 批发	

window shopping   guàng shāngdiàn 逛商店

E2 *At the bank* zài yínháng 在银行
The world's major currencies
shìjiè zhǔyào huòbì míngchēng
世界主要货币名称

Australian Dollar (AUD $ A)	Àodàlìyàyuán 澳大利亚元
Canadian Dollar (CAD Can $)	Jiānádàyuán 加拿大元
Euro (EUR €)	Ōuyuán 欧元
foreign currency	wàibì 外币
Hong Kong Dollar (HKD HK $)	Gǎngbì 港币
Japanese Yen (JPY ¥)	Rìyuán 日元
New Zealand Dollar (NZD $ NZ)	Xīnxīlányuán 新西兰元
Pound Sterling (GBP £)	Yīngbàng 英镑
Renminbi Yuan (CNY ¥)	Rénmínbì (yuán) 人民币(元)
Singapore Dollar (SGD S $)	Xīnjiāpōyuán 新加坡元
US Dollar (USD US $)	Měiyuán 美元

Unit of Chinese currency
Zhōngguó huòbì dānwèi 中国货币单位

money	qián 钱
yuan	yuán 元，kuài 块 (*The basic unit of Chinese currency similar to the dollar.* kuài 块 *is used in spoken language.*)
jiao	jiǎo 角，máo 毛 (*One-tenth of one* yuan, *similar to 10 cents.* máo 毛 *is used in spoken language.*)

Banking yínháng 银行

account	zhànghù 账户
ATM (automated teller machine)	zìdòng tíkuǎnjī 自动提款机
ATM card	zìdòng tíkuǎnkǎ 自动提款卡
balance	yú'é 余额
bankbook	cúnzhé 存折
borrow	jièrù 借入，jièyòng 借用
cash a check	duìxiàn 兑现
cash	xiànjīn 现金
check	zhīpiào 支票
check account	zhīpiào zhànghù 支票账户
credit card	xìnyòngkǎ 信用卡
deposit account	cúnkuǎn zhànghù 存款账户
deposit	cún qián 存钱，cún kuǎn 存款
electronic transfer	diànhuì 电汇
exchange	(duì)huàn （兑）换
exchange rate	duìhuànlǜ 兑换率
invest	tóuzī 投资
interest rate	lìlǜ 利率
interest	lìxi 利息
lend	bǎ…jiègěi 把……借给
loan	dài kuǎn 贷款，jiè kuǎn 借款
mortgage	dǐyā dàikuǎn 抵押贷款
open an account	kāihù 开户
overdraw	tòuzhī 透支
overdue	guòqī wèi fù de 过期未付的
owe	qiàn 欠
pay back, repay	guīhuán 归还
savings account	huóqī cúnkuǎn zhànghù 活期存款账户
statement	jiésuànbiǎo 结算表，zhàngdān 账单
transfer	zhuǎn zhàng 转账
withdraw	qǔ qián 取钱，qǔ kuǎn 取款

E3 At the post office zài yóujú 在邮局

air mail	hángkōngxìn 航空信
birthday card	shēngrìkǎ 生日卡
cashing a remittance	qǔ huìkuǎn 取汇款
envelope	xìnfēng 信封
express post	kuàidì 快递
parcel	bāoguǒ 包裹
parcel form	bāoguǒdān 包裹单
fill in the parcel form	tiánxiě bāoguǒdān 填写包裹单
letter box	xìnxiāng 信箱
letter	xìn 信
post office box	yóuzhèng xìnxiāng 邮政信箱
postage	yóufèi 邮费
postcard	míngxìnpiàn 明信片
printed matter	yìnshuāpǐn 印刷品
registered mail	guàhàoxìn 挂号信
send	(yóu)jì （邮）寄
send a letter	jì xìn 寄信
send a remittance	jì qián 寄钱，huìkuǎn 汇款
stamp	yóupiào 邮票
ordinary mail	píngxìn 平信
stick a stamp on the envelope	tiē yóupiào 贴邮票
writing paper	xìnzhǐ 信纸

E4 At the photo studio zài zhàoxiàngguǎn 在照相馆

camera	(zhào)xiàngjī （照）相机
develop film	chōngxǐ jiāojuǎnr 冲洗胶卷儿
digital camera	shùmǎ xiàngjī 数码相机
enlarge	fàngdà 放大
film	jiāojuǎn 胶卷
negative	dǐpiàn 底片
photograph	zhàopiàn 照片，xiàngpiàn 相片
photographer	shèyǐngshī 摄影师

photographic studio	shèyǐngshì 摄影室	
develop and print photos		
	xǐ yìn zhàopiàn 洗印照片	
snapshot	kuàizhào 快照	

E5 *At the hairdresser's* zài lǐfàdiàn 在理发店

perm	tàng fà 烫发
shave, cut hair off the face	

	guā húzi 刮胡子，xiū miàn 修面
dye one's hair	rǎn fà 染发
hair drier	chuīfēngjī 吹风机
hair style	fàxíng 发型
hair	tóufa 头发
haircut	jiǎn fà 剪发，lǐ fà 理发
hairdresser, barber	lǐfàshī 理发师，lǐfàyuán 理发员
moustache, beard	húzi 胡子，húxū 胡须
shampoo	xǐ fà 洗发，xǐ tóu 洗头

F *Traffic* jiāotōng 交通

F1 *Means of transportation* zhǔyào jiāotōng gōngjù 主要交通工具

airplane	fēijī 飞机
bicycle	zìxíngchē 自行车
boat, ship, yacht, etc.	chuán 船
bus	gōnggòng qìchē 公共汽车，gōngjiāochē 公交车
car	qìchē 汽车
coach	chángtú qìchē 长途汽车
express train	tè kuài lièchē 特快列车
fast train	kuàichē 快车
ferry	dùchuán 渡船
high-speed railway	gāosù tiělù 高速铁路
motorbike	mótuōchē 摩托车
powered ship	jīdòngchuán 机动船
steamer	lúnchuán 轮船
subway	dìtiě 地铁
taxi	chūzūchē 出租车
train	huǒchē 火车
vehicle	chē 车

F2 *Public transportation* gōnggòng jiāotōng 公共交通

boarding gate	dēngjīmén 登机门
business class	shāngwùcāng 商务舱
carriage	huǒchē chēxiāng 火车车厢
dining car	cānchē 餐车
economy class	jīngjìcāng 经济舱
hard seat	yìngzuò 硬座，yìngxí 硬席
hard sleeper	yìngwò 硬卧
lower berth	xiàpù 下铺
luggage van	(huǒchē) xínglichē （火车）行李车
middle berth	zhōngpù 中铺
platform	yuètái 月台，zhàntái 站台
quay, wharf	mǎtóu 码头，tíngbóchù 停泊处
sleeper	wòpù 卧铺
soft seat	ruǎnzuò 软座，ruǎnxí 软席
soft sleeper	ruǎnwò 软卧
ticket office	shòupiàochù 售票处
upper berth	shàngpù 上铺
waiting room	hòuchēshì 候车室，hòujīshì 候机室，hòuchuánshì 候船室

F3 Ticket　piào 票
Luggage　xíngli 行李

airplane ticket	jīpiào 机票
book	dìng 订
bus ticket	(qì)chēpiào （汽）车票
buying ticket	mǎi piào 买票
platform ticket	zhàntáipiào 站台票
self-service ticketing	wú rén shòu piào 无人售票
senior citizen card	lǎoniánkǎ 老年卡
steamer ticket, ferry ticket	
	chuánpiào 船票
card for one month	yuèpiào 月票
card for one year	niánpiào 年票
train ticket	(huǒ)chēpiào （火）车票
transportation card	chéngchēkǎ 乘车卡
left luggage office, checkroom	
	xíngli jìcúnchù 行李寄存处
luggage label	xíngli biāoqiān 行李标签
luggage rack	xínglijià 行李架
pick luggage up	qǔ xíngli 取行李
registered luggage	tuōyùn xíngli 托运行李

F4 Travel by means of transportation
shǐyòng jiāotōng gōngjù 使用交通工具

alight from a plane	xià fēijī 下飞机
arrival	dàodá 到达
board a plane	dēngjī 登机
by bus	zuò qìchē 坐汽车
by car	zuò xiǎoqìchē 坐小汽车
by motorcycle	qí mótuōchē 骑摩托车
by plane	zuò fēijī 坐飞机
by train	zuò huǒchē 坐火车
by subway	zuò dìtiě 坐地铁
departure	chūfā 出发
disembark	xià chuán 下船
drive car	kāi chē 开车

embark	shàng chuán 上船
get off a bus/car	xià chē 下车
get on a bus, get in a car	
	shàng chē 上车
go on board	shàng chuán 上船
land	jiàngluò 降落，zhuólù 着陆，
	dēng àn 登岸
lift	dā chē 搭车
return to port	fǎnháng 返航
ride a bicycle	qí zìxíngchē 骑自行车
ride a horse	qí mǎ 骑马
set sail	qǐháng 启航
take off	qǐfēi 起飞
traffic jam	dǔchē 堵车

F5 Direction　fāngwèi 方位

front	qiánbian 前边，qiánmiàn 前面
behind	hòubian 后边，hòumiàn 后面
left	zuǒbian 左边，zuǒmiàn 左面
right	yòubian 右边，yòumiàn 右面
above	shàngbian 上边，
	shàngmiàn 上面
under	xiàbian 下边，xiàmiàn 下面
inside	lǐbian 里边，lǐmiàn 里面
outside	wàibian 外边，wàimiàn 外面
next to	páng(biān) 旁（边）
between	zhōngjiān 中间
opposite	duìmiàn 对面
nearby	fùjìn 附近
east (side)	dōngbian 东边，
	dōngmiàn 东面
west (side)	xībian 西边，xīmiàn 西面
south (side)	nánbian 南边，nánmiàn 南面
north (side)	běibian 北边，běimiàn 北面

266

F6 *Entry and exit*   chū-rùjìng 出入境

apply for	shēnqǐng 申请
arrival card	rùjìngkǎ 入境卡
boarding card	dēngjīkǎ 登机卡
customs	hǎiguān 海关
declare	shēnbào 申报
departure card	chūjìngkǎ 出境卡
destination	mùdìdì 目的地

certificate	zhèngjiàn 证件
import duty	jìnkǒushuì 进口税
one way ticket	dānchéngpiào 单程票
passport	hùzhào 护照
return ticket	wǎng-fǎnpiào 往返票
security check	ānjiǎn 安检
visa	qiānzhèng 签证

G   Going away chū yuǎn mén 出远门

G1 *Travel*   lǚyóu 旅游

camping	yěyíng 野营
go tramping	yuǎnzú 远足,
	túbù lǚxíng 徒步旅行
picnic	yěcān 野餐
see and enjoy	guānshǎng 观赏
visit, sight-seeing	yóulǎn 游览 (*It is used when visiting a scenic or historical site.*)
visit	cānguān 参观 (*It is used when visiting a historical site, building, school, factory, museum and exhibition, etc.*)

G2 *In hotel*   zhù lǚguǎn 住旅馆

double room	shuāngrénfáng 双人房
fill in the form	tián biǎo 填表
occupied	kè mǎn 客满
overnight	guò yè 过夜
safe	bǎoxiǎnxiāng 保险箱
single room	dānrénfáng 单人房
suite	tàojiān 套间
vacancy	kòng fáng 空房, kòng wèi 空位

G3 *Meteorology*   qìxiàng 气象

air temperature	qìwēn 气温
below zero	líng xià 零下

blow	guā fēng 刮风
Centigrade (℃)	Shèshì 摄氏
change, turn	zhuǎn 转
climate	qìhòu 气候
cloud	yún 云
cloudy	duōyún 多云, yīn(tiān) 阴(天)
dew	lù 露, lùshuǐ 露水
Fahrenheit (℉)	Huáshì 华氏
fog	wù 雾
forecast	yùbào 预报
frost	shuāng 霜, jié shuāng 结霜
hail	bīngbáo 冰雹
ice	bīng 冰, jié bīng 结冰
lightning	shǎndiàn 闪电
rain	yǔ 雨, xià yǔ 下雨
rainbow	hóng 虹
sleet	yǔ jiā xuě 雨夹雪
snow	xuě 雪, xià xuě 下雪
sunny	qíng(tiān) 晴(天)
temperature	wēndù 温度
thunder	léi 雷, léishēng 雷声, dǎléi 打雷
weather	tiānqì 天气
wind	fēng 风

cold	lěng 冷	swamp	zhǎozé 沼泽，shīdì 湿地
comfortable	shūfu 舒服	plant	zhíwù 植物
cool	liángkuai 凉快，	bloom	kāi(huā) 开(花)
	liángshuǎng 凉爽	branch	zhītiáo 枝条
dry	gānzào 干燥	flower	huā 花
hot	rè 热	fruit	guǒshí 果实
sultry	mēnrè 闷热	grass	cǎo 草
uncomfortable	nánshòu 难受	harvest	shōuhuò 收获
warm	wēnnuǎn 温暖，nuǎnhuo 暖和	leaf	yè 叶
wet	cháoshī 潮湿	ripe	chéngshú 成熟
		root	gēn 根

G4 *Natural scenery* zìrán jǐngguān 自然景观

		sprout	fā yá 发芽
		stem	jīng 茎
nature	dàzìrán 大自然	tree	shù 树
all over the mountain	màn shān 漫山	animal	dòngwù 动物
bay	hǎiwān 海湾	bear	xióng 熊
beach	hǎitān 海滩，hétān 河滩，	camel	luòtuo 骆驼
	hútān 湖滩，tāndì 滩地	cat	māo 猫
desert	shāmò 沙漠	cattle	niú 牛
earth	dìqiú 地球	deer	lù 鹿
farm	nóngchǎng 农场	dog	gǒu 狗
grassland	cǎoyuán 草原	donkey	lú 驴
ground, land	(dà)dì （大)地	dragon	lóng 龙
hill, mountain	shān 山	elephant	xiàng 象
lake	hú 湖	giant panda	dàxióngmāo 大熊猫
lawn	cǎodì 草地	horse	mǎ 马
meadow	mùchǎng 牧场	leopard	bào 豹
moon	yuèliang 月亮	lion	shīzi 狮子
river	hé 河，jiāng 江	mouse	lǎoshǔ 老鼠
scenery	fēngjǐng 风景	pig	zhū 猪
sea	hǎi 海	rabbit	tù 兔
seaside	hǎibiān 海边	sheep	yáng 羊
sky	tiān(kōng) 天(空)	snake	shé 蛇
soil	tǔrǎng 土壤，nítǔ 泥土	tiger	hǔ 虎
star	xīng 星	wolf	láng 狼
sun	tàiyáng 太阳	bird	niǎo 鸟

chicken	jī 鸡	peacock	kǒngquè 孔雀
crow	wūyā 乌鸦	pigeon	gēzi 鸽子
duck	yā 鸭	sparrow	máquè 麻雀
goose	é 鹅	swallow	yànzi 燕子
magpie	xǐquè 喜鹊	swan	tiān'é 天鹅
ostrich	tuóniǎo 鸵鸟		

H   *Leisure* xiūxián 休闲

H1 *Sports*   tǐyù 体育，yùndòng 运动

badminton	yǔmáoqiú 羽毛球
baseball	bàngqiú 棒球
basketball	lánqiú 篮球
billiards	táiqiú 台球
cricket	bǎnqiú 板球
football	zúqiú 足球
golf	gāo'ěrfūqiú 高尔夫球
hockey	qūgùnqiú 曲棍球
rugby	gǎnlǎnqiú 橄榄球
table tennis	pīngpāngqiú 乒乓球
tennis	wǎngqiú 网球
volleyball	páiqiú 排球
ball game	qiú lèi yùndòng 球类运动
boxing	quánjī 拳击
bronze medal	tóngpái 铜牌
exercise	duànliàn 锻炼
fishing	diào yú 钓鱼
gold medal	jīnpái 金牌
high jump	tiào gāo 跳高
ice skating	huá bīng 滑冰
long jump	tiào yuǎn 跳远
match, event, race	bǐsài 比赛
mountain climbing	pá shān 爬山
Olympic Games	Àolínpǐkè yùndònghuì 奥林匹克运动会，Àoyùnhuì 奥运会
roller skating	huá hànbīng 滑旱冰

rowing	huá chuán 划船
running	pǎobù 跑步
silver medal	yínpái 银牌
skiing	huá xuě 滑雪
swimming	yóuyǒng 游泳
swimming pool	yóuyǒngchí 游泳池
tai chi	tàijíquán 太极拳
track and field sports	tiánjìng yùndòng 田径运动

H2 *Entertainment*   yúlè 娱乐

ballet	bālěiwǔ 芭蕾舞
Beijing opera	jīngjù 京剧，jīngxì 京戏
circus	mǎxì 马戏
concert	yǎnchànghuì 演唱会，yīnyuèhuì 音乐会
crosstalk	xiàngsheng 相声
dance drama	wǔjù 舞剧
dance party	wǔhuì 舞会
dance	wǔdǎo 舞蹈，tiào wǔ 跳舞
disco	dísīkē 迪斯科
film	diànyǐng 电影
folk dance	mínjiān wǔdǎo 民间舞蹈
magic	móshù 魔术
music	yīnyuè 音乐
opera	gējù 歌剧，xìqǔ 戏曲，xìjù 戏剧
pantomime	yǎjù 哑剧

sing	chàng (gē) 唱(歌)	organ	fēngqín 风琴
song	gēqǔ 歌曲	piano	gāngqín 钢琴
storytelling	píngshū 评书	cards	pūkèpái 扑克牌
accordion	shǒufēngqín 手风琴	chess	guójì xiàngqí 国际象棋
erhu	èrhú 二胡	Chinese checkers	tiàoqí 跳棋
pipa (a kind of Chinese string musical instrument)		Chinese chess	Zhōngguó xiàngqí 中国象棋
	pípa 琵琶	mahjong	májiàng 麻将

I Visiting a doctor kàn yīshēng 看医生

I1 *Main parts of the human body*
réntǐ zhǔyào bùwèi 人体主要部位

abdomen	fù 腹，dùzi 肚子	intestine	cháng 肠
ankle	jiǎohuái 脚踝	joint	guānjié 关节
arm	bì 臂，gēbo 胳膊	kidney	shèn 肾
back	bèi 背	knee	xīgài 膝盖
blood	xiě/xuè 血	leg	tuǐ 腿
body	shēntǐ 身体	lip	(zuǐ)chún (嘴)唇
bottom, buttocks	tún(bù) 臀(部)，pìgu 屁股	liver	gān 肝
breast	rǔfáng 乳房	lung	fèi 肺
calf	xiǎotuǐ 小腿	mouth	zuǐ 嘴
cheek	miànjiá 面颊	neck	jǐng 颈，bózi 脖子
chest	xiōng 胸	nose	bí(zi) 鼻(子)
chin	xiàba 下巴	shoulder	jiān(bǎng) 肩(膀)
ear	ěrduo 耳朵	stomach	wèi 胃
eye	yǎn(jing) 眼(睛)	thigh	dàtuǐ 大腿
eyebrow	méimao 眉毛	throat	hóulong 喉咙，sǎngzi 嗓子
face	liǎn 脸	tongue	shétou 舌头
finger	shǒuzhǐ 手指	tooth	yá(chǐ) 牙(齿)
foot	jiǎo 脚	vessel	xuèguǎn 血管
gum	yáyín 牙龈	waist	yāo 腰
hair	tóufa 头发	wrist	shǒuwàn 手腕
hand	shǒu 手		
head	tóu 头，nǎodai 脑袋		
heart	xīn(zàng) 心(脏)		
heel	jiǎogēn 脚跟		

I2 *Disease* jíbìng 疾病
Symptom zhèngzhuàng 症状

blood pressure	xuèyā 血压
bronchitis	zhīqìguǎnyán 支气管炎
enteritis	chángyán 肠炎

flu	liúgǎn 流感	acupuncture	zhēnjiǔ 针灸
have a cold	gǎnmào 感冒	CT Scan	CT sǎomiáo CT扫描
heart disease	xīnzàngbìng 心脏病	course	liáochéng 疗程
hepatitis	gānyán 肝炎	cupping	bá huǒguàn 拔火罐
infectious disease	chuánrǎnbìng 传染病	diagnosis	zhěnduàn 诊断
patient	bìngrén 病人	ECG	zuò xīndiàntú 做心电图
pneumonia	fèiyán 肺炎	feel sb's pulse	hào mài 号脉
tuberculosis	fèijiéhé 肺结核	give an injection	dǎzhēn 打针
burn	shāoshāng 烧伤	have blood tested	yàn xiě 验血
cough	késou 咳嗽	have stool tested	yàn biàn 验便
have diarrhoea	lā dùzi 拉肚子	have urine tested	yàn niào 验尿
dizzy	tóuyūn 头晕	massage	tuīná 推拿，ànmó 按摩
fever	fāshāo 发烧	medical insurance	yībǎo 医保
have a fall	diēshāng 跌伤	nurse	hùshi 护士
headache	tóuténg 头疼	operation	shǒushù 手术
infection	chuánrǎn 传染，gǎnrǎn 感染	pharmacy	yàofáng 药房
nausea	ěxin 恶心，fǎnwèi 反胃	physical examination	tǐjiǎn 体检
perspire	chū hàn 出汗	qigong	qìgōng 气功
runny nose	liú bítì 流鼻涕	stay in hospital	zhùyuàn 住院
snot	bítì 鼻涕	take temperature	liáng tǐwēn 量体温
sore throat	sǎngzi téng 嗓子疼	taking X-ray	zhào X guāng 照X光
sore, pain, ache	téng 疼，tòng 痛	ultrasound	zhào chāoshēngbō 照超声波，
sputum	tán 痰		zuò B chāo 做B超
stuffy nose	bízi bù tōng 鼻子不通	waiting room	hòuzhěnshì 候诊室
swell	zhǒngzhàng 肿胀		
tear	yǎnlèi 眼泪		
tired all over	húnshēn méi jìn 浑身没劲，fá lì 乏力	**I4 Medication**	yàowù zhìliáo 药物治疗
		Chinese herbs	zhōngcǎoyào 中草药
trouble breathing	hūxī kùnnan 呼吸困难	Chinese medicine	zhōngyào 中药
vomit	(ǒu)tù (呕)吐	medicine	yào 药
watery eyes	liú yǎnlèi 流眼泪	pill	yàowán 药丸
		powder	yàofěn 药粉
		prescribe	kāi yàofāng 开药方

I3 Consultation and medical treatment
wènzhěn hé yīliáo 问诊和医疗

body temperature	tǐwēn 体温	prescription	yàofāng 药方
		tablet	yàopiàn 药片

J *Dealing with people* rénjì jiāowǎng 人际交往

J1 *Family*   jiātíng 家庭
     Relative   qīnshǔ 亲属
     Friend   péngyou 朋友

father	bàba 爸爸，fùqīn 父亲
mother	māma 妈妈，mǔqīn 母亲
elder brother	gēge 哥哥
elder brother's wife, sister-in-law	
	sǎozi 嫂子
younger brother	dìdi 弟弟
younger brother's wife, sister-in-law	
	dìxí 弟媳
elder sister	jiějie 姐姐
elder sister's husband, brother-in-law	
	jiěfu 姐夫
younger sister	mèimei 妹妹
younger sister's husband, brother-in-law	
	mèifu 妹夫
father's father, grandfather	
	yéye 爷爷，zǔfù 祖父
father's mother, grandmother	
	nǎinai 奶奶，zǔmǔ 祖母
mother's father, grandfather	
	wàigōng 外公，lǎoye 姥爷，
	wàizǔfù 外祖父
mother's mother, grandmother	
	wàipó 外婆，lǎolao 姥姥，
	wàizǔmǔ 外祖母
husband	zhàngfu 丈夫，lǎogōng 老公，
	àiren 爱人
wife	qīzi 妻子，lǎopo 老婆，
	xífu 媳妇，àiren 爱人
son	érzi 儿子
daughter-in-law	érxí 儿媳

daughter	nǚ'ér 女儿
son-in-law	nǚxu 女婿
son's son, grandson	sūnzi 孙子
son's daughter, granddaughter	
	sūnnǚ 孙女
daughter's son, grandson	
	wàisūn 外孙
daughter's daughter, granddaughter	
	wàisūnnǚ 外孙女
father's elder brother, uncle	
	bófù 伯父，dàye 大爷
father's elder brother's wife, aunt	
	bómǔ 伯母，dàmā 大妈
father's younger brother, uncle	
	shūfù 叔父，shūshu 叔叔
father's younger brother's wife, aunt	
	shěnmǔ 婶母，shěnzi 婶子，
	shěnshen 婶婶
father's sister, aunt	gūmǔ 姑母，gūmā 姑妈，
	gūgu 姑姑
father's sister's husband, uncle	
	gūfu 姑父
mother's brother, uncle	
	jiùfù 舅父，jiùjiu 舅舅
mother's brother's wife, aunt	
	jiùmǔ 舅母，jiùmā 舅妈
mother's sister, aunt	yímǔ 姨母，yímā 姨妈
mother's sister's husband, uncle	
	yífu 姨父
brother's son, nephew	zhí'er 侄儿，zhízi 侄子
brother's son's wife, nephew's wife	
	zhíxífu 侄媳妇
brother's daughter, niece	

zhínǚ 侄女

brother's daughter's husband, niece's husband

zhínǚxu 侄女婿

sister's son, nephew   wàisheng 外甥

sister's son's wife, nephew's wife

wàisheng xífu 外甥媳妇

sister's daughter, niece

wàishengnǚ 外甥女

sister's daughter's husband, niece's husband

wàisheng nǚxu 外甥女婿

acquaintance	shúrén 熟人	
apprentice	túdì 徒弟	
boyfriend	nánpéngyou 男朋友	
classmate	tóngxué 同学，	
	tóngchuāng 同窗	
colleague	tóngshì 同事	
companion, partner	tóngbàn 同伴，	huǒbàn 伙伴
familiar	mìyǒu 密友	
girlfriend	nǚpéngyou 女朋友	

junior fellow apprentice

shīdì 师弟

lover	qíngrén 情人	
master	shīfu 师傅	
neighbor	línjū 邻居	
roommate	shìyǒu 室友	

senior fellow apprentice

shīxiōng 师兄

student	xuésheng 学生
teacher	lǎoshī 老师
teacher's wife	shīmǔ 师母
townsman	tóngxiāng 同乡

J2 Manner   lǐmào 礼貌，lǐjié 礼节

regard, greeting	wènhòu 问候
good evening	wǎnshang hǎo 晚上好
good morning	zǎoshang hǎo 早上好，

---

nín zǎo 您早

good night	wǎn'ān 晚安
hello, how are you	nǐ hǎo 你好
nice to meet you	xìnghuì 幸会
welcome	huānyíng 欢迎
please	qǐng 请

please take your time to enjoy the meal

qǐng màn yòng 请慢用

excuse me...	qǐngwèn… 请问……
come in please	qǐng jìn 请进
sit down please	qǐng zuò 请坐
here is your tea	qǐng hē chá 请喝茶，
	qǐng yòng chá 请用茶

could you help me please

nǐ néng bāng wǒ ma
你能帮我吗

excuse me please	duìbuqǐ 对不起，	láojià 劳驾
give way please	qǐng ràng yi ràng 请让一让	
I can't	bù xíng 不行	
may I trouble you	láojià 劳驾，	máfan nǐ 麻烦你

never mind, don't worry

méi guānxi 没关系，

bú yòng xiè 不用谢，

bú yàojǐn 不要紧

no trouble	bù máfan 不麻烦	
sorry	bàoqiàn 抱歉，	duìbuqǐ 对不起
tell me please	qǐng gàosù wǒ 请告诉我	
thanks	xièxie 谢谢	
thanks so much	fēicháng gǎnxiè 非常感谢	
wait a minute please	qǐng shāo děng 请稍等	
yes, you can	kěyǐ 可以，	xíng 行
you are welcome	bú kèqi 不客气	
goodbye	zàijiàn 再见	
see you tomorrow	míngtiān jiàn 明天见	

take care (a polite expression used when seeing a

guest off)   màn zǒu 慢走

273

stop here please	qǐng liú bù 请留步	*happy Spring Festival*	xīn chūn kuàilè 新春快乐
have a safe trip	yílù-píng'ān 一路平安	*health and longevity*	jiànkāng chángshòu 健康长寿
have a smooth journey		*lucky new (, rabbit, dragon,...) year*	
	yílù-shùnfēng 一路顺风		xīn (, tù, lóng, …) nián jíxiáng
congratulations	zhùhè 祝贺		新(、兔、龙、……)年吉祥
congratulations for making a fortune		*young forever*	qīngchūn yǒng zhù 青春永驻
	gōngxǐ fācái 恭喜发财		
everything as one wishes		**J3** *Title* chēngwèi 称谓	
	wàn shì rúyì 万事如意	*Mr, gentleman*	xiānsheng 先生
good luck for you	zhù nǐ hǎo yùn 祝你好运	*Mrs*	fūren 夫人，tàitai 太太
happy birthday	shēngrì kuàilè 生日快乐	*madam, lady*	nǚshì 女士
happy new year	xīnnián hǎo 新年好,	*Miss*	xiǎojiě 小姐
	guò nián hǎo 过年好	*comrade*	tóngzhì 同志

K *Others* qítā 其他

K1 *Dates, seasons, periods of time and measuring units* rìqī 日期、jìjié 季节、shíjiānduàn yǔ shíjiān dānwèi 时间段与时间单位

year	nián 年	*December*	Shí'èryuè 十二月
this year	jīnnián 今年	*this month*	zhè(ge) yuè 这(个)月
next year	míngnián 明年	*next month*	xià (gè) yuè 下(个)月
last year	qùnián 去年	*last month*	shàng (gè) yuè 上(个)月
month	yuè 月	*week*	xīngqī 星期，zhōu 周
January	Yīyuè 一月	*Sunday*	Xīngqīrì 星期日，Lǐbàitiān 礼拜天
February	Èryuè 二月	*Monday*	Xīngqīyī 星期一
March	Sānyuè 三月	*Tuesday*	Xīngqī'èr 星期二
April	Sìyuè 四月	*Wednesday*	Xīngqīsān 星期三
May	Wǔyuè 五月	*Thursday*	Xīngqīsì 星期四
June	Liùyuè 六月	*Friday*	Xīngqīwǔ 星期五
July	Qīyuè 七月	*Saturday*	Xīngqīliù 星期六
August	Bāyuè 八月	*weekend*	zhōumò 周末
September	Jiǔyuè 九月	*this week*	zhè(ge) xīngqī 这(个)星期,
October	Shíyuè 十月		zhè zhōu 这周
November	Shíyīyuè 十一月	*next week*	xià (gè) xīngqī 下(个)星期,
			xià zhōu 下周
		last week	shàng (gè) xīngqī 上(个)星期,
			shàng zhōu 上周
		date	rì 日，hào 号

day, date	tiān 天	
today	jīntiān 今天	
tomorrow	míngtiān 明天	
the day after tomorrow		
	hòutiān 后天	
yesterday	zuótiān 昨天	
the day before yesterday		
	qiántiān 前天	
season	jì(jié) 季(节)	
spring	chūn(tiān) 春(天)	
summer	xià(tiān) 夏(天)	
autumn	qiū(tiān) 秋(天)	
winter	dōng(tiān) 冬(天)	
the four seasons	sìjì 四季	
time	shíhou 时候, shíjiān 时间	
early morning	zǎoshang 早上,	
	zǎochen 早晨	
morning	shàngwǔ 上午	
noon	zhōngwǔ 中午	
afternoon	xiàwǔ 下午	
evening	wǎnshang 晚上	
daytime	báitiān 白天	
night	yè(li) 夜(里)	
hour	xiǎoshí 小时	
o'clock	diǎn 点	
quarter	kè 刻	
minute	fēn 分	
second	miǎo 秒	

K2 Festival jiérì 节日
Holiday jiàrì 假日

New Year	xīnnián 新年	
New Year's Day	Yuándàn 元旦	
Christmas	Shèngdàn 圣诞	
Spring Festival	Chūnjié 春节	
Tomb Sweeping Day	Qīngmíngjié 清明节 (about the

fifth of April)

Labor Day	Láodòngjié 劳动节	
Dragon Boat Festival	Duānwǔjié 端午节 (Lunar

calendar: fifth day of the fifth month.)

Mid-Autumn Festival Zhōngqiūjié 中秋节 (Lunar
calendar: fifteenth of the eighth month.)

National Day Guóqìngjié 国庆节 (the first of
October)

have a holiday	fàng jià 放假	
summer holiday	shǔjià 暑假	
winter holiday	hánjià 寒假	

K3 Country guójiā 国家
Nationality guójí 国籍

person	rén 人	
Africa	Fēizhōu 非洲	
African	Fēizhōurén 非洲人	
Egypt	Āijí 埃及	
Egyptian	Āijírén 埃及人	
Ethiopia	Āisài'ébǐyà 埃塞俄比亚	
Ethiopian	Āisài'ébǐyàrén 埃塞俄比亚人	
Nigeria	Nírìlìyà 尼日利亚	
Nigerian	Nírìlìyàrén 尼日利亚人	
South Africa	Nánfēi 南非	
South African	Nánfēirén 南非人	
Tanzania	Tǎnsāngníyà 坦桑尼亚	
Tanzanian	Tǎnsāngníyàrén 坦桑尼亚人	
Zambia	Zànbǐyà 赞比亚	
Zambian	Zànbǐyàrén 赞比亚人	
America	Měizhōu 美洲	
American	Měizhōurén 美洲人	
North America	Běiměizhōu 北美洲	
Canada	Jiānádà 加拿大	
Canadian	Jiānádàrén 加拿大人	
Mexico	Mòxīgē 墨西哥	
Mexican	Mòxīgērén 墨西哥人	

United States	Měiguó 美国	Saudi Arabian	Shātè'ālābórén 沙特阿拉伯人
American	Měiguórén 美国人	Singapore	Xīnjiāpō 新加坡
South America	Nánměizhōu 南美洲	Singaporean	Xīnjiāpōrén 新加坡人
Argentina	Āgēntíng 阿根廷	South Korea	Hánguó 韩国
Argentine	Āgēntíngrén 阿根廷人	South Korean	Hánguórén 韩国人
Brazil	Bāxī 巴西	Syria	Xùlìyà 叙利亚
Brazilian	Bāxīrén 巴西人	Syrian	Xùlìyàrén 叙利亚人
Chile	Zhìlì 智利	Turkey	Tǔ'ěrqí 土耳其
Chilean	Zhìlìrén 智利人	Turk	Tǔ'ěrqírén 土耳其人
Colombia	Gēlúnbǐyà 哥伦比亚	Vietnam	Yuènán 越南
Colombian	Gēlúnbǐyàrén 哥伦比亚人	Vietnamese	Yuènánrén 越南人
Venezuela	Wěinèiruìlā 委内瑞拉	Oceania	Dàyángzhōu 大洋洲
Venezuelan	Wěinèiruìlārén 委内瑞拉人	Australia	Àodàlìyà 澳大利亚
Asia	Yàzhōu 亚洲	Australian	Àodàlìyàrén 澳大利亚人
Asian	Yàzhōurén 亚洲人	New Zealand	Xīnxīlán 新西兰
Afghanistan	Āfùhàn 阿富汗	New Zealander	Xīnxīlánrén 新西兰人
Afghan	Āfùhànrén 阿富汗人	Europe	Ōuzhōu 欧洲
China	Zhōngguó 中国	European	Ōuzhōurén 欧洲人
Chinese	Zhōngguórén 中国人	Belgium	Bǐlìshí 比利时
India	Yìndù 印度	Belgian	Bǐlìshírén 比利时人
Indian	Yìndùrén 印度人	France	Fǎguó 法国
Indonesia	Yìndùníxīyà 印度尼西亚	French	Fǎguórén 法国人
Indonesian	Yìndùníxīyàrén 印度尼西亚人	Germany	Déguó 德国
Iran	Yīlǎng 伊朗	German	Déguórén 德国人
Iranian	Yīlǎngrén 伊朗人	Greece	Xīlà 希腊
Iraq	Yīlākè 伊拉克	Greek	Xīlàrén 希腊人
Iraqi	Yīlākèrén 伊拉克人	Italy	Yìdàlì 意大利
Israel	Yǐsèliè 以色列	Italian	Yìdàlìrén 意大利人
Israeli	Yǐsèlièrén 以色列人	Russia	Éluósī 俄罗斯
Japan	Rìběn 日本	Russian	Éluósīrén 俄罗斯人
Japanese	Rìběnrén 日本人	Spain	Xībānyá 西班牙
Pakistan	Bājīsītǎn 巴基斯坦	Spanish	Xībānyárén 西班牙人
Pakistani	Bājīsītǎnrén 巴基斯坦人	the Netherlands	Hélán 荷兰
Palestine	Bālèsītǎn 巴勒斯坦	Dutch	Hélánrén 荷兰人
Palestinian	Bālèsītǎnrén 巴勒斯坦人	United Kingdom	Yīngguó 英国
Saudi Arabia	Shātè'ālābó 沙特阿拉伯	British	Yīngguórén 英国人

K4 *Occupation* zhíyè 职业

accountant	kuàijì 会计
actor, actress	yǎnyuán 演员
agronomist	nóngxuéjiā 农学家
architect	jiànzhùshī 建筑师
baker	miànbāoshī 面包师
businessman	shāngrén 商人
cashier	chūnà 出纳
chef	chúshī 厨师
cleaner	qīngjiégōng 清洁工
dancer	wǔdǎojiā 舞蹈家
designer	shèjìshī 设计师
doctor	yīshēng 医生
driver	jiàshǐyuán 驾驶员
engineer	gōngchéngshī 工程师
farm owner	nóngchǎngzhǔ 农场主
farmer	nóngmín 农民
film star	diànyǐng míngxīng 电影明星
fireman	xiāofángyuán 消防员
flower grower	huānóng 花农
gardener	yuányìshī 园艺师
hairdresser, barber	lǐfàshī 理发师
interpreter	fānyì 翻译
manager	jīnglǐ 经理
nurse	hùshi 护士
officer	guānyuán 官员, gōngwùyuán 公务员
painter	huàjiā 画家, yóuqīgōng 油漆工
pilot	fēixíngyuán 飞行员, lǐnghángyuán 领航员
poet	shīrén 诗人
police	jǐngchá 警察
postman	yóudìyuán 邮递员
receptionist	jiēdàiyuán 接待员
reporter	jìzhě 记者
scientist	kēxuéjiā 科学家
secretary	mìshū 秘书
singer	gēshǒu 歌手
student	xuésheng 学生
taxi driver	chūzūchē sījī 出租车司机
teacher	lǎoshī 老师, jiàoshī 教师
ticket seller	shòupiàoyuán 售票员
tourist guide	dǎoyóu 导游
TV presenter	diànshì jiémù zhǔchírén 电视节目主持人, bōyīnyuán 播音员
waiter, waitress	fúwùyuán 服务员
worker	gōngrén 工人
writer	zuòjiā 作家

K5 *Useful verbs* chángyòng dòngcí 常用动词

be	shì 是
can	néng 能, huì 会
have	yǒu 有
want	yào 要, xiǎng 想
chew	jiáo 嚼
drink	hē 喝
eat	chī 吃
spit	tǔ 吐
swallow	yàn 咽
taste	cháng 尝
crawl	pá 爬
fly	fēi 飞
jump	tiào 跳
lie	tǎng 躺
run	pǎo 跑
sit	zuò 坐
stand	zhàn 站
walk	zǒu 走
answer	dá 答
ask	wèn 问
cry	kū 哭

draw	huà 画
learn	xué 学
listen	tīng 听
pass	chuán(dì) 传(递)
pick	zhāi 摘
sing	chàng 唱
smile, laugh	xiào 笑
speak	shuō 说
take	ná 拿
teach	jiāo 教
watch, see, look	kàn 看
write	xiě 写
borrow, lend	jiè 借
brush	shuā 刷
close	guān 关
hang	guà 挂
help	bāng(zhù) 帮(助)
return	huán 还
live	zhù 住
open	kāi 开
receive	shōu 收
send	fā 发
take off	tuō 脱
wash	xǐ 洗
wear, put on	chuān 穿, dài 戴
back, return	huí 回
come	lái 来
cross	chuānguò 穿过
follow	suí 随, gēn 跟
go to	dào 到, wǎng 往

go	qù 去
pass	jīngguò 经过
turn	guǎi 拐, zhuǎnwān 转弯

K6 Measurement words for distances, capacities and weights dù-liàng-héng 度量衡

Distance chángdù 长度

fen (0.3333 centimeter)	
	fēn 分
cun (0.3333 decimeter)	
	cùn 寸
chi (0.3333 meter)	chǐ 尺
zhang (3.333 meters)	zhàng 丈
li (0.5 kilometer)	lǐ 里
centimeter (cm)	límǐ 厘米, gōngfēn 公分
meter (m)	mǐ 米
kilometer (km)	qiānmǐ 千米, gōnglǐ 公里

Capacity róngliàng 容量

milliliter (ml)	háoshēng 毫升
liter (l)	shēng 升

Weight zhòngliàng 重量

liang (50 grams)	liǎng 两
jin (0.5 kilogram)	jīn 斤
gram (g)	kè 克
kilogram (kg)	qiānkè 千克, gōngjīn 公斤
tonne (t)	dūn 吨